POETRY OF THE AMERICAN RENAISSANCE

A Diverse Anthology from the Romantic Period

POETRY OF THE AMERICAN RENAISSANCE

A Diverse Anthology from the Romantic Period

Edited and with an Introduction by
PAUL KANE

GEORGE BRAZILLER • NEW YORK

For my parents

Since this page cannot legibly accommodate all copyright notices, page 383 constitutes an extension of this copyright page.

First published in 1995 by George Braziller, Inc.
Introduction, headnotes, and explanatory notes copyright © 1995 by Paul Kane
All rights reserved.
For information, please address the publisher:

GEORGE BRAZILLER, INC.
277 Broadway, Suite 708
New York, NY 10007
www.georgebraziller.com

Library of Congress Cataloging-in-Publication Data:

Poetry of the American Renaissance: a diverse anthology from the romantic period/
edited and with an introduction by Paul Kane.
     p.   cm.
   ISBN 0-8076-1398-3
    1. American poetry—19th century. 2. Romanticism—United States.
  I. Kane, Paul, 1950-
PS607.P638 1995   95-17681
811'.308—dc20   CIP

Designed by RITA LASCARO
Printed and bound in the United States
First edition

CONTENTS

INTRODUCTION

I.

This anthology offers a selection of poetry from the half century between 1820 and 1870, a time of unusual literary ferment and accomplishment in the United States. Although I have stretched it chronologically at both ends, this period embraces what is generally known as the American Renaissance, the era in which American literature seemed to come of age. Many of the writers associated with the traditional canon belong to this span of years: Washington Irving, James Fenimore Cooper, Ralph Waldo Emerson, Nathaniel Hawthorne, Edgar Allan Poe, Henry David Thoreau, Walt Whitman, Herman Melville, and Emily Dickinson. They are not, of course, the only writers of interest from that time, and all the standard anthologies offer a broader and more diverse spectrum than those canonical few. And yet, in the jostling for precious space in such books many admirable writers are inevitably shunted into obscurity, and generations of readers never encounter their work. This anthology seeks to address that problem in the realm of poetry; it allows the reader to encounter writers from both the canon and, as it were, the apocrypha: the familiar poets are all here, but so are some long-overlooked ones, as well as others who have simply fallen out of sight. While anthologies are always retrospective, this one also wishes to suggest how we might look upon the poetry of the American Renaissance in the future.

There is something quizzical about the notion of an American Renaissance, since the term denotes a "rebirth" of our literature at a time when many were still calling for it to be born. As one British reviewer put it in 1820, "In the four quarters of the globe, who reads an American book?" And as late as 1844 Emerson, in his essay "The Poet," declared, "I look in vain for the poet whom I describe." If by the great half decade of 1850–1855 (which saw the publication of Emerson's *Representative Men*, Hawthorne's *The Scarlet Letter*, Melville's *Moby-Dick*, Thoreau's *Walden*, and Whitman's *Leaves of Grass*) the United States was furnished with a new and impressive body of literature, why speak of it as a rebirth? In one sense such a locution is entirely typical, for America was forever being reborn— from the beginnings of European exploration to the founding of colonies to British ascendancy and its subsequent overthrow to the creation of a revolutionary democracy, America kept being reinvented, reestablished on new footings. Moreover, a tradition of renewal was set early on by the Puritans in the jeremiads that sought to reaffirm the special covenant that was to be America's destiny; in politics the Jeffersonian appeal to agrarian principles and the Jacksonian egalitarian revolution were all couched in the language of regeneration. Thus we could say that the pattern simply continued: our literary rebirth was yet another beginning, brought about this time by the advent of an American version of romanticism (which would lead into the radical valences of New England transcendentalism). Other considerations, however, pertain.

In considering the notion of a rebirth, it is useful to know that the actual phrase "American Renaissance" is an invention of the critic F. O. Matthiessen, who published in 1941—on the eve of America's coming-of-age as a world power—a magisterial study of five writers (Emerson, Thoreau, Hawthorne, Melville, and Whitman), whom he designated as those "who bulk largest in stature." Thus was born simultaneously our "classic" period and our "renaissance." Matthiessen's book, *American Renaissance: Art and Expression in the Age of Emerson and Whitman*, was instrumental in legitimizing American studies in the academy, and his title has denominated our mid-nineteenth-century literature ever since. Matthiessen thought of this period as a renaissance in the sense of "coming to its first maturity and affirming its rightful heritage in the whole expanse of art and culture." He went on to quote André Malraux: "Every civilization is like the Renaissance, and creates its own heritage out of everything in the past that helps it to surpass itself." But if the term *renaissance* names not so much a fixed historical period as it does a timeless strategy for creating civilization (*"A heritage is not transmitted;"* says Malraux; *"it must be conquered"*), then the same is true for our other period term, *romanticism*—by all accounts a notoriously slippery word.

Romanticism, like the Renaissance, has a historical referent and a conceptual one, and both entail the idea of a return or rebirth. In the case of the Renaissance there was a revaluation or "rediscovery" of the classical world (whereby it was reborn in Europe), while with romanticism there was a turn toward the romance tradition of medieval Europe. But in fact romanticism arose from a complex conjunction of various philosophic, scientific, religious, and economic changes that had profound cultural and political extensions in the late eighteenth and early nineteenth centuries. In that sense romanticism comprises a discrete set of historical events that can eventually be mapped out—in the case of American literature—as coordinate with the rise of the sentimental novel, the gothic and historical romance, primitivism, antiquarianism, the celebration of individualism, the cult of nature, and so on. Small wonder, we might conclude, that romanticism seemed to mark a new moment in history or that transcendentalism would come to be called the "Newness."

But romanticism can also name a tendency, a recursive movement in human thought and action that is not confined to one historical period but operates whenever there is an overriding emphasis on imagination or freedom or on the irrational, the ideal, the transcendent. As such, the romantic is often contrasted with the cool restraint and reasonableness of the classic, which constitutes its opposite. And yet some would maintain that all true art is romantic in impulse, since it seeks to move beyond the confines of the given and return us to sources of imaginative power (which is the import of Emerson's account of transcendentalism as "Idealism as it appears in 1842"). While these thumbnail definitions are reductive (and it should be noted that the study of romanticism has generated a highly sophisticated critical literature), they nonetheless can serve a salutary purpose, for if we keep in mind the uses to which such terms are put, we can see not only the ways in which the American Renaissance is coterminous with nineteenth-century romanticism but also, more importantly, that it is a twentieth-century construction—or fiction—that serves to mythologize our past in order to establish the basis for a distinctively national literature and identity. That precisely the same concerns were also being pursued during the American Renaissance itself is one of the points of interest encountered in the poetry. And if the American Renaissance is regarded as the true founding moment for our canonical literature, then it should come as no surprise that romantic concepts of art and society continue to dominate our thinking about American culture today.

II.

Poetry in the nineteenth century occupied an important position in the culture: it was still a popular literary form and was valued as entertainment or stimulus or consolation. It was considered the highest literary art, though already fiction was the dominant genre in the marketplace. Poetry had a public profile: it appeared in newspapers, magazines, and broadsheets. In this the nineteenth contrasts starkly with the late twentieth century, where poetry seems to have fulfilled Milton's prophecy of finding a "fit audience . . .

though few" (unless the burgeoning of poetry readings may be taken as a contemporary sign of renewed interest). In particular, the proliferation of poetry anthologies in the nineteenth century attests to poetry's continued prestige. Among the best-known anthologies were two edited by the critic Rufus Griswold, *The Poets and Poetry of America* (1842) and *The Female Poets of America* (1848). Both were large undertakings, the first almost six hundred pages long and the second four hundred, together representing a total of almost two hundred fifty poets, most of them Griswold's contemporaries. The high art of poetry, one could surmise, had attracted many votaries.

For the decade 1800 to 1810 the *Annals of American Literature* lists twenty-two prominent books of verse published; between 1840 and 1850 it lists eighty-four books. This upsurge in the publication of poetry had various causes, some of them obviously economic. One crucial factor is that, as the United States moved from an agrarian to a market economy, it became possible for publishing to develop into a full-fledged industry. This resulted from an interplay of factors: technological innovations in printing and binding, improvements in interstate transportation and hence distribution, a dramatic increase in the population (it more than tripled between 1820 and 1860), and by 1850 a literacy rate (among white Americans) of almost 90 percent. All these factors added up to a set of conditions that made publishing a lucrative business and authorship a viable profession. Few poets could earn their livelihood from poetry alone, but the rapid increase in the number of magazines and newspapers offered poets additional publishing opportunities—articles, reviews, and stories—and provided them with editing or journalism work as well. For women writers, especially, publishing could be an important source of income. Indeed, most of the best-selling novels of the period were written by women (giving rise to Hawthorne's intemperate remark about "that damned mob of scribbling women" stifling his career).

For many of the poets in this anthology the lyceum movement proved to be another important development in the growth of the profession of letters. The lyceum (named after Aristotle's philosophic school) was an educational society that brought lecturers to speak to local communities. The first "American Lyceum" was established in 1826 in Millbury, Massachusetts, but by midcentury there were more than three thousand lyceums throughout the country, and a number of writers (Emerson in particular) helped support themselves by traveling the lyceum circuit. Not only did such adult programs spur interest in higher education, they also acted as forums for the dissemination of writers' views and works, which in turn stimulated sales of books. Many of the poets in this anthology spent time touring the lyceums, primarily in New England, but also in the mid-Atlantic region and in the West, where they often spoke to large audiences. The lyceum was a popular institution, and it underscored the fact that, if the poet had a rival for literary preeminence and prestige in the mid-nineteenth century, it was certainly the orator. In ways that may be difficult to imagine now, when so many of our public speakers are either bumblers or buffoons, oratory in the nineteenth century was an art form taken seriously by speaker and listener alike, whether it was in the lyceum hall or the pulpit or the revival tent. Public speaking was rightfully regarded at the time as a genuine American cultural achievement. This undoubtedly affected the way poets wrote, and we might trace the rhetorical and didactic element so prominent in the poetry of the period to filiations between poetry and oratory, to the recognition that the poet spoke to a public that expected edification.

Much of the literature of the American Renaissance was written in the Northeast, to the extent that the movement is generally thought to be primarily a New England phenomenon (the notable exceptions being Poe, Whitman, and Melville). And while there can be no doubt that the Boston–Concord axis functions as the strongest regional marker of the time, the range of poets in this anthology suggests that some readjustment of perspective may be called for. More than half the poets represented here lived and worked outside New England; at least ten were active in New York City at some point, and nine had significant ties to the South or West. Admittedly, with so many available poets to choose from, such figures could be skewed easily enough, but the main point is simple: the verse of this period was a diverse phenomenon, and its riches are worth celebrating.

In this context it merits mentioning the obvious: that the present anthology is limited to American poetry in English and to poets whose work was published in some form during the period 1820 to 1870. What may not be obvious at first is what is left out. Thus, poetry composed in Spanish or in various Native American languages is not included, nor is the vibrant oral tradition of folk songs, spirituals, and *corridos*. Such work—valuable as it is—simply falls outside the scope of this anthology. To include all the poetry one would wish to make available would require a library, not a book.

III.

There are a number of groupings of poets from this era that are traditional among scholars or otherwise useful to point out. The first is known as the Fireside Poets, or the Schoolroom Poets (since their works were often memorized), which include William Cullen Bryant, Henry Wadsworth Longfellow, John Greenleaf Whittier, Oliver Wendell Holmes, and James Russell Lowell. During their own time and for generations after they were regarded as the most accomplished poets, and their poems were considered both memorable and—in the minds of schoolteachers—worth memorizing for recitation. It is instructive to note that these poets, once seemingly secure in their reputations, have now been largely eclipsed by other poets whom they may have regarded as minor, if not actually inept (Whitman and Dickinson especially). In any given period the writers who loom largest are not necessarily those who survive the sifting of time. We like to think of this as a sort of quality check, whereby the truly good are finally separated from the merely popular, and to some degree that is certainly the case.

But there are other factors involved, especially when the writers are only a century removed: the dynamics of literary change are such that previous poets and styles are often denigrated in order to clear a space for newer or more "original" ones. At a certain point in the twentieth century the Fireside Poets seemed hopelessly old-fashioned and overrated; their poetry could not be further from the new orthodoxies of modernism. Framed pictures of gray-bearded bards were soon removed from the schoolroom walls. While there is little chance that their reputations will ever be dusted off and burnished again, there are signs that the poetry of the Fireside Poets is once again being read with genuine critical attention. To read them without prejudice is to open ourselves to their actual merits. As with many poets from this period they have the virtues of their vices: what we might read as formal, stiff, and exceedingly regular in style, their contemporaries considered elegant, dignified, and well crafted; what we may deem tendentious and sentimental, they would have read as profound or emotionally affecting. The careful reader will probably split the difference. Indeed, if we refrain from elevating our contemporary preferences into timeless aesthetic principles, we may yet recover what is best in a poetry from so different a historical time.

The second traditional grouping is the transcendentalists. This includes—in the present anthology—Emerson, Thoreau, Margaret Fuller, Ellen Sturgis Hooper, Christopher Pearse Cranch, Jones Very, and William Ellery Channing. (Whitman and Dickinson are sometimes associated with them as well.) The acknowledged leader of this group was Emerson, and in many ways he was both the most conventional and the most experimental among them. While much of Emerson's poetry shares the formal features of the Fireside Poets and others like them, his poems are unusual for their combined clarity of expression and subtlety of thought. At the same time one can see in certain poems stylistic alternations that move between principles of compression and expansion—modes that influenced the subsequent poetry of Dickinson and Whitman. For the most part the other transcendentalist poets wrote heterodox poems in orthodox styles, creating at times interesting internal tensions (such as Very's mystical raptures expressed in sonnets). While they all shared certain fundamental philosophic tenets, the transcendentalists did not subscribe to any sharply delineated creed or system. This gave the movement a certain vagueness in the minds of many, as when one follower defined transcendentalism, with a wave of her hand, as *a little beyond.* At the very least transcendentalism was an explosive mixture of beliefs, including the virtue of self-reliance, the presence of the divinity within, the innate capacity to intuit truth directly, and the redemptive potential for individual and societal growth. Transcendentalism was read by many as a provocation. Thus Emerson's declaration in "The Poet" that "America is a poem in our eyes; its ample geography dazzles the imagination, and it will not wait long for meters" is usually read as prophesying Whitman's poetry. Whitman himself described the onset of his poetic career in this way: "I was simmering, simmering, simmering; Emerson brought me to a boil." From a transcendentalist point of view the capaciousness of Whitman's verse could be taken as a natural outgrowth of impulses then stirring in America. Emerson described the literature of transcendentalism as being in the optative mood—that is, expressing a wish or desire and often a hope. However, the genial optimism that seemed part and parcel of transcendentalism did not, as is sometimes thought, blind its followers to the darker aspects of life, though it did make them—in Emerson's formulation—the party of hope. In the end transcendentalism's legacy appears to have been mainly literary—which is another way of saying that its effects are felt everywhere.

As already noted, this period saw the emergence of women's writing on a new scale. Not only were women writing a large percentage of what was being published (possibly as much as half), they were also major consumers of literature. In the case of women poets this led to something of a closed system, whereby women read what other women wrote. Certainly there were men who read their work, but the notion of the women's sphere often extended to the realm of poetry as well. Nonetheless, next to Longfellow, the most popular poet of the time was Lydia Huntley

Sigourney, and the names of other women were quite literally household words, such as Frances Osgood, Phoebe and Alice Carey, Julia Ward Howe, and Frances Harper. The impact of their poetry is hard to gauge, but it would be difficult to overestimate, since many of the social movements of the time—embracing abolitionism, women's rights, temperance leagues, and a host of other reform causes—were directly influenced by the writings of women. We might take Lincoln's remark to the novelist Harriet Beecher Stowe, author of *Uncle Tom's Cabin*, as indicative: "So this is the little lady who made this big war." It is one of the remarkable features of subsequent literary history that by the early twentieth century the impressive achievements of women's writing during the preceding century had been almost completely blotted out. For reasons not dissimilar to those that brought about the demise of the Fireside Poets, women's poetry was seen as uniformly sentimental or sententious and therefore mediocre. Emily Dickinson, of course, could be pointed to as the exception—and indeed she was exceptional—but she only served to prove the case, or so it seemed. To read nineteenth-century women's poetry now is to engage in an act of recovery and, perhaps, restoration. One poet likely to see increasing attention is Maria Gowen Brooks, whose highly romantic imaginings are unusually powerful.

This anthology includes three African-American poets: George Moses Horton, James Monroe Whitfield, and Frances Harper. There were certainly others writing at the time, but for obvious reasons the usual avenues for publication were not available to them. And since even for free blacks there were few educational opportunities, the rich tradition of oral literature in African-American culture may have absorbed a good deal of poetic activity. In most cases it was the abolitionist press that published African-American work, and most of what was written would have appeared in periodicals. The most popular form of black literature during this time was the slave narrative, which was so often electrifying and polarizing. Accounts by Frederick Douglass, Lunsford Lane, Harriet Jacobs, and thousands of others in newspapers, magazines, and books created in effect a separate American genre. That so many of these writings had to be authorized or vouched for by white editors in order to assure readers of their authenticity suggests that the few African-American poets we know of must have had a keen sense of what they were accomplishing in the face of so much resistance.

Although it would not have been thought of as ethnic poetry at the time, the work of John Rollin Ridge, Adah Isaacs Menken, and Emma

Lazarus offers a glimpse of the dynamics of cultural identity among Jewish writers and—more problematically—Native American writers. Ridge, a controversial member of the Cherokee Nation (and also the first Native American novelist), writes with a sense of the need to assimilate into white culture. At the time, Native American literature remained primarily oral; it was not until the twentieth century that a significant body of it was written in English. The same holds true for Mexican-American literature, which could be said to begin in 1848 when Mexico was forced to cede large tracts of land to the United States. Until late in the century Mexican-American literature was written almost exclusively in Spanish. The post–Civil War influx of immigrants would give rise to strong ethnic traditions in American writing, but at midcentury we see mainly their beginnings. Turning to Jewish writing, a strong sense of the value of Hebrew culture is evident in the work of Adah Menken, a convert to Judaism, and Emma Lazarus, a prominent activist for Jewish causes in New York. The words from Lazarus's poem "The New Colossus," inscribed on the Statue of Liberty, are probably among the best-known lines of American poetry.

As might be expected, national themes loom large in the poetry from these years. Whitman is perhaps the prime example, but many other poets took up similar concerns of national identity and purpose. In the case of poetry from the Civil War a thematic intensification occurs. Again, Whitman is important here, but so are Melville, Julia Ward Howe, and Henry Howard Brownell in the North and Henry Timrod in the South. The cataclysm of the war radically reshaped America, and by 1870 not only was a new literary period (realism) underway but a new national ethos was in place. The Gilded Age, as Mark Twain called it, brought quite a different set of assumptions to bear on the social, political, and cultural life of the country. By then the American Renaissance was truly over.

Finally, two poets who seem to stand separate from the rest, Emily Dickinson and Frederick Goddard Tuckerman, should be noted. They might be termed poets of seclusion, for both lived reclusive lives and both wrote in relative obscurity. Though Tuckerman published a book of poems, he was all but unknown as a poet in his time. With Dickinson, the case is even more extreme: her work became known only after her death, and not until the twentieth century was she regarded as among the best poets to have written in English. Tuckerman, too, has had his share of critical encomiums in this century; taken together, he and Dickinson seem both atypical and yet somehow indicative of the surprising ferment, or newness, that pervaded the period.

In looking back on the poetry of the American Renaissance two general observations might be offered. First, to read the poetry of the past requires an act of sympathetic imagination. Not all the poetry in this anthology is of equal quality, but it is all of more than antiquarian or scholarly interest. The poetry will speak to us if we wish to hear it. And second, to read this poetry is to realize once again that the past is never simply past, for we are constantly reinventing and reevaluating it, and those acts of judgment help shape our present moment and fix the trajectory of our future.

—Paul Kane

THE POEMS

The poems selected for this volume use, as far as possible, first printed versions from editions published with the author's participation. When that policy has proved inexpedient, standard scholarly editions have been consulted. Original spelling and punctuation are retained throughout, and except in cases of obvious typographical error, texts have not been changed.

LYDIA HUNTLEY SIGOURNEY

Lydia Huntley Sigourney (1791–1865) was among the most popular poets of her time and one of the most prolific: she published sixty-seven books in her lifetime, ranging from volumes of poetry to travel accounts, advice manuals, and memoirs. The daughter of a groundskeeper in Hartford, she was taken up by the family employing her father and encouraged in her literary leanings. She later taught school but gave it up reluctantly when she married Charles Sigourney, a prominent hardware merchant in Hartford and a widower with three children. The marriage produced two more children, though of the five only two survived to adulthood. From the beginning Charles Sigourney strongly objected to his wife's career as a public author, and the issue was a source of long-standing conflict in the marriage. However, her husband relented somewhat when his business declined and Sigourney's increasing popularity became crucial to their economic prosperity. As Sigourney's fame spread, she came into contact with many famous writers and public figures, including overseas luminaries such as William Wordsworth, Thomas Carlyle, the Marquis de Lafayette, and Louis Philippe, the king of the French. But her real concerns were closer to home, and she advocated in her prose and poetry many of the progressive causes of the period, embracing women's education, the abolition of slavery, and the humane, Christian treatment of Native Americans.

Sigourney (known as the "sweet singer of Hartford") was a popular and conventional writer of the sort later stigmatized as "sentimental" by critics for whom such a style and manner had become outdated. But at her best Sigourney could engage her readers with striking images, a strong narrative impulse and—as in "To a Shred of Linen"—a wit that charmed.

Indian Names

"How can the red men be forgotten, while so many of our states and territories, bays, lakes and rivers, are indelibly stamped by names of their giving?"

Ye say they all have passed away,
    That noble race and brave,
That their light canoes have vanished
    From off the crested wave;
That 'mid the forests where they roamed
    There rings no hunter shout,
But their names is on your waters,
    Ye may not wash it out.

'Tis where Ontario's billow
    Like Ocean's surge is curled,
Where strong Niagara's thunders wake
    The echo of the world.
Where red Missouri bringeth
    Rich tribute from the west,
And Rappahannock sweetly sleeps
    On green Virginia's breast.

Ye say their cone-like cabins,
    That clustered o'er the vale,
Have fled away like withered leaves
    Before the autumn gale,
But their memory liveth on your hills,
    Their baptism on your shore,
Your everlasting rivers speak
    Their dialect of yore.

Old Massachusetts wears it,
    Within her lordly crown,
And broad Ohio bears it,
    Amid his young renown;
Connecticut hath wreathed it
    Where her quiet foliage waves,
And bold Kentucky breathed it hoarse
    Through all her ancient caves.

Wachuset hides its lingering voice
    Within his rocky heart,
And Alleghany graves its tone
    Throughout his lofty chart;
Monadnock on his forehead hoar
    Doth seal the sacred trust,
Your mountains build their monument,
    Though ye destroy their dust.

Ye call these red-browed brethren
    The insects of an hour,
Crushed like the noteless worm amid
    The regions of their power;
Ye drive them from their father's lands,
    Ye break of faith the seal,
But can ye from the court of Heaven
    Exclude their last appeal?

Ye see their unresisting tribes,
    With toilsome step and slow,
On through the trackless desert pass,
    A caravan of woe;
Think ye the Eternal's ear is deaf?
    His sleepless vision dim?
Think ye the *soul's blood* may not cry
    From that far land to him?

To a Shred of Linen

Would they swept cleaner!—
                    Here's a littering shred
Of linen left behind—a vile reproach
To all good housewifery. Right glad am I,
That no neat lady, train'd in ancient times
Of pudding-making, and of sampler-work,
And speckless sanctity of household care,
Hath happened here, to spy thee. She, no doubt,
Keen looking through her spectacles, would say,
"This comes of reading books:"—or some spruce beau,

Essenc'd and lily-handed, had he chanc'd
To scan thy slight superficies, 'twoud be
"This comes of writing poetry."—Well—well—
Come forth—offender!—hast thou aught to say?
Canst thou by merry thought, or quaint conceit,
Repay this risk, that I have run for thee?
————Begin at alpha, and resolve thyself
Into thine elements. I see the stalk
And bright, blue flower of flax, which erst o'erspread
That fertile land, where mighty Moses stretch'd
His rod miraculous. I see thy bloom
Tinging, too scantly, these New England vales.
But, lo! the sturdy farmer lifts his flail,
To crush thy bones unpitying, and his wife
With 'kerchief'd head, and eyes brimful of dust,
Thy fibrous nerves, with hatchel-tooth divides.
————I hear a voice of music—and behold!
The ruddy damsel singeth at her wheel,
While by her side the rustic lover sits.
Perchance, his shrewd eye secretly doth count
The mass of skeins, which, hanging on the wall,
Increaseth day by day. Perchance his thought,
(For men have deeper minds than women—sure!)
Is calculating what a thrifty wife
The maid will make; and how his dairy shelves
Shall groan beneath the weight of golden cheese,
Made by her dexterous hand, while many a keg
And pot of butter, to the market borne,
May, transmigrated, on his back appear,
In new thanksgiving coats.
                    Fain would I ask,
Mine own New England, for thy once loved wheel,
By sofa and piano quite displac'd.
Why dost thou banish from thy parlor-hearth
That old Hygeian harp, whose magic rul'd
Dyspepsia, as the minstrel-shepherd's skill
Exorcis'd Saul's ennui? There was no need,
In those good times, of trim calisthenics,
And there was less of gadding, and far more

Of home-born, heart-felt comfort, rooted strong
In industry, and bearing such rare fruit,
As wealth might never purchase.
                     But come back,
Thou shred of linen. I did let thee drop,
In my harangue, as wiser ones have lost
The thread of their discourse. What was thy lot
When the rough battery of the loom had stretch'd
And knit thy sinews, and the chemist sun
Thy brown complexion bleach'd?
                     Methinks I scan
Some idiosyncrasy, that marks thee out
A defunct pillow-case.—Did the trim guest,
To the best chamber usher'd, e'er admire
The snowy whiteness of thy freshen'd youth
Feeding thy vanity? or some sweet babe
Pour its pure dream of innocence on thee?
Say, hast thou listen'd to the sick one's moan,
When there was none to comfort?—or shrunk back
From the dire tossings of the proud man's brow?
Or gather'd from young beauty's restless sigh
A tale of untold love?
                  Still, close and mute!—
Wilt tell no secrets, ha?—Well then, go down,
With all thy churl-kept hoard of curious lore,
In majesty and mystery, go down
Into the paper-mill, and from its jaws,
Stainless and smooth, emerge.—Happy shall be
The renovation, if on thy fair page
Wisdom and truth, their hallow'd lineaments
Trace for posterity. So shall thine end
Be better than thy birth, and worthier bard
Thine apotheosis immortalise.

WILLIAM CULLEN BRYANT

William Cullen Bryant (1794–1878) wrote his most famous and enduring poem, "Thanatopsis," before the age of twenty. Although success was slow in coming, he did eventually enjoy a long and distinguished career as a prominent poet and as the magisterial editor of an influential newspaper. For almost fifty years Bryant edited the *Evening Post* in New York, where he espoused many and various causes. Bryant was a leading voice in the abolitionist movement and an early supporter of Abraham Lincoln; he campaigned on behalf of free speech and the labor movement, opposed the death penalty, fought corruption in politics, and urged the creation of Central Park in New York. Bryant had a wide acquaintanceship at home and abroad and was active in numerous organizations. At the time of his death in 1878 he was a prodigiously famous American.

Bryant was born in rural Cummington, Massachusetts. His father was a physician whose Unitarianism and love of Greek and Latin classics helped shape Bryant's early tastes and attitudes. Owing to financial considerations Bryant spent only a year at Williams College and was unable to transfer, as he had hoped, to Yale College. Instead, he left school and studied law, eventually practicing in Great Barrington in the Berkshires. There he married and settled down, becoming a town clerk and a justice of the peace. At the age of thirty, however, he moved his family to New York to become a journalist and pursue a literary career. Although never prolific as a poet, Bryant published numerous volumes of poetry in his lifetime (though many were essentially reissues of a collected *Poems*), and he wrote extensively on topics of literature, travel, and politics. At the age of seventy-six Bryant brought out his verse translation of Homer's *Iliad*, followed a year later by the *Odyssey*. A tireless public man, he died from a fall following an oration in Central Park.

Bryant's first poems were in the satiric manner of the English poet Alexander Pope. Soon, however, he began writing poems under the influence of the later eighteenth-century English Graveyard Poets (especially Thomas Gray); and, after encountering William Wordsworth's nature poetry, he adopted a lush meditative style that often employed an elevated and sonorous blank verse. His many poems in this mode helped introduce the American public to a romantic appreciation of the landscape; indeed, a famous painting by Asher B. Durand *(Kindred Spirits)* appropriately shows Bryant and the Hudson River School painter Thomas Cole together in a sublime setting in the Catskill Mountains. Bryant's verse tends to take up natural scenes and imbue them with a somber dignity. As a poet Bryant is a moralist, and his linking of nature and humanity always articulates a simple and deeply felt belief in the necessary virtues.

Thanatopsis

To him who in the love of nature holds
Communion with her visible forms, she speaks
A various language; for his gayer hours
She has a voice of gladness, and a smile
And eloquence of beauty, and she glides
Into his darker musings, with a mild
And gentle sympathy, that steals away
Their sharpness, ere he is aware. When thoughts
Of the last bitter hour come like a blight
Over thy spirit, and sad images
Of the stern agony, and shroud, and pall,
And breathless darkness, and the narrow house,
Make thee to shudder, and grow sick at heart;—
Go forth, under the open sky, and list
To Nature's teachings, while from all around—
Earth and her waters, and the depths of air,—
Comes a still voice—Yet a few days, and thee
The all-beholding sun shall see no more
In all his course; nor yet in the cold ground,
Where thy pale form was laid, with many tears,
Nor in the embrace of ocean shall exist
Thy image. Earth, that nourished thee, shall claim
Thy growth, to be resolved to earth again;
And, lost each human trace, surrendering up
Thine individual being, shalt thou go
To mix forever with the elements,
To be a brother to the insensible rock
And to the sluggish clod, which the rude swain
Turns with his share, and treads upon. The oak
Shall send his roots abroad, and pierce thy mould.
Yet not to thy eternal resting place
Shalt thou retire alone—nor couldst thou wish
Couch more magnificent. Thou shalt lie down

With patriarchs of the infant world—with kings,
The powerful of the earth—the wise, the good,
Fair forms, and hoary seers of ages past,
All in one mighty sepulchre.—The hills
Rock-ribbed and ancient as the sun,—the vales
Stretching in pensive quietness between;
The venerable woods—rivers that move
In majesty, and the complaining brooks
That make the meadows green; and poured round all,
Old ocean's gray and melancholy waste,—
Are but the solemn decorations all
Of the great tomb of man. The golden sun,
The planets, all the infinite host of heaven,
Are shining on the sad abodes of death,
Through the still lapse of ages. All that tread
The globe are but a handful to the tribes
That slumber in its bosom.—Take the wings
Of morning—and the Barcan desert pierce,
Or lose thyself in the continuous woods
Where rolls the Oregan, and hears no sound,
Save his own dashings—yet—the dead are there,
And millions in those solitudes, since first
The flight of years began, have laid them down
In their last sleep—the dead reign there alone.
So shalt thou rest—and what if thou shalt fall
Unheeded by the living—and no friend
Take note of thy departure? All that breathe
Will share thy destiny. The gay will laugh
When thou art gone, the solemn brood of care
Plod on, and each one as before will chase
His favorite phantom; yet all these shall leave
Their mirth and their employments, and shall come,
And make their bed with thee. As the long train
Of ages glide away, the sons of men,
The youth in life's green spring, and he who goes
In the full strength of years, matron, and maid,
And the sweet babe, and the gray-headed man,—
Shall one by one be gathered to thy side,
By those, who in their turn shall follow them.

So live, that when thy summons comes to join
The innumerable caravan, that moves
To that mysterious realm, where each shall take
His chamber in the silent halls of death,
Thou go not, like the quarry-slave at night,
Scourged to his dungeon, but sustained and soothed
By an unfaltering trust, approach thy grave,
Like one who wraps the drapery of his couch
About him, and lies down to pleasant dreams.

To a Waterfowl

Whither, 'midst falling dew,
While glow the heavens with the last steps of day
Far, through their rosy depths, dost thou pursue
Thy solitary way?

Vainly the fowler's eye
Might mark thy distant flight to do thee wrong,
As, darkly painted on the crimson sky,
Thy figure floats along.

Seek'st thou the plashy brink
Of weedy lake, or marge of river wide,
Or where the rocking billows rise and sink
On the chafed ocean side?

There is a Power whose care
Teaches thy way along that pathless coast,—
The desert and illimitable air,—
Lone wandering, but not lost.

All day thy wings have fanned,
At that far height, the cold thin atmosphere,
Yet stoop not, weary, to the welcome land,
Though the dark night is near.

And soon that toil shall end,
Soon shalt thou find a summer home, and rest,
And scream among thy fellows; reeds shall bend,
Soon, o'er thy sheltered nest.

Thou'rt gone, the abyss of heaven
Hath swallow'd up thy form; yet, on my heart
Deeply hath sunk the lesson thou hast given,
    And shall not soon depart.

    He, who, from zone to zone,
Guides through the boundless sky thy certain flight,
In the long way that I must tread alone,
    Will lead my steps aright.

Sonnet—To an American Painter Departing for Europe

Thine eyes shall see the light of distant skies:
    Yet, Cole! thy heart shall bear to Europe's strand
    A living image of thy native land,
Such as on thy own glorious canvass lies.
Lone lakes—savannahs where the bison roves—
    Rocks rich with summer garlands—solemn streams—
    Skies, where the desert eagle wheels and screams—
Spring bloom and autumn blaze of boundless groves.
Fair scenes shall greet thee where thou goest—fair,
    But different—every where the trace of men,
    Paths, homes, graves, ruins, from the lowest glen
To where life shrinks from the fierce Alpine air.
    Gaze on them, till the tears shall dim thy sight,
    But keep that earlier, wilder image bright.

To the Fringed Gentian

Thou blossom bright with autumn dew,
And colored with the heaven's own blue,
That openest, when the quiet light
Succeeds the keen and frosty night.

Thou comest not when violets lean
O'er wandering brooks and springs unseen,
Or columbines, in purple drest,
Nod o'er the ground bird's hidden nest.

Thou waitest late, and com'st alone,
When woods are bare and birds are flown,
And frosts and shortening days portend
The aged year is near its end.

Then doth thy sweet and quiet eye
Look through its fringes to the sky,
Blue—blue—as if that sky let fall
A flower from its cerulean wall.

I would that thus, when I shall see
The hour of death draw near to me,
Hope, blossoming within my heart,
May look to heaven as I depart.

The Prairies

These are the Gardens of the Desert, these
The unshorn fields, boundless and beautiful,
For which the speech of England has no name—
The Prairies. I behold them for the first,
And my heart swells, while the dilated sight
Takes in the encircling vastness. Lo! they stretch
In airy undulations, far away,
As if the ocean, in his gentlest swell,
Stood still, with all his rounded billows fixed,
And motionless for ever.—Motionless?—
No—they are all unchained again. The clouds
Sweep over with their shadows, and, beneath,
The surface rolls and fluctuates to the eye;
Dark hollows seem to glide along and chase
The sunny ridges. Breezes of the South!
Who toss the golden and the flame-like flowers,
And pass the prairie-hawk that, poised on high,
Flaps his broad wings, yet moves not—ye have played
Among the palms of Mexico and vines
Of Texas, and have crisped the limpid brooks
That from the fountains of Sonora glide
Into the calm Pacific—have ye fanned

A nobler or a lovelier scene than this?
Man hath no part in all this glorious work:
The hand that built the firmament hath heaved
And smoothed these verdant swells, and sown their slopes
With herbage, planted them with island groves,
And hedged them round with forests. Fitting floor
For this magnificent temple of the sky—
With flowers whose glory and whose multitude
Rival the constellations! The great heavens
Seem to stoop down upon the scene in love,—
A nearer vault, and of a tenderer blue,
Than that which bends above the eastern hills.

    As o'er the verdant waste I guide my steed,
Among the high rank grass that sweeps his sides,
The hollow beating of his footstep seems
A sacrilegious sound. I think of those
Upon whose rest he tramples. Are they here—
The dead of other days?—and did the dust
Of these fair solitudes once stir with life
And burn with passion? Let the mighty mounds
That overlook the rivers, or that rise
In the dim forest crowded with old oaks,
Answer. A race, that long has passed away,
Built them;—a disciplined and populous race
Heaped, with long toil, the earth, while yet the Greek
Was hewing the Pentelicus to forms
Of symmetry, and rearing on its rock
The glittering Parthenon. These ample fields
Nourished their harvests, here their herds were fed,
When haply by their stalls the bison lowed,
And bowed his maned shoulder to the yoke.
All day this desert murmured with their toils,
Till twilight blushed and lovers walked, and wooed
In a forgotten language, and old tunes,
From instruments of unremembered form,
Gave the soft winds a voice. The red man came—
The roaming hunter tribes, warlike and fierce,
And the mound-builders vanished from the earth.
The solitude of centuries untold

Has settled where they dwelt. The prairie wolf
Hunts in their meadows, and his fresh-dug den
Yawns by my path. The gopher mines the ground
Where stood their swarming cities. All is gone—
All—save the piles of earth that hold their bones—
The platforms where they worshiped unknown gods—
The barriers which they builded from the soil
To keep the foe at bay—till o'er the walls
The wild beleaguerers broke, and, one by one,
The strongholds of the plain were forced, and heaped
With corpses. The brown vultures of the wood
Flocked to those vast uncovered sepulchres,
And sat, unscared and silent, at their feast.
Haply some solitary fugitive,
Lurking in marsh and forest, till the sense
Of desolation and of fear became
Bitterer than death, yielded himself to die.
Man's better nature triumphed. Kindly words
Welcomed and soothed him; the rude conquerors
Seated the captive with their chiefs; he chose
A bride among their maidens, and at length
Seemed to forget,—yet ne'er forgot,—the wife
Of his first love, and her sweet little ones
Butchered, amid their shrieks, with all his race.
　　Thus change the forms of being. Thus arise
Races of living things, glorious in strength,
And perish, as the quickening breath of God
Fills them, or is withdrawn. The red man too—
Has left the blooming wilds he ranged so long,
And, nearer to the Rocky Mountains, sought
A wider hunting-ground. The beaver builds
No longer by these streams, but far away,
On waters whose blue surface ne'er gave back
The white man's face—among Missouri's springs,
And pools whose issues swell the Oregan,
He rears his little Venice. In these plains
The bison feeds no more. Twice twenty leagues
Beyond remotest smoke of hunter's camp,
Roams the majestic brute, in herds that shake

The earth with thundering steps—yet here I meet
His ancient footprints stamped beside the pool.
    Still this great solitude is quick with life.
Myriads of insects, gaudy as the flowers
They flutter over, gentle quadrupeds,
And birds, that scarce have learned the fear of man,
Are here, and sliding reptiles of the ground,
Startlingly beautiful. The graceful deer
Bounds to the wood at my approach. The bee,
A more adventurous colonist than man,
With whom he came across the eastern deep,
Fills the savannas with his murmurings,
And hides his sweets, as in the golden age,
Within the hollow oak. I listen long
To his domestic hum, and think I hear
The sound of that advancing multitude
Which soon shall fill these deserts. From the ground
Comes up the laugh of children, the soft voice
Of maidens, and the sweet and solemn hymn
Of Sabbath worshippers. The low of herds
Blends with the rustling of the heavy grain
Over the dark-brown furrows. All at once
A fresher wind sweeps by, and breaks my dream,
And I am in the wilderness alone.

MARIA GOWEN BROOKS

Maria Gowen Brooks (1794?–1845) was dubbed "Maria of the West" by the English romantic poet Robert Southey, who praised her first volume of poems, *Judith, Esther, and Other Poems* (1820). Brooks took up the nickname and used it in translation as a pseudonym for her later work, calling herself "Maria del Occidente." Rufus Griswold, editor of *The Female Poets of America* (1854), doubted that there would be "many names that will shine with a clearer, steadier, and more enduring lustre than that of Maria del Occidente." Although her reputation all but vanished in the twentieth century, she has been rediscovered recently by poets and critics. Her life and work are highly unusual, and together they convey to us something of the intense and passionate strain that runs through this period.

Left an orphan at the age of fourteen, she married her fifty-year-old legal guardian, John Brooks, two years later. They had two sons, but the marriage was an unhappy one for Brooks. During the War of 1812 her husband suffered financial losses and the family moved from Boston to Portland, Maine. There she apparently fell in love with a Canadian officer but remained with her husband. Of this period she wrote that "fortitude became faint" and "I wept and prayed in agony." In 1823 John Brooks died and Maria Brooks moved her family to Matanzas, Cuba, where her uncle owned a coffee plantation. Brooks grew to love Cuba and while there completed her epic poem, *Zóphiël, or the Bride of Seven*, based on the Apocryphal Book of Tobit. Upon publication of the first canto in 1825 Robert Southey called Brooks "the most impassioned and most imaginative of all poetesses," comparing her to the Greek poet Sappho. Upon inheriting her uncle's plantation in 1829 Brooks accompanied her eldest son to New Hampshire, where he attended Dartmouth College and she studied in the library. After travels in Europe, where she met Southey, Washington Irving, and the Marquis de Lafayette, she followed her son to West Point and later to New York City. In 1838 her younger son died, as did a stepson in 1839. *Idomen, or the Vale of Yamuri*, an autobiographical romance, was published privately in 1843. Two years later Brooks returned to Cuba, where she fell ill with tropical fever and died.

Brooks is best known for her epic *Zóphiël*, set in biblical times, in which she recounts the adventures of a young Hebrew woman, Egla, who is pursued by the fallen angel, Zóphiël. It is a wild and exuberant tale, richly romantic in narrative and style. All of Brooks's poetry is similarly marked with a vibrancy of feeling that her many readers admired and embraced.

from *Zóphiël, or the Bride of Seven*

Canto First: Grove of Acacias

I.

Shade of Columbus, here thy relics rest;
    Here, while these numbers to the desert ring,
The self-same breeze that passes o'er thy breast,
    Salutes me, as with panting heart, I sing.

II.

Madoc! my ancient father's bones repose
    Where their bold harps thy country's bards enwreathed;
And this warm blood once coursed the veins of those
    Who flourished where thy first faint sigh was breathed.

III.

Heroes departed both, if still ye love
    These realms to which on earth, ye oped the way,
Amid the joys that crown your deeds, above,
    One moment pause and deign to bless my lay!

. . .

L.

It chanced, that day, lured by the verdure, came
    Zóphiël, a spirit sometimes ill; but ere
He fell, a heavenly angel. The faint flame
    Of dying embers on an altar, where

Zorah, fair Egla's sire, in secret bowed
    And sacrificed to the great unseen God,
While friendly shades the sacred rites enshroud,
    The spirit saw; his inmost soul was awed,

And he bethought him of the forfeit joys
    Once his in Heaven; deep in a darkling grot
He sat him down; the melancholy noise
    Of leaf and creeping vine accordant with his thought.

40

LI.

When fiercer spirits howled, he but complained
    Ere yet 'twas his to roam the pleasant earth.
His heaven-invented harp he still retained,
    Though tuned to bliss no more; and had its birth

Of him, beneath some black, infernal clift,
    The first drear song of woe; and torment wrung
The restless spirit less, when he might lift
    His plaining voice, and frame the like as now he sung.

LII.

"Woe to thee, wild ambition! I employ
    Despair's low notes thy dread effects to tell;
Born in high heaven, her peace thou couldst destroy;
    And, but for thee, there had not been a Hell.

"Through the celestial domes thy clarion pealed;
    Angels, entranced, beneath thy banners ranged,
And straight were fiends; hurled from the shrinking field,
    They waked in agony to wail the change.

"Darting through all her veins the subtle fire,
    The world's fair mistress first inhaled thy breath;
To lot of higher beings learnt to aspire;
    Dared to attempt, and doomed the world to death.

"The thousand wild desires, that still torment
    The fiercely struggling soul, where peace once dwelt,
But perished; feverish hope; drear discontent,
    Impoisoning all possest,—Oh! I have felt

"As spirits feel,—yet not for man we moan,
    Scarce o'er the silly bird in state were he,
That builds his nest, loves, sings the morn's return,
    And sleeps at evening; save by aid of thee.

"Fame ne'er had roused, nor song her records kept;
    The gem, the ore, the marble breathing life,
The pencil's colours, all in earth had slept,
    Now see them mark with death his victim's strife.

"Man found thee, death: but Death and dull decay,
  Baffling, by aid of thee, his mastery proves;
By mighty works he swells his narrow day,
  And reigns, for ages, on the world he loves.

"Yet what the price? With stings that never cease
  Thou goad'st him on; and when too keen the smart,
His highest dole he'd barter but for peace,
  Food thou wilt have, or feast upon his heart."

LIII.

Thus Zóphiël still, though now the infernal crew
  Had gained, by sin, a privilege in the world,
Allayed their torments in the cool night dew,
  And by the dim starlight again their wings unfurled.

LIV.

And now, regretful of the joys his birth
  Had promised, deserts, mounts, and streams he crost,
To find, amid the loveliest spots of earth,
  Faint semblance of the heaven he had lost.

LV.

And oft, by unsuccessful searching pained,
  Weary he fainted through the toilsome hours;
And then his mystic nature he sustained
  On steam of sacrifices, breath of flowers.

LVI.

Sometimes he gave out oracles, amused
  With mortal folly; resting on the shrines,
Or, all in some fair Sybyl's form infused,
  Spoke from her trembling lips, or traced her mystic lines.

LVII.

And now he wanders on from glade to glade
    To where more precious shrubs diffuse their balms;
And gliding through the thickly-woven shade
    Where the soft captive lay in all her charms,

He caught a glimpse. The colours in her face,
    Her bare white arms, her lips, her shining hair,
Burst on his view. He would have flown the place;
    Fearing some faithful angel rested there,

Who'd see him, 'reft of glory, lost to bliss,
    Wandering, and miserably panting, fain
To glean a joy e'en from a place like this:
    The thought of what he once had been was pain

Ineffable. But what assailed his ear?
    A sigh! Surprised, another glance he took;
Then doubting—fearing—softly coming near—
    He ventured to her side and dared to look;

Whispering, "Yes, 'tis of earth! So, new-found life
    Refreshing, looked sweet Eve, with purpose fell,
When first sin's sovereign gazed on her, and strife
    Had with his heart, that grieved with arts of hell,

Stern as it was, to win her o'er to death.
    Most beautiful of all in earth or heaven!
"Oh, could I quaff for aye that fragrant breath!
    Couldst thou, or being like thee, be given

"To bloom for ever for me thus! Still true
    To one dear theme, my full soul, flowing o'er,
Would find no room for thought of what it knew,
    Nor picturing forfeit transport, curse me more.

LVIII.

"But, oh! severest curse! I cannot be
    In what I love, blest e'en the little span
(With all a spirit's keen capacity
    For bliss) permitted the poor insect, man.

LIX.

"The few I've seen, and deemed of worth to win,
  Like some sweet flowret, mildewed in my arms,
Withered to hideousness as foul as sin,
  Grew fearful hags; and then, with potent charm

"Of muttered word and harmful drug, did learn
  To force me to their will. Down the damp grave,
Loathing I went, at Endor, and uptorn,
  Brought back the dead; when tortured Saul did crave

"To view his lowering fate. Fair, nay, as this
  Young slumberer, that dread witch; when, I arrayed
In lovely shape, to meet my guileful kiss.
  She yielded first her lip. And thou, sweet maid—
What is't I see?—a recent tear has strayed,
  And left its stain upon her cheek of bliss.

LX.

"She has fall'n to sleep in grief; haply been chid,
  Or by rude mortal wrong'd. So let it prove
Meet for my purpose: 'mid these blossoms hid,
  I'll gaze; and when she wakes, with all that love

"And art can lend, come forth. He who would gain
  A fond, full heart, in love's soft surgery skill'd,
Should seek it when 'tis sore; allay its pain
  With balm by pity prest: 'tis all his own so heal'd.

LXI.

"She may be mine a little year; e'en fair
  And sweet as now. Oh! respite! while possest
I lose the dismal sense of my despair:
  But then—I will not think upon the rest!

LXII.

"And wherefore grieve to cloud her little day
    Of fleeting life? What doom from power divine
I bear eternally: pity—away!
    Wake, petty fly! and, while thou mayst, be mine,

"'Though but an hour; so thou supply'st thy looms
    With shining silk, and in the cruel snare
See'st the fond bird entrapped, but for his plumes,
    To work thy robes, or twine amidst thy hair."

LXIII.

To whisper softly in her ear he bent,
    But draws him back restrained: a higher power,
That loved her, and would keep her innocent,
    Repelled his evil touch. And from her bower,

To lead the maid, Sephora comes; the sprite,
    Half baffled, followed, hovering on unseen,
Till Meles, fair to see and nobly dight,
    Received his pensive bride. Gentle of mien,

She meekly stood. He fastened round her arms
    Rings of refulgent ore; low and apart
Murmuring, "So, beauteous captive, shall thy charms
    For ever thrall and clasp thy captive's heart."

LXIV.

The air's light touch seemed softer as she moved,
    In languid resignation; his quick eye
Spoke in black glances how she was approved,
    Who shrank reluctant from his ardency.

LXV.

'Twas sweet to look upon the goodly pair
    In their contrasted loveliness: her height
Might almost vie with his, but heavenly fair,
    Of soft proportion she, and sunny hair;
He cast in manliest mould, with ringlets murk as night.

LXVI.

And oft her drooping and resigned blue eye
    She'd wistful raise to read his radiant face;
But then, why shrunk her heart?—a secret sigh
    Told her it most required what there it could not trace.

LXVII.

Now fair had fall'n the night. The damsel mused
    At her own window, in the pearly ray
Of the full moon; her thoughtful soul infused
    Thus in her words; left lone awhile to pray.

LXVIII.

"What bliss for her who lives her little day
    In blest obedience, like to those divine,
Who to her loved, her earthly lord can say,
    'God is thy law,' most just, and thou art mine.

"To every blast she bends in beauty meek;—
    Let the storm beat,—his arms her shelter kind,—
And feels no need to blanch her rosy cheek
    With thoughts befitting his superior mind.

"Who only sorrows when she sees him pained,
    Then knows to pluck away pain's keenest dart;
Or bid love catch it ere its goal be gained,
    And steal its venom ere it reach his heart.

"'Tis the soul's food: the fervid must adore.—
    For this the heathen, unsufficed with thought,
Moulds him an idol of the glittering ore,
    And shrines his smiling goddess, marble-wrought.

"What bliss for her, ev'n in this world of woe,
    Oh! Sire who mak'st yon orb-strewn arch thy throne;
That sees thee in thy noblest work below
    Shrine undefaced, adored, and all her own!

"This I had hoped; but hope too dear, too great,
  Go to thy grave!—I feel thee blasted, now.
Give me fate's sovereign, well to bear the fate
  Thy pleasure sends; this, my sole prayer, allow!"

Composed at the Request of a Lady, and Descriptive of Her Feelings

She Returned to the North, and Died Soon After

Adieu, fair isle! I love thy bowers,
  I love thy dark-eyed daughters there;
The cool pomegranate's scarlet flowers
  Look brighter in their jetty hair.

They praised my forehead's stainless white;
  And when I thirsted, gave a draught
From the full clustering cocoa's height,
  And smiling, blessed me as I quaff'd.

Well pleased, the kind return I gave,
  And, clasped in their embraces' twine,
Felt the soft breeze, like Lethe's wave,
  Becalm this beating heart of mine.

Why will my heart so wildly beat?
  Say, Seraphs, is my lot too blest,
That thus a fitful, feverish heat
  Must rifle me of health and rest?

Alas! I fear my native snows—
  A clime too cold, a heart too warm—
Alternate chills—alternate glows—
  Too fiercely threat my flower-like form.

The orange-tree has fruit and flowers;
  The grenadilla, in its bloom,
Hangs o'er its high, luxuriant bowers,
  Like fringes from a Tyrian loom.

When the white coffee-blossoms swell,
    The fair moon full, the evening long,
I love to hear the warbling bell,
    And sun-burnt peasant's wayward song.

Drive gently on, dark muleteer,
    And the light seguidilla frame;
Fain would I listen still, to hear
    At every close thy mistress' name.

Adieu, fair isle! the waving palm
    Is pencilled on the purest sky;
Warm sleeps the bay, the air is balm,
    And, soothed to languor, scarce a sigh

Escapes for those I love so well,
    For those I've loved and left so long,
On me their fondest musings dwell,
    To them alone my sighs belong.

On, on, my bark! blow southern breeze!
    No longer would I lingering stay;
'Twere better far *to die* with these
    Than *live in pleasure* far away.

GEORGE MOSES HORTON

George Moses Horton (1798?–1883?), an African-American slave who sought to earn his freedom by writing poetry, worked for years on the campus of the University of North Carolina at Chapel Hill, where students would pay him to dictate love poems for them. Horton, befriended by students and by the president of the university, gradually learned to read and write and, with the help of Caroline Lee Hentz, the wife of a faculty member, published his first book of poems, *Hope of Liberty*, in 1829. The book was intended to raise sufficient money for Horton to buy his freedom and sail to Liberia in Africa, but his hopes were disappointed, despite subsequent reprintings in 1837 and 1838 (retitled *Poems by a Slave*). Horton's work attracted the attention of abolitionists in the North, where several of his poems were published in magazines, including William Lloyd Garrison's *Liberator*. Despite his pleas for assistance in his poems and letters, Horton was constrained to continue toiling as a slave, working at various menial jobs on the college campus. In 1845 he published his second volume, *The Poetical Works of George M. Horton, the Colored Bard of North Carolina*, which carried an autobiographical preface. Already an old man by the time of the Civil War, Horton escaped to Sherman's army at Raleigh in 1865. In Raleigh he published his final volume of poems, *Naked Genius*. After the war Horton moved to Philadelphia, where he apparently wrote short stories to support himself. He is thought to have died in Philadelphia in 1883.

Horton's poetry displays many of the features often developed in oral composition: metrical regularity, the prevalence of end rhyme, and formulaic repetitions. But Horton also studied his written models carefully, drawing upon the work of Lord Byron and the Wesleyan hymnal in particular. While his subjects and his treatment of them are often conventional, his poems pleading for freedom carry a genuine force and pathos that breaks through the decorous pattern of the verse.

On Liberty and Slavery

Alas! and am I born for this,
    To wear this slavish chain?
Deprived of all created bliss,
    Through hardship, toil and pain!

How long have I in bondage lain,
    And languished to be free!
Alas! and must I still complain—
    Deprived of liberty.

Oh, Heaven! and is there no relief
    This side the silent grave—
To soothe the pain—to quell the grief
    And anguish of a slave?

Come Liberty, thou cheerful sound,
    Roll through my ravished ears!
Come, let my grief in joys be drowned,
    And drive away my fears.

Say unto foul oppression, Cease:
    Ye tyrants rage no more,
And let the joyful trump of peace,
    Now bid the vassal soar.

Soar on the pinions of that dove
    Which long has cooed for thee,
And breathed her notes from Afric's grove,
    The sound of Liberty.

Oh, Liberty! thou golden prize,
    So often sought by blood—
We crave thy sacred sun to rise,
    The gift of nature's God!

Bid Slavery hide her haggard face,
    And barbarism fly:
I scorn to see the sad disgrace
    In which enslaved I lie.

Dear Liberty! upon thy breast,
    I languish to respire;
And like the Swan unto her nest,
    I'd to thy smiles retire.

Oh, blest asylum—heavenly balm!
    Unto thy boughs I flee—
And in thy shades the storm shall calm,
    With songs of Liberty!

On Hearing of the Intention of a Gentleman To Purchase the Poet's Freedom

When on life's ocean first I spread my sail,
I then implored a mild auspicious gale;
And from the slippery strand I took my flight,
And sought the peaceful haven of delight.

Tyrannic storms arose upon my soul,
And dreadful did their mad'ning thunders roll;
The pensive muse was shaken from her sphere,
And hope, it vanish'd in the clouds of fear.

At length a golden sun broke thro' the gloom,
And from his smiles arose a sweet perfume—
A calm ensued, and birds began to sing,
And lo! the sacred muse resumed her wing.

With frantic joy she chaunted as she flew,
And kiss'd the clement hand that bore her thro'
Her envious foes did from her sight retreat,
Or prostrate fall beneath her burning feet.

'Twas like a proselyte, allied to Heaven—
Or rising spirits' boast of sins forgiven,
Whose shout dissolves the adamant away
Whose melting voice the stubborn rocks obey.

'Twas like the salutation of the dove,
Borne on the zephyr thro' some lonesome grove,
When Spring returns, and Winter's chill is past,
And vegetation smiles above the blast.

'Twas like the evening of a nuptial pair,
When love pervades the hour of sad despair—
'Twas like fair Helen's sweet return to Troy,
When every Grecian bosom swell'd with joy.

The silent harp which on the osiers hung,
Was then attuned, and manumission sung:
Away by hope the clouds of fear were driven,
And music breathed my gratitude to heaven.

Hard was the race to reach the distant goal,
The needle oft was shaken from the pole;
In such distress, who could forbear to weep?
Toss'd by the headlong billows of the deep!

The tantalizing beams which shone so plain,
Which turn'd my former pleasures into pain—
Which falsely promised all the joys of fame,
Gave way, and to a more substantial flame.

Some philanthropic souls as from afar,
With pity strove to break the slavish bar;
To whom my floods of gratitude shall roll,
And yield with pleasure to their soft control.

And sure of Providence this work begun—
He shod my feet this rugged race to run;
And in despite of all the swelling tide,
Along the dismal path will prove my guide.

Thus on the dusky verge of deep despair,
Eternal Providence was with me there;
When pleasure seemed to fade on life's gay dawn,
And the last beam of hope was almost gone.

RALPH WALDO EMERSON

Ralph Waldo Emerson (1803–1882), who is best known for his essays and often thought to be the most influential American thinker and writer of his time, is also a poet of remarkable originality and subtlety. He is sometimes cast in the role of a poet's poet (his impact can be traced in the work of many nineteenth- and twentieth-century poets), but his unusual verse was also widely admired (and puzzled over) by the reading public on both sides of the Atlantic.

Emerson was born on Election Day (May 25) into an old and prominent Boston family. His father, who died when Emerson was eight, was a Unitarian minister who came from a long line of ministers. Emerson was sent to the Boston Latin School, where at the age of eight he began writing verses. In 1817 he entered Harvard, where he won prizes for his essays and oratory but was otherwise undistinguished as a scholar. Graduating in 1821, Emerson took up teaching, but soon returned to Harvard to enroll in the new Divinity School. He began preaching in 1826 and became pastor of the Second Church of Boston in 1829. In that year he married Ellen Tucker, who died of tuberculosis sixteen months later. Up to that point Emerson had led an entirely conventional life, and there was little to suggest his future eminence. Now, in his grief, coupled with doubts about administering communion as a sacrament, Emerson resigned his position at the Second Church and traveled to Europe. While overseas he met Wordsworth, Coleridge, and Carlyle (with whom he began a lengthy correspondence) and returned at the end of 1831 to take up a new career as a writer and lecturer. Settling in Concord, Massachusetts, Emerson married again in 1835 and entered upon the life's work that would make him famous.

Emerson's first book, *Nature*, was published in 1836. It was followed by a series of influential and controversial lectures, including "The American Scholar" and the "Divinity School Address" (for which he was banned from Harvard for almost thirty years). During this time the transcendentalist circle formed around Emerson; it included Fuller, Thoreau, Very, Channing, and others. In 1840 Emerson and Fuller founded the *Dial*, the transcendentalist journal; in 1842 he took over the editing. *Essays*, based on his lectures (which were mined from his journals), appeared in 1841, and *Essays: Second Series* was published in 1844. During this time Emerson continued to write poetry, and in 1846 he brought out his first collection, *Poems*, which went through four printings in the first year. Emerson lectured extensively and was a very popular speaker on the lyceum circuit. His increasing involvement in the abolitionist movement, however, continued to make him controversial, as did his championing of certain younger writers such as Thoreau, Channing, and Whitman.

In 1847 Emerson undertook a successful lecture tour in England and Scotland and later traveled on the Continent. While overseas he visited, among others, Dickens, Tennyson, Eliot, de Tocqueville, and Chopin, as well as Wordsworth, Carlyle, and De Quincey. In America, in addition to his lecturing in the East, Emerson traveled in the West (once as far as California) and in Canada. A man of considerable reputation by then, Emerson's books were eagerly read: in 1849 *Nature; Addresses, and Lectures* appeared, followed by *Representative Men* (1850), *English Traits* (1856), and *The Conduct of Life* (1860).

As the Civil War approached, Emerson became more involved in antislavery activities; and, when the war came, he was an ardent supporter of the Union cause. In 1862 he was introduced to President Lincoln in Washington and later wrote in support of the Emancipation Proclamation. *May-Day and Other Pieces*, Emerson's second collection of poems, was published in 1867, and in 1870 another volume of prose writings appeared, *Society and Solitude*. Emerson was now approaching old age, and his health and memory began to trouble him. After a fire at his home in Concord, Emerson and his daughter, Ellen, traveled to Europe and Egypt, and once again he was feted by many prominent writers. After his return in 1873 Emerson slowly began to decline. With help from a friend, James Cabot, Emerson brought out *Letters and Social Aims* (1875), and in the following year his *Selected Poems* was published. However, a weakening ability to concentrate soon brought an end to any new writing. Emerson lingered a long time in his twilight years, dying finally of pneumonia in 1882.

Each and All

Little thinks, in the field, yon red-cloaked clown,
Of thee from the hill-top looking down;
The heifer that lows in the upland farm,
Far-heard, lows not thine ear to charm;
The sexton, tolling his bell at noon,
Deems not that great Napoleon
Stops his horse, and lists with delight,
Whilst his files sweep round yon Alpine height;
Nor knowest thou what argument
Thy life to thy neighbor's creed has lent.
All are needed by each one;
Nothing is fair or good alone.
I thought the sparrow's note from heaven,
Singing at dawn on the alder bough;
I brought him home, in his nest, at even;
He sings the song, but it pleases not now,
For I did not bring home the river and sky;—
He sang to my ear,—they sang to my eye.
The delicate shells lay on the shore;
The bubbles of the latest wave
Fresh pearls to their enamel gave;
And the bellowing of the savage sea
Greeted their safe escape to me.
I wiped away the weeds and foam,
I fetched my sea-born treasures home;
But the poor, unsightly, noisome things
Had left their beauty on the shore,
With the sun, and the sand, and the wild uproar.
The lover watched his graceful maid,
As 'mid the virgin train she strayed,
Nor knew her beauty's best attire
Was woven still by the snow-white choir.
At last she came to his hermitage,
Like the bird from the woodlands to the cage;—
The gay enchantment was undone,
A gentle wife, but fairy none.
Then I said, 'I covet truth;

55

Beauty is unripe childhood's cheat;
I leave it behind with the games of youth.'—
As I spoke, beneath my feet
The ground-pine curled its pretty wreath,
Running over the club-moss burrs;
I inhaled the violet's breath;
Around me stood the oaks and firs;
Pine-cones and acorns lay on the ground,
Over me soared the eternal sky,
Full of light and of deity;
Again I saw, again I heard,
The rolling river, the morning bird;—
Beauty through my senses stole;
I yielded myself to the perfect whole.

The Problem

I like a church; I like a cowl;
I love a prophet of the soul;
And on my heart monastic aisles
Fall like sweet strains, or pensive smiles;
Yet not for all his faith can see
Would I that cowled churchman be.

Why should the vest on him allure,
Which I could not on me endure?

Not from a vain or shallow thought
His awful Jove young Phidias brought;
Never from lips of cunning fell
The thrilling Delphic oracle;
Out from the heart of nature rolled
The burdens of the Bible old;
The litanies of nations came,
Like the volcano's tongue of flame,
Up from the burning core below,—
The canticles of love and woe;
The hand that rounded Peter's dome,
And groined the aisles of Christian Rome,

Wrought in a sad sincerity;
Himself from God he could not free;
He builded better than he knew;—
The conscious stone to beauty grew.

Know'st thou what wove yon woodbird's nest
Of leaves, and feathers from her breast?
Or how the fish outbuilt her shell,
Painting with morn each annual cell?
Or how the sacred pine-tree adds
To her old leaves new myriads?
Such and so grew these holy piles,
Whilst love and terror laid the tiles.
Earth proudly wears the Parthenon,
As the best gem upon her zone;
And Morning opes with haste her lids,
To gaze upon the Pyramids;
O'er England's abbeys bends the sky,
As on its friends, with kindred eye;
For, out of Thought's interior sphere,
These wonders rose to upper air;
And Nature gladly gave them place,
Adopted them into her race,
And granted them an equal date
With Andes and with Ararat.

These temples grew as grows the grass;
Art might obey, but not surpass.
The passive Master lent his hand
To the vast soul that o'er him planned;
And the same power that reared the shrine,
Bestrode the tribes that knelt within.
Ever the fiery Pentecost
Girds with one flame the countless host,
Trances the heart through chanting choirs,
And through the priest the mind inspires.
The word unto the prophet spoken
Was writ on tables yet unbroken;
The word by seers or sibyls told,
In groves of oak, or fanes of gold,

Still floats upon the morning wind,
Still whispers to the willing mind.
One accent of the Holy Ghost
The heedless world hath never lost.
I know what say the fathers wise,—
The Book itself before me lies,
Old *Chrysostom*, best Augustine,
And he who blent both in his line,
The younger *Golden Lips* or mines,
Taylor, the Shakspeare of divines.
His words are music in my ear,
I see his cowled portrait dear;
And yet, for all his faith could see,
I would not the good bishop be.

The Visit

Askest, 'How long thou shalt stay,'
Devastator of the day?
Know, each substance, and relation,
Thorough nature's operation,
Hath its unit, bound, and metre;
And every new compound
Is some product and repeater,—
Product of the early found.
But the unit of the visit,
The encounter of the wise,—
Say, what other metre is it
Than the meeting of the eyes?
Nature poureth into nature
Through the channels of that feature.
Riding on the ray of sight,
More fleet than waves or whirlwinds go,
Or for service, or delight,
Hearts to hearts their meaning show,
Sum their long experience,
And import intelligence.
Single look has drained the breast;
Single moment years confessed.

The duration of a glance
Is the term of covenance,
And, though thy rede be church or state,
Frugal multiples of that.
Speeding Saturn cannot halt;
Linger,—thou shalt rue the fault;
If Love his moment overstay,
Hatred's swift repulsions play.

Uriel

It fell in the ancient periods,
    Which the brooding soul surveys,
Or ever the wild Time coined itself
    Into calendar months and days.

This was the lapse of Uriel,
Which in Paradise befell.
Once, among the Pleiads walking,
SAID overheard the young gods talking;
And the treason, too long pent,
To his ears was evident.
The young deities discussed
Laws of form, and metre just,
Orb, quintessence, and sunbeams,
What subsisteth, and what seems.
One, with low tones that decide,
And doubt and reverend use defied,
With a look that solved the sphere,
And stirred the devils everywhere,
Gave his sentiment divine
Against the being of a line.
'Line in nature is not found;
Unit and universe are round;
In vain produced, all rays return;
Evil will bless, and ice will burn.'
As Uriel spoke with piercing eye,
A shudder ran around the sky;
The stern old war-gods shook their heads;

59

The seraphs frowned from myrtle-beds;
Seemed to the holy festival
The rash word boded ill to all;
The balance-beam of Fate was bent;
The bounds of good and ill were rent;
Strong Hades could not keep his own,
But all slid to confusion.

A sad self-knowledge, withering, fell
On the beauty of Uriel;
In heaven once eminent, the god
Withdrew, that hour, into his cloud;
Whether doomed to long gyration
In the sea of generation,
Or by knowledge grown too bright
To hit the nerve of feebler sight.
Straightway, a forgetting wind
Stole over the celestial kind,
And their lips the secret kept,
If in ashes the fire-seed slept.
But now and then, truth-speaking things
Shamed the angels' veiling wings;
And, shrilling from the solar course,
Or from fruit of chemic force,
Procession of a soul in matter,
Or the speeding change of water,
Or out of the good of evil born,
Came Uriel's voice of cherub scorn,
And a blush tinged the upper sky,
And the gods shook, they knew not why.

Hamatreya

Minott, Lee, Willard, Hosmer, Meriam, Flint
Possessed the land which rendered to their toil
Hay, corn, roots, hemp, flax, apples, wool, and wood.
Each of these landlords walked amidst his farm,
Saying, ''Tis mine, my children's, and my name's:
How sweet the west wind sounds in my own trees!

How graceful climb those shadows on my hill!
I fancy these pure waters and the flags
Know me, as does my dog: we sympathize;
And, I affirm, my actions smack of the soil.'
Where are these men? Asleep beneath their grounds;
And strangers, fond as they, their furrows plough.
Earth laughs in flowers, to see her boastful boys
Earth-proud, proud of the earth which is not theirs;
Who steer the plough, but cannot steer their feet
Clear of the grave.
They added ridge to valley, brook to pond,
And sighed for all that bounded their domain.
'This suits me for a pasture; that's my park;
We must have clay, lime, gravel, granite-ledge,
And misty lowland, where to go for peat.
The land is well,—lies fairly to the south.
'Tis good, when you have crossed the sea and back,
To find the sitfast acres where you left them.'
Ah! the hot owner sees not Death, who adds
Him to his land, a lump of mould the more.
Hear what the Earth says:—

EARTH-SONG

'Mine and yours;
Mine, not yours.
Earth endures;
Stars abide—
Shine down in the old sea;
Old are the shores;
But where are old men?
I who have seen much,
Such have I never seen.

'The lawyer's deed
Ran sure,
In tail,
To them, and to their heirs
Who shall succeed,
Without fail,
Forevermore.

'Here is the land,
Shaggy with wood,
With its old valley,
Mound, and flood.
But the heritors?
Fled like the flood's foam,—
The lawyer, and the laws,
And the kingdom,
Clean swept herefrom.

'They called me theirs,
Who so controlled me;
Yet every one
Wished to stay, and is gone.
How am I theirs,
If they cannot hold me,
But I hold them?'

When I heard the Earth-song,
I was no longer brave;
My avarice cooled
Like lust in the chill of the grave.

The Rhodora:

On Being Asked, Whence Is the Flower?

In May, when sea-winds pierced our solitudes,
I found the fresh Rhodora in the woods,
Spreading its leafless blooms in a damp nook,
To please the desert and the sluggish brook.
The purple petals, fallen in the pool,
Made the black water with their beauty gay;
Here might the red-bird come his plumes to cool,
And court the flower that cheapens his array.
Rhodora! if the sages ask thee why
This charm is wasted on the earth and sky,
Tell them, dear, that if eyes were made for seeing,
Then Beauty is its own excuse for being:
Why thou wert there, O rival of the rose!

I never thought to ask, I never knew;
But, in my simple ignorance, suppose
The self-same Power that brought me there brought you.

The Snow-Storm

Announced by all the trumpets of the sky,
Arrives the snow, and, driving o'er the fields,
Seems nowhere to alight: the whited air
Hides hills and woods, the river, and the heaven,
And veils the farm-house at the garden's end.
The sled and traveller stopped, the courier's feet
Delayed, all friends shut out, the housemates sit
Around the radiant fireplace, enclosed
In a tumultuous privacy of storm.

Come see the north wind's masonry.
Out of an unseen quarry evermore
Furnished with tile, the fierce artificer
Curves his white bastions with projected roof
Round every windward stake, or tree, or door.
Speeding, the myriad-handed, his wild work
So fanciful, so savage, nought cares he
For number or proportion. Mockingly,
On coop or kennel he hangs Parian wreaths;
A swan-like form invests the hidden thorn;
Fills up the farmer's lane from wall to wall,
Maugre the farmer's sighs; and, at the gate,
A tapering turret overtops the work.
And when his hours are numbered, and the world
Is all his own, retiring, as he were not,
Leaves, when the sun appears, astonished Art
To mimic in slow structures, stone by stone,
Built in an age, the mad wind's night-work,
The frolic architecture of the snow.

Ode,
Inscribed to W. H. Channing

Though loath to grieve
The evil time's sole patriot,
I cannot leave
My honied thought
For the priest's cant,
Or statesman's rant.

If I refuse
My study for their politique,
Which at the best is trick,
The angry Muse
Puts confusion in my brain.

But who is he that prates
Of the culture of mankind,
Of better arts and life?
Go, blindworm, go,
Behold the famous States
Harrying Mexico
With rifle and with knife!

Or who, with accent bolder,
Dare praise the freedom-loving mountaineer?
I found by thee, O rushing Contoocook!
And in thy valleys, Agiochook!
The jackals of the negro-holder.

The God who made New Hampshire
Taunted the lofty land
With little men;—
Small bat and wren
House in the oak:—
If earth-fire cleave
The upheaved land, and bury the folk,
The southern crocodile would grieve.

Virtue palters; Right is hence;
Freedom praised, but hid;
Funeral eloquence
Rattles the coffin-lid.

What boots thy zeal,
O glowing friend,
That would indignant rend
The northland from the south?
Wherefore? to what good end?
Boston Bay and Bunker Hill
Would serve things still;—
Things are of the snake.

The horseman serves the horse,
The neatherd serves the neat,
The merchant serves the purse,
The eater serves his meat;
'Tis the day of the chattel,
Web to weave, and corn to grind;
Things are in the saddle,
And ride mankind.

These are two laws discrete,
Not reconciled,—
Law for man, and law for thing;
The last builds town and fleet,
But it runs wild,
And doth the man unking.

'Tis fit the forest fall,
The steep be graded,
The mountain tunnelled,
The sand shaded,
The orchard planted,
The glebe tilled,
The prairie granted,
The steamer built.

Let man serve law for man;
Live for friendship, live for love,
For truth's and harmony's behoof;
The state may follow how it can,
As Olympus follows Jove.

    Yet do not I invite
The wrinkled shopman to my sounding woods,
Nor bid the unwilling senator
Ask votes of thrushes in the solitudes.
Every one to his chosen work;—
Foolish hands may mix and mar;
Wise and sure the issues are.
Round they roll till dark is light,
Sex to sex, and even to odd;—
The over-god
Who marries Right to Might,
Who peoples, unpeoples,—
He who exterminates
Races by stronger races,
Black by white faces,—
Knows to bring honey
Out of the lion;
Grafts gentlest scion
On pirate and Turk.

The Cossack eats Poland,
Like stolen fruit;
Her last noble is ruined,
Her last poet mute:
Straight, into double band
The victors divide;
Half for freedom strike and stand;—
The astonished Muse finds thousands at her side.

Merlin I

Thy trivial harp will never please
Or fill my craving ear;
Its chords should ring as blows the breeze,
Free, peremptory, clear.
No jingling serenader's art,
Nor tinkle of piano strings,
Can make the wild blood start
In its mystic springs.
The kingly bard
Must smite the chords rudely and hard,
As with hammer or with mace;
That they may render back
Artful thunder, which conveys
Secrets of the solar track,
Sparks of the supersolar blaze.
Merlin's blows are strokes of fate,
Chiming with the forest tone,
When boughs buffet boughs in the wood;
Chiming with the gasp and moan
Of the ice-imprisoned flood;
With the pulse of manly hearts;
With the voice of orators;
With the din of city arts;
With the cannonade of wars;
With the marches of the brave;
And prayers of might from martyrs' cave.

Great is the art,
Great be the manners, of the bard.
He shall not his brain encumber
With the coil of rhythm and number;
But, leaving rule and pale forethought,
He shall aye climb
For his rhyme.
'Pass in, pass in,' the angels say,
'In to the upper doors,

Nor count compartments of the floors,
But mount to paradise
By the stairway of surprise.'

Blameless master of the games,
King of sport that never shames,
He shall daily joy dispense
Hid in song's sweet influence.
Things more cheerly live and go,
What time the subtle mind
Sings aloud the tune whereto
Their pulses beat,
And march their feet,
And their members are combined.

By Sybarites beguiled,
He shall no task decline;
Merlin's mighty line
Extremes of nature reconciled,—
Bereaved a tyrant of his will,
And made the lion mild.
Songs can the tempest still,
Scattered on the stormy air,
Mould the year to fair increase,
And bring in poetic peace.

He shall not seek to weave,
In weak, unhappy times,
Efficacious rhymes;
Wait his returning strength.
Bird, that from the nadir's floor
To the zenith's top can soar,
The soaring orbit of the muse exceeds that journey's length.
Nor profane affect to hit
Or compass that, by meddling wit,
Which only the propitious mind
Publishes when 'tis inclined.
There are open hours
When the God's will sallies free,
And the dull idiot might see

The flowing fortunes of a thousand years;—
Sudden, at unawares,
Self-moved, fly-to the doors,
Nor sword of angels could reveal
What they conceal.

Merlin II

The rhyme of the poet
Modulates the king's affairs;
Balance-loving Nature
Made all things in pairs.
To every foot its antipode;
Each color with its counter glowed;
To every tone beat answering tones,
Higher or graver;
Flavor gladly blends with flavor;
Leaf answers leaf upon the bough;
And match the paired cotyledons.
Hands to hands, and feet to feet,
Coeval grooms and brides;
Eldest rite, two married sides
In every mortal meet.
Light's far furnace shines,
Smelting balls and bars,
Forging double stars,
Glittering twins and trines.
The animals are sick with love,
Lovesick with rhyme;
Each with all propitious time
Into chorus wove.

Like the dancers' ordered band,
Thoughts come also hand in hand;
In equal couples mated,
Or else alternated;
Adding by their mutual gage,
One to other, health and age.
Solitary fancies go

Short-lived wandering to and fro,
Most like to bachelors,
Or an ungiven maid,
Not ancestors,
With no posterity to make the lie afraid,
Or keep truth undecayed.
Perfect-paired as eagle's wings,

Justice is the rhyme of things;
Trade and counting use
The self-same tuneful muse;
And Nemesis,
Who with even matches odd,
Who athwart space redresses
The partial wrong,
Fills the just period,
And finishes the song.

Subtle rhymes, with ruin rife,
Murmur in the house of life,
Sung by the Sisters as they spin;
In perfect time and measure they
Build and unbuild our echoing clay,
As the two twilights of the day
Fold us music-drunken in.

Bacchus

Bring me wine, but wine which never grew
In the belly of the grape,
Or grew on vine whose tap-roots, reaching through
Under the Andes to the Cape,
Suffered no savor of the earth to scape.

Let its grapes the morn salute
From a nocturnal root,
Which feels the acrid juice
Of Styx and Erebus;
And turns the woe of Night,
By its own craft, to a more rich delight.

We buy ashes for bread;
We buy diluted wine;
Give me of the true,—
Whose ample leaves and tendrils curled
Among the silver hills of heaven,
Draw everlasting dew;
Wine of wine,
Blood of the world,
Form of forms, and mould of statures,
That I intoxicated,
And by the draught assimilated,
May float at pleasure through all natures;
The bird-language rightly spell,
And that which roses say so well.

Wine that is shed
Like the torrents of the sun
Up the horizon walls,
Or like the Atlantic streams, which run
When the South Sea calls.

Water and bread,
Food which needs no transmuting,
Rainbow-flowering, wisdom-fruiting
Wine which is already man,
Food which teach and reason can.

Wine which Music is,—
Music and wine are one,—
That I, drinking this,
Shall hear far Chaos talk with me;
Kings unborn shall walk with me;
And the poor grass shall plot and plan
What it will do when it is man.
Quickened so, will I unlock
Every crypt of every rock.

I thank the joyful juice
For all I know;—
Winds of remembering

Of the ancient being blow,
And seeming-solid walls of use
Open and flow.

Pour, Bacchus! the remembering wine;
Retrieve the loss of me and mine!
Vine for vine be antidote,
And the grape requite the lote!
Haste to cure the old despair,—
Reason in Nature's lotus drenched,
The memory of ages quenched;
Give them again to shine;
Let wine repair what this undid;
And where the infection slid,
A dazzling memory revive;
Refresh the faded tints,
Recut the aged prints,
And write my old adventures with the pen
Which on the first day drew,
Upon the tablets blue,
The dancing Pleiads and eternal men.

Musketaquid

Because I was content with these poor fields,
Low, open meads, slender and sluggish streams,
And found a home in haunts which others scorned,
The partial wood-gods overpaid my love,
And granted me the freedom of their state,
And in their secret senate have prevailed
With the dear, dangerous lords that rule our life,
Made moon and planets parties to their bond,
And through my rock-like, solitary wont
Shot million rays of thought and tenderness.
For me, in showers, in sweeping showers, the spring
Visits the valley;—break away the clouds,—
I bathe in the morn's soft and silvered air,
And loiter willing by yon loitering stream.
Sparrows far off, and nearer, April's bird,

Blue-coated,—flying before from tree to tree,
Courageous, sing a delicate overture
To lead the tardy concert of the year.
Onward and nearer rides the sun of May;
And wide around, the marriage of the plants
Is sweetly solemnized. Then flows amain
The surge of summer's beauty; dell and crag,
Hollow and lake, hill-side, and pine arcade,
Are touched with genius. Yonder ragged cliff
Has thousand faces in a thousand hours.

Beneath low hills, in the broad interval
Through which at will our Indian rivulet
Winds mindful still of sannup and of squaw,
Whose pipe and arrow oft the plough unburies,
Here in pine houses built of new fallen trees,
Supplanters of the tribe, the farmers dwell.
Traveller, to thee, perchance, a tedious road,
Or, it may be, a picture; to these men,
The landscape is an armory of powers,
Which, one by one, they know to draw and use.
They harness beast, bird, insect, to their work;
They prove the virtues of each bed of rock,
And, like the chemist mid his loaded jars,
Draw from each stratum its adapted use
To drug their crops or weapon their arts withal.
They turn the frost upon their chemic heap,
They set the wind to winnow pulse and grain,
They thank the spring-flood for its fertile slime,
And, on cheap summit-levels of the snow,
Slide with the sledge to inaccessible woods
O'er meadows bottomless. So, year by year,
They fight the elements with elements,
(That one would say, meadow and forest walked,
Transmuted in these men to rule their like,)
And by the order in the field disclose
The order regnant in the yeoman's brain.

What these strong masters wrote at large in miles,
I followed in small copy in my acre;

For there's no rood has not a star above it;
The cordial quality of pear or plum
Ascends as gladly in a single tree
As in broad orchards resonant with bees;
And every atom poises for itself,
And for the whole. The gentle deities
Showed me the lore of colors and of sounds,
The innumerable tenements of beauty,
The miracle of generative force,
Far-reaching concords of astronomy
Felt in the plants, and in the punctual birds;
Better, the linked purpose of the whole,
And, chiefest prize, found I true liberty
In the glad home plain-dealing nature gave.
The polite found me impolite; the great
Would mortify me, but in vain; for still
I am a willow of the wilderness,
Loving the wind that bent me. All my hurts
My garden spade can heal. A woodland walk,
A quest of river-grapes, a mocking thrush,
A wild-rose, or rock-loving columbine,
Salve my worst wounds.
For thus the wood-gods murmured in my ear:
'Dost love our manners? Canst thou silent lie?
Canst thou, thy pride forgot, like nature pass
Into the winter night's extinguished mood?
Canst thou shine now, then darkle,
And being latent feel thyself no less?
As, when the all-worshipped moon attracts the eye,
The river hill, stems, foliage are obscure
Yet envies none, none are unenviable.'

Hymn:

Sung at the Completion of the Concord Monument, April 19, 1836

By the rude bridge that arched the flood,
   Their flag to April's breeze unfurled,
Here once the embattled farmers stood,
    And fired the shot heard round the world.

The foe long since in silence slept;
　　Alike the conqueror silent sleeps;
And Time the ruined bridge has swept
　　Down the dark stream which seaward creeps.

On this green bank, by this soft stream,
　　We set to-day a votive stone;
That memory may their deed redeem,
　　When, like our sires, our sons are gone.

Spirit, that made those heroes dare
　　To die, or leave their children free,
Bid Time and Nature gently spare
　　The shaft we raise to them and thee.

Brahma

If the red slayer think he slays,
　　Or if the slain think he is slain,
They know not well the subtle ways
　　I keep, and pass, and turn again.

Far or forgot to me is near;
　　Shadow and sunlight are the same;
The vanished gods to me appear;
　　And one to me are shame and fame.

They reckon ill who leave me out;
　　When me they fly, I am the wings;
I am the doubter and the doubt,
　　And I the hymn the Brahmin sings.

The strong gods pine for my abode,
　　And pine in vain the sacred Seven;
But thou, meek lover of the good!
　　Find me, and turn thy back on heaven.

Days

Daughters of Time, the hypocritic Days,
Muffled and dumb like barefoot dervishes,
And marching single in an endless file,
Bring diadems and fagots in their hands.
To each they offer gifts after his will,
Bread, kingdoms, stars, and sky that holds them all.
I, in my pleached garden, watched the pomp,
Forgot my morning wishes, hastily
Took a few herbs and apples, and the Day
Turned and departed silent. I, too late,
Under her solemn fillet saw the scorn.

Waldeinsamkeit

I do not count the hours I spend
In wandering by the sea;
The forest is my loyal friend,
Like God it useth me.

In plains that room for shadows make
Of skirting hills to lie,
Bound in by streams which give and take
Their colors from the sky;

Or on the mountain-crest sublime,
Or down the oaken glade,
O what have I to do with time?
For this the day was made.

Cities of mortals woe-begone
Fantastic care derides,
But in the serious landscape lone
Stern benefit abides.

Sheen will tarnish, honey cloy,
And merry is only a mask of sad,
But, sober on a fund of joy,
The woods at heart are glad.

There the great Planter plants
Of fruitful worlds the grain,
And with a million spells enchants
The souls that walk in pain.

Still on the seeds of all he made
The rose of beauty burns;
Through times that wear, and forms that fade,
Immortal youth returns.

The black ducks mounting from the lake,
The pigeon in the pines,
The bittern's boom, a desert make
Which no false art refines.

Down in yon watery nook,
Where bearded mists divide,
The gray old gods whom Chaos knew,
The sires of Nature, hide.

Aloft, in secret veins of air,
Blows the sweet breath of song,
O, few to scale those uplands dare,
Though they to all belong!

See thou bring not to field or stone
The fancies found in books;
Leave authors' eyes, and fetch your own,
To brave the landscape's looks.

And if, amid this dear delight,
My thoughts did home rebound,
I well might reckon it a slight
To the high cheer I found.

Oblivion here thy wisdom is,
Thy thrift, the sleep of cares;
For a proud idleness like this
Crowns all thy mean affairs.

Compensation

I.

The wings of Time are black and white,
Pied with morning and with night.
Mountain tall and ocean deep
Trembling balance duly keep.
In changing moon and tidal wave
Glows the feud of Want and Have.
Gauge of more and less through space,
Electric star or pencil plays,
The lonely Earth amid the balls
That hurry through the eternal halls,
A makeweight flying to the void,
Supplemental asteroid,
Or compensatory spark,
Shoots across the neutral Dark.

II.

Man's the elm, and Wealth the vine;
Stanch and strong the tendrils twine:
Though the frail ringlets thee deceive,
None from its stock that vine can reave.
Fear not, then, thou child infirm,
There's no god dare wrong a worm;
Laurel crowns cleave to deserts,
And power to him who power exerts.
Hast not thy share? On winged feet,
Lo! it rushes thee to meet;
And all that Nature made thy own,
Floating in air or pent in stone,
Will rive the hills and swim the sea,
And, like thy shadow, follow thee.

"Awed I behold once more"

Awed I behold once more
My old familiar haunts; here the blue river
The same blue wonder that my infant eye
Admired, sage doubting whence the traveller came,—
Whence brought his sunny bubbles ere he washed
The fragrant flag roots in my father's fields,
And where thereafter in the world he went.
Look, here he is unaltered, save that now
He hath broke his banks & flooded all the vales
With his redundant waves.

Here is the rock where yet a simple child
I caught with bended pin my earliest fish,
Much triumphing,—And these the fields
Over whose flowers I chased the butterfly,
A blooming hunter of a fairy fine.
And hark! where overhead the ancient crows
Hold their sour conversation in the sky.
        These are the same, but I am not the same
But wiser than I was, & wise enough
Not to regret the changes, tho' they cost
Me many a sigh. Oh call not Nature dumb;
These trees & stones are audible to me,
These idle flowers, that tremble in the wind,
I understand their faery syllables,
And all their sad significance. This wind,
That rustles down the well-known forest road—
It hath a sound more eloquent than speech.
The stream, the trees, the grass, the sighing wind,
All of them utter sounds of admonishment
And grave parental love.

They are not of our race, they seem to say,
And yet have knowledge of our moral race,
And somewhat of majestic sympathy,
Something of pity for the puny clay,
That holds & boasts the immeasureable mind.

I feel as if I were welcome to these trees
After long months of weary wandering,
Acknowledged by their hospitable boughs;
They know me as their son, for side by side,
They were coeval with my ancestors,
Adorned with them my country's primitive times,
And soon may give my dust their funeral shade.

"Teach me I am forgotten by the dead"

Teach me I am forgotten by the dead
And that the dead is by herself forgot
And I no longer would keep terms with me.
I would not murder, steal, or fornicate,
Nor with ambition break the peace of towns
But I would bury my ambition
The hope & action of my sovereign soul
In miserable ruin. Nor a hope
Should ever make a holiday for me
I would not be the fool of accident
I would not have a project seek an end
That needed aught
Beyond the handful of my present means
The sun of Duty drop from his firmament
To be a rushlight for each petty end
I would not harm my fellow men
On this low argument, *'twould harm myself*

Maia

Illusion works impenetrable,
Weaving webs innumerable,
Her gay pictures never fail,
Crowds each on other, veil on veil,
Charmer who will be believed
By Man who thirsts to be deceived.

NATHANIEL HAWTHORNE

Nathaniel Hawthorne (1804–1864) was once described by James Russell Lowell as "the greatest poet, though he wrote in prose . . . that America has given the world." Indeed, Hawthorne is best remembered for his novels and stories, but his few poems (there are only twenty-nine extant) cast a curious light on his sensibility, revealing a brooding intensity that similarly marks his rich prose.

Hawthorne was born in Salem, Massachusetts, the son of a sea captain who died when Hawthorne was four years old. After a childhood spent with his reclusive mother, Hawthorne eventually went on to Bowdoin College in Maine, where he was befriended by classmates Henry Wadsworth Longfellow and Franklin Pierce (the future president). After a brief and unlikely stay at the transcendentalist utopian community, Brook Farm, Hawthorne married Sophia Peabody of Salem in 1842 and settled for three years in Concord, where he rented Emerson's ancestral home, the Old Manse.

Although Hawthorne became a famous writer in his own time, his career developed slowly and not without some shrewd self-promotion. The work that clinched his fame, *The Scarlet Letter* (1850), was published late in his life when he was forty-six. In 1852 Hawthorne wrote the campaign biography for Franklin Pierce and was subsequently rewarded with a consulship at Liverpool, England (1853–1857). After various travels in Europe he and his family returned to Concord in 1860, where he worked on a number of literary projects, many of which were left unfinished at the time of his death. Hawthorne cultivated the public image of a shy and sensitive loner, but his many acquaintances included prominent writers of the period, among them Emerson, Melville, Holmes, Longfellow, Thoreau, and Lowell—all of whom admired his work.

"Oh could I raise the darken'd veil"

Oh could I raise the darken'd veil,
Which hides my future life from me,
Could unborn ages slowly sail,
Before my view—and could I see
My every action painted there,
To cast one look I would not dare.
There poverty and grief might stand,
And dark Despair's corroding hand,
Would make me seek the lonely tomb
To slumber in its endless gloom.
Then let me never cast a look,
Within Fate's fix'd mysterious book.

The Ocean

The Ocean has its silent caves,
Deep, quiet and alone;
Though there be fury on the waves,
Beneath them there is none. — peace
The awful spirits of the deep
Hold their communion there;
And there are those for whom we weep,
The young, the bright, the fair.

Calmly the wearied seamen rest
Beneath their own blue sea
The ocean solitudes are blest,
For there is purity.
The earth has guilt, the earth has care,
Unquiet are its graves;
But peaceful sleep is ever there,
Beneath the dark blue waves.

"Oh, Man can seek the downward glance"

Oh, Man can seek the downward glance,
    And each kind word—affection's spell—
Eye, voice, its value can enhance;
    For eye may speak, and tongue can tell.

But Woman's love, it waits the while
    To echo to another's tone,
To linger on another's smile
    Ere dare to answer with its own.

HENRY WADSWORTH LONGFELLOW

Henry Wadsworth Longfellow (1807–1882) was a remarkably prolific writer and translator and the most famous American poet of his time. For generations students grew up memorizing and reciting his poems, some of which have entered into the fabric of American culture, particularly his historical narratives (including *Evangeline, The Song of Hiawatha*, "The Courtship of Miles Standish," and "The Midnight Ride of Paul Revere"). The popularity of Longfellow's work was itself a phenomenon, and his seventy-fifth birthday was cause for national celebration. Longfellow's success in bringing a wide readership to a wide range of poetry should not be underestimated for the cultural work it accomplished. Poetry was a vibrant and popular medium in his day in part because he made it so.

Longfellow attended Bowdoin College in Maine, where he was a classmate of Nathaniel Hawthorne. Longfellow's aptitude for foreign languages quickly became evident, and after his graduation Bowdoin hired him to fill the newly instituted chair of modern languages. Sent to Europe for further studies by the college, Longfellow spent three years in France, Spain, Italy, and Germany. Soon after his return he married and settled down to teach and write textbooks and scholarly articles. In 1835 he was appointed to the chair of modern languages at Harvard and again went to Europe for additional studies. During a stay in Holland his wife suffered a miscarriage and died from complications. Grieving for his wife, he continued on to Germany, where he met William Cullen Bryant and, later, his future second wife, Fanny Appleton.

Upon his return to Harvard he began to publish poems and to attain some fame (particularly for "The Psalm of Life"). Thereafter Longfellow's poetic output accelerated, and he published numerous volumes between 1841 and 1882 (the year of his death). During his lifetime Longfellow published more than forty books, which included language grammars, translations, travel books, plays, collections of verse, and individual book-length poems. Longfellow's second marriage in 1843 made him a wealthy man and allowed him, twelve years later, to resign his position at Harvard and concentrate solely on his writing. Craigie House in Cambridge, where the Longfellows lived, became a meeting place for many eminent writers, scholars, and politicians. In 1861 his wife died after her dress caught on fire while she was working with candle wax. Longfellow himself was badly burned in his attempt to save her. To assuage his grief, Longfellow began a translation of Dante's *Divine Comedy*, which remains one of the best verse translations in English. For the next fifteen years Longfellow continued writing a steady flow of poetry. After a period of illness he died at the age of seventy-five.

Longfellow's reputation as a poet rose to rare heights (he is one of the few Americans honored with a bust in the Poet's Corner at Westminster Abbey), but in the twentieth century his fame fell to an almost equivalent degree: he simply plummeted out of fashion. When a more judicious appraisal of his work finally prevails, Longfellow will undoubtedly be seen as a major American poet whose narrative gifts and mastery of poetic technique place him at the junction between the popular forms of fiction and poetry. His readership was immense and his influence on nineteenth-century American culture virtually incalculable.

A Psalm of Life

What the Heart of the Young Man Said to the Psalmist

Tell me not, in mournful numbers,
    Life is but an empty dream!
For the soul is dead that slumbers,
    And things are not what they seem.

Life is real! Life is earnest!
    And the grave is not its goal;
Dust thou art, to dust returnest,
    Was not spoken of the soul.

Not enjoyment, and not sorrow,
    Is our destined end or way;
But to act, that each to-morrow
    Find us farther than to-day.

Art is long, and Time is fleeting,
    And our hearts, though stout and brave,
Still, like muffled drums, are beating
    Funeral marches to the grave.

In the world's broad field of battle,
    In the bivouac of Life,
Be not like dumb, driven cattle!
    Be a hero in the strife!

Trust no Future, howe'er pleasant!
    Let the dead Past bury its dead!
Act,—act in the living Present!
    Heart within, and God o'erhead!

Lives of great men all remind us
    We can make our lives sublime,
And, departing, leave behind us
    Footprints on the sands of time;

Footprints, that perhaps another,
    Sailing o'er life's solemn main,
A forlorn and shipwrecked brother,
    Seeing, shall take heart again.

Let us, then, be up and doing,
    With a heart for any fate;
Still achieving, still pursuing,
    Learn to labor and to wait.

The Wreck of the Hesperus

It was the schooner Hesperus,
    That sailed the wintry sea;
And the skipper had taken his little daughtèr,
    To bear him company.

Blue were her eyes as the fairy-flax,
    Her cheeks like the dawn of day,
And her bosom white as the hawthorn buds,
    That ope in the month of May.

The skipper he stood beside the helm,
    His pipe was in his mouth,
And he watched how the veering flaw did blow
    The smoke now West, now South.

Then up and spake an old Sailòr,
    Had sailed the Spanish Main,
"I pray thee, put into yonder port,
    For I fear a hurricane.

"Last night, the moon had a golden ring,
    And to-night no moon we see!"
The skipper, he blew a whiff from his pipe,
    And a scornful laugh laughed he.

Colder and louder blew the wind,
    A gale from the Northeast;
The snow fell hissing in the brine,
    And the billows frothed like yeast.

Down came the storm, and smote amain,
    The vessel in its strength;
She shuddered and paused, like a frighted steed,
    Then leaped her cable's length.

"Come hither! come hither! my little daughtèr,
    And do not tremble so;
For I can weather the roughest gale,
    That ever wind did blow."

He wrapped her warm in his seaman's coat
    Against the stinging blast;
He cut a rope from a broken spar,
    And bound her to the mast.

"O father! I hear the church-bells ring,
    O say, what may it be?"
"'T is a fog-bell on a rock-bound coast!"—
    And he steered for the open sea.

"O father! I hear the sound of guns,
    O say, what may it be?"
"Some ship in distress, that cannot live
    In such an angry sea!"

"O father! I see a gleaming light,
    O say, what may it be?"
But the father answered never a word,
    A frozen corpse was he.

Lashed to the helm, all stiff and stark,
    With his face turned to the skies,
The lantern gleamed through the gleaming snow
    On his fixed and glassy eyes.

Then the maiden clasped her hands and prayed
    That savèd she might be;
And she thought of Christ, who stilled the wave
    On the Lake of Galilee.

And fast through the midnight dark and drear,
    Through the whistling sleet and snow,
Like a sheeted ghost, the vessel swept
    Towards the reef of Norman's Woe.

And ever the fitful gusts between
    A sound came from the land;
It was the sound of the trampling surf,
    On the rocks and the hard sea-sand.

The breakers were right beneath her bows,
    She drifted a dreary wreck,
And a whooping billow swept the crew
    Like icicles from her deck.

She struck where the white and fleecy waves
    Looked soft as carded wool,
But the cruel rocks, they gored her side
    Like the horns of an angry bull.

Her rattling shrouds, all sheathed in ice,
    With the masts went by the board;
Like a vessel of glass, she stove and sank,
    Ho! ho! the breakers roared!

At daybreak, on the bleak sea-beach,
    A fisherman stood aghast,
To see the form of a maiden fair,
    Lashed close to a drifting mast.

The salt-sea was frozen on her breast,
    The salt tears in her eyes;
And he saw her hair, like the brown sea-weed,
    On the billows fall and rise.

Such was the wreck of the Hesperus,
    In the midnight and the snow!
Christ save us all from a death like this,
    On the reef of Norman's Woe!

The Village Blacksmith

Under a spreading chestnut tree
    The village smithy stands;
The smith, a mighty man is he,
    With large and sinewy hands;
And the muscles of his brawny arms
    Are strong as iron bands.

His hair is crisp, and black, and long,
    His face is like the tan;
His brow is wet with honest sweat,
    He earns whate'er he can,
And looks the whole world in the face,
    For he owes not any man.

Week in, week out, from morn till night,
    You can hear his bellows blow;
You can hear him swing his heavy sledge,
    With measured beat and slow,
Like a sexton ringing the village bell,
    When the evening sun is low.

And children coming home from school
    Look in at the open door;
They love to see the flaming forge,
    And hear the bellows roar,
And catch the burning sparks that fly
    Like chaff from a threshing floor.

He goes on Sunday to the church,
    And sits among his boys;
He hears the parson pray and preach,
    He hears his daughter's voice,
Singing in the village choir,
    And it makes his heart rejoice.

It sounds to him like her mother's voice,
    Singing in Paradise!
He needs must think of her once more,
    How in the grave she lies;
And with his hard, rough hand he wipes
    A tear out of his eyes.

Toiling,—rejoicing,—sorrowing,
    Onward through life he goes;
Each morning sees some task begin,
    Each evening sees it close;
Something attempted, something done,
    Has earned a night's repose.

Thanks, thanks to thee, my worthy friend,
    For the lesson thou hast taught!
Thus at the flaming forge of life
    Our fortunes must be wrought;
Thus on its sounding anvil shaped
    Each burning deed and thought!

The Warning

Beware! The Israelite of old, who tore
    The lion in his path,—when, poor and blind,
He saw the blessed light of heaven no more,
    Shorn of his noble strength and forced to grind
In prison, and at last led forth to be
A pander to Philistine revelry,—

Upon the pillars of the temple laid
    His desperate hands, and in its overthrow
Destroyed himself, and with him those who made
    A cruel mockery of his sightless woe;
The poor, blind Slave, the scoff and jest of all,
Expired, and thousands perished in the fall!

There is a poor, blind Samson in this land,
    Shorn of his strength, and bound in bonds of steel,
Who may, in some grim revel, raise his hand,
    And shake the pillars of this Commonweal,
Till the vast Temple of our liberties
A shapeless mass of wreck and rubbish lies.

Mezzo Cammin

Boppard on the Rhine. August 25, 1842.

Half of my life is gone, and I have let
    The years slip from me and have not fulfilled
    The aspiration of my youth, to build
    Some tower of song with lofty parapet.
Not indolence, nor pleasure, nor the fret
    Of restless passions that would not be stilled,
    But sorrow, and a care that almost killed,
    Kept me from what I may accomplish yet;
Though, half-way up the hill, I see the Past
    Lying beneath me with its sounds and sights,—
    A city in the twilight dim and vast,
With smoking roofs, soft bells, and gleaming lights,—
    And hear above me on the autumnal blast
    The cataract of Death far thundering from the heights.

The Jewish Cemetery at Newport

How strange it seems! These Hebrews in their graves,
    Close by the street of this fair seaport town,
Silent beside the never-silent waves,
    At rest in all this moving up and down!

The trees are white with dust, that o'er their sleep
    Wave their broad curtains in the south-wind's breath,
While underneath such leafy tents they keep
    The long, mysterious Exodus of Death.

And these sepulchral stones, so old and brown,
    That pave with level flags their burial-place,
Seem like the tablets of the Law, thrown down
    And broken by Moses at the mountain's base.

The very names recorded here are strange,
    Of foreign accent, and of different climes;
Alvares and Rivera interchange
    With Abraham and Jacob of old times.

"Blessed be God! for he created Death!"
    The mourners said, "and Death is rest and peace";
Then added, in the certainty of faith,
    "And giveth Life that never more shall cease."

Closed are the portals of their Synagogue,
    No Psalms of David now the silence break,
No Rabbi reads the ancient Decalogue
    In the grand dialect the Prophets spake.

Gone are the living, but the dead remain,
    And not neglected; for a hand unseen,
Scattering its bounty, like a summer rain,
    Still keeps their graves and their remembrance green.

How came they here? What burst of Christian hate,
    What persecution, merciless and blind,
Drove o'er the sea—that desert desolate—
    These Ishmaels and Hagars of mankind?

They lived in narrow streets and lanes obscure,
    Ghetto and Judenstrass, in mirk and mire;
Taught in the school of patience to endure
    The life of anguish and the death of fire.

All their lives long, with the unleavened bread
    And bitter herbs of exile and its fears,
The wasting famine of the heart they fed,
    And slaked its thirst with marah of their tears.

Anathema maranatha! was the cry
    That rang from town to town, from street to street;
At every gate the accursed Mordecai
    Was mocked and jeered, and spurned by Christian feet.

Pride and humiliation hand in hand
    Walked with them through the world where'er they went;
Trampled and beaten were they as the sand,
    And yet unshaken as the continent.

For in the background figures vague and vast
    Of patriarchs and of prophets rose sublime,
And all the great traditions of the Past
    They saw reflected in the coming time.

And thus for ever with reverted look
    The mystic volume of the world they read,
Spelling it backward, like a Hebrew book,
    Till life became a Legend of the Dead.

But ah! what once has been shall be no more!
    The groaning earth in travail and in pain
Brings forth its races, but does not restore,
    And the dead nations never rise again.

My Lost Youth

Often I think of the beautiful town
    That is seated by the sea;
Often in thought go up and down
The pleasant streets of that dear old town,
    And my youth comes back to me.
        And a verse of a Lapland song
        Is haunting my memory still:
    "A boy's will is the wind's will,
And the thoughts of youth are long, long thoughts."

I can see the shadowy lines of its trees,
    And catch, in sudden gleams,
The sheen of the far-surrounding seas,
And islands that were the Hesperides
    Of all my boyish dreams.
      And the burden of that old song,
      It murmurs and whispers still:
   "A boy's will is the wind's will,
And the thoughts of youth are long, long thoughts."

I remember the black wharves and the slips,
    And the sea-tides tossing free;
And Spanish sailors with bearded lips,
And the beauty and mystery of the ships,
    And the magic of the sea.
      And the voice of that wayward song
      Is singing and saying still:
   "A boy's will is the wind's will,
And the thoughts of youth are long, long thoughts."

I remember the bulwarks by the shore,
    And the fort upon the hill;
The sun-rise gun, with its hollow roar,
The drum-beat repeated o'er and o'er,
    And the bugle wild and shrill.
      And the music of that old song
      Throbs in my memory still:
   "A boy's will is the wind's will,
And the thoughts of youth are long, long thoughts."

I remember the sea-fight far away,
    How it thundered o'er the tide!
And the dead captains, as they lay
In their graves, o'erlooking the tranquil bay,
    Where they in battle died.
      And the sound of that mournful song
      Goes through me with a thrill:
   "A boy's will is the wind's will,
And the thoughts of youth are long, long thoughts."

I can see the breezy dome of groves,
    The shadows of Deering's Woods;
And the friendships old and the early loves
Come back with a sabbath sound, as of doves
      In quiet neighborhoods.
        And the verse of that sweet old song,
        It flutters and murmurs still:
    "A boy's will is the wind's will,
And the thoughts of youth are long, long thoughts."

I remember the gleams and glooms that dart
    Across the schoolboy's brain;
The song and the silence in the heart,
That in part are prophecies, and in part
      Are longings wild and vain.
        And the voice of that fitful song
        Sings on, and is never still:
    "A boy's will is the wind's will,
And the thoughts of youth are long, long thoughts."

There are things of which I may not speak;
    There are dreams that cannot die;
There are thoughts that make the strong heart weak,
And bring a pallor into the cheek,
      And a mist before the eye.
        And the words of that fatal song
        Come over me like a chill:
    "A boy's will is the wind's will,
And the thoughts of youth are long, long thoughts."

Strange to me now are the forms I meet
    When I visit the dear old town;
But the native air is pure and sweet,
And the trees that o'ershadow each well-known street,
      As they balance up and down,
        Are singing the beautiful song,
        Are sighing and whispering still:
    "A boy's will is the wind's will,
And the thoughts of youth are long, long thoughts."

And Deering's Woods are fresh and fair,
    And with joy that is almost pain
My heart goes back to wander there,
And among the dreams of the days that were,
    I find my lost youth again.
      And the strange and beautiful song,
      The groves are repeating it still:
    "A boy's will is the wind's will,
And the thoughts of youth are long, long thoughts."

Aftermath

When the Summer fields are mown,
When the birds are fledged and flown,
    And the dry leaves strew the path;
With the falling of the snow,
With the cawing of the crow,
Once again the fields we mow
    And gather in the aftermath.

Not the sweet, new grass with flowers
Is this harvesting of ours;
    Not the upland clover bloom;
But the rowen mixed with weeds,
Tangled tufts from marsh and meads,
Where the poppy drops its seeds
    In the silence and the gloom.

The Bells of San Blas

What say the Bells of San Blas
To the ships that southward pass
    From the harbor of Mazatlan?
To them it is nothing more
Than the sound of surf on the shore,—
    Nothing more to master or man.

But to me, a dreamer of dreams,
To whom what is and what seems
    Are often one and the same,—
The Bells of San Blas to me
Have a strange, wild melody,
    And are something more than a name.

For bells are the voice of the church;
They have tones that touch and search
    The hearts of young and old;
One sound to all, yet each
Lends a meaning to their speech,
    And the meaning is manifold.

They are a voice of the Past,
Of an age that is fading fast,
    Of a power austere and grand;
When the flag of Spain unfurled
Its folds o'er this western world,
    And the Priest was lord of the land.

The chapel that once looked down
On the little seaport town
    Has crumbled into the dust;
And on oaken beams below
The bells swing to and fro,
    And are green with mould and rust.

"Is, then, the old faith dead,"
They say, "and in its stead
    Is some new faith proclaimed,
That we are forced to remain
Naked to sun and rain,
    Unsheltered and ashamed?

"Once in our tower aloof
We rang over wall and roof
    Our warnings and our complaints;
And round about us there
The white doves filled the air,
    Like the white souls of the saints.

"The saints! Ah, have they grown
Forgetful of their own?
    Are they asleep, or dead,
That open to the sky
Their ruined Missions lie,
    No longer tenanted?

"Oh, bring us back once more
The vanished days of yore,
    When the world with faith was filled;
Bring back the fervid zeal,
The hearts of fire and steel,
    The hands that believe and build.

"Then from our tower again
We will send over land and main
    Our voices of command,
Like exiled kings who return
To their thrones, and the people learn
    That the Priest is lord of the land!"

O Bells of San Blas, in vain
Ye call back the Past again!
    The Past is deaf to your prayer:
Out of the shadows of night
The world rolls into light;
    It is daybreak everywhere.

JOHN GREENLEAF WHITTIER

John Greenleaf Whittier (1807–1892) might well be regarded as the quintessential activist poet: having dedicated himself utterly to the abolition of slavery, this cause became the subject matter of much of his poetry, and his poetry became a means of furthering that cause. Whittier was raised a devout Quaker, and his social conscience, nurtured in that religious environment, became the bedrock of his life and work. More than once Whittier risked his life for his views, enduring threats from mobs and physical attacks. But Whittier was never simply a political or didactic poet; his verse is rooted in a rural existence, detailing its values and modes of living. In the end it was for his faithful rendering of village and country life that he was beloved by his many readers.

Whittier was born in 1807 near Haverhill, Massachusetts, and grew up working on the family farm. His was not an easy childhood, and he received little formal education. However, William Lloyd Garrison, who published Whittier's first poem in a local paper, helped convince Whittier's father to let his son attend Haverhill Academy. Whittier supported himself initially as a shoemaker and schoolteacher but later worked as editor of various newspapers and magazines. His first book, *Legends of New England*—a collection of stories in prose and poetry—was published in 1831. In 1835 he was elected to the Massachusetts legislature, where he became active in the Whig party and in the national antislavery movement. That year he was stoned by a mob in Concord, New Hampshire, for his abolitionist views. In the midst of this activity Whittier published *Narrative of James Williams* and *Poems* (both in 1838), the same year in which the offices of his paper, the *Pennsylvania Freeman*, were attacked and burned by a mob. Whittier founded the Liberty party (1840) and ran for Congress two years later. He helped set up the Republican party and supported the election of Abraham Lincoln. In 1857 Whittier helped found the *Atlantic Monthly*, the magazine where many of his poems subsequently appeared. Between 1840 and the end of the Civil War in 1865 Whittier published eighteen books, but it was *Snow-Bound* in 1866 that made him truly famous. That poem sold twenty thousand copies and gave him a measure of financial security. With the abolitionist cause behind him Whittier became known more for his regionalist writing than for his political stances. He was an early proponent of Sarah Orne Jewett's work, and the postwar interest in literary regionalism took some of its cues from Whittier's accomplishments. Whittier's friends included the poets

Sigourney, Emerson, Longfellow, Holmes, and Lowell, as well as Mark Twain and other important writers of the period. Whittier never married.

Whittier's literary output was both substantial and diverse, and, as with most important writers, each age seems to take a different aspect of his work as representative of the whole. For years, as one of the venerable Fireside Poets, Whittier's homiletic and regional verse was most prized. More recently his abolitionist writings have drawn the attention of critics.

The Hunters of Men

Have ye heard of our hunting, o'er mountain and glen,
Through cane-brake and forest,—the hunting of men?
The lords of our land to this hunting have gone,
As the fox-hunter follows the sound of the horn;
Hark! the cheer and the hallo! the crack of the whip,
And the yell of the hound as he fastens his grip!
All blithe are our hunters, and noble their match,
Though hundreds are caught, there are millions to catch.
So speed to their hunting, o'er mountain and glen,
Through cane-brake and forest,—the hunting of men!

Gay luck to our hunters! how nobly they ride
In the glow of their zeal, and the strength of their pride!
The priest with his cassock flung back on the wind,
Just screening the politic statesman behind;
The saint and the sinner, with cursing and prayer,
The drunk and the sober, ride merrily there.
And woman, kind woman, wife, widow, and maid,
For the good of the hunted, is lending her aid:
Her foot's in the stirrup, her hand on the rein,
How blithely she rides to the hunting of men!

Oh, goodly and grand is our hunting to see,
In this "land of the brave and this home of the free."
Priest, warrior, and statesman, from Georgia to Maine,
All mounting the saddle, all grasping the rein;
Right merrily hunting the black man, whose sin
Is the curl of his hair and the hue of his skin!
Woe, now, to the hunted who turns him at bay!
Will our hunters be turned from their purpose and prey?
Will their hearts fail within them? their nerves tremble, when
All roughly they ride to the hunting of men?

Ho! alms for our hunters! all weary and faint,
Wax the curse of the sinner and prayer of the saint.
The horn is wound faintly, the echoes are still,
Over cane-brake and river, and forest and hill.
Haste, alms for our hunters! the hunted once more
Have turned from their flight with their backs to the shore:
What right have they here in the home of the white,
Shadowed o'er by our banner of Freedom and Right?
Ho! alms for the hunters! or never again
Will they ride in their pomp to the hunting of men!

Alms, alms for our hunters! why will ye delay,
When their pride and their glory are melting away?
The parson has turned; for, on charge of his own,
Who goeth a warfare, or hunting, alone?
The politic statesman looks back with a sigh,
There is doubt in his heart, there is fear in his eye.
Oh, haste, lest that doubting and fear shall prevail,
And the head of his steed take the place of the tail.
Oh, haste, ere he leave us! for who will ride then,
For pleasure or gain, to the hunting of men?

Ichabod!

So fallen! so lost! the light withdrawn
    Which once he wore!
The glory from his gray hairs gone
    Forevermore!

Revile him not—the Tempter hath
    A snare for all;
And pitying tears, not scorn and wrath,
    Befit his fall!

Oh! dumb be passion's stormy rage,
    When he who might
Have lighted up and led his age,
    Falls back in night.

Scorn! would the angels laugh, to mark
    A bright soul driven,
Fiend-goaded, down the endless dark,
    From hope and heaven!

Let not the land, once proud of him,
    Insult him now,
Nor brand with deeper shame his dim,
    Dishonored brow.

But let its humbled sons, instead,
    From sea to lake,
A long lament, as for the dead,
    In sadness make.

Of all we loved and honored, nought
    Save power remains—
A fallen angel's pride of thought,
    Still strong in chains.

All else is gone; from those great eyes
    The soul has fled:
When faith is lost, when honor dies,
    The man is dead!

Then, pay the reverence of old days
    To his dead fame;
Walk backward, with averted gaze,
    And hide the shame!

Telling the Bees

Here is the place; right over the hill
    Runs the path I took;
You can see the gap in the old wall still,
    And the stepping-stones in the shallow brook.

There is the house, with the gate red-barred,
    And the poplars tall;
And the barn's brown length, and the cattle-yard,
    And the white horns tossing above the wall.

There are the bee-hives ranged in the sun;
　　And down by the brink
Of the brook are her poor flowers, weed-o'errun,
　　Pansy and daffodil, rose and pink.

A year has gone, as the tortoise goes,
　　Heavy and slow;
And the same rose blows, and the same sun glows,
　　And the same brook sings of a year ago.

There's the same sweet clover-smell in the breeze;
　　And the June sun warm
Tangles his wings of fire in the trees,
　　Setting, as then, over Fernside farm.

I mind me how with a lover's care
　　From my Sunday coat
I brushed off the burs, and smoothed my hair,
　　And cooled at the brook-side my brow and throat.

Since we parted, a month had passed,—
　　To love, a year;
Down through the beeches I looked at last
　　On the little red gate and the well-sweep near.

I can see it all now,—the slantwise rain
　　Of light through the leaves,
The sundown's blaze on her window-pane,
　　The bloom of her roses under the eaves.

Just the same as a month before,—
　　The house and the trees,
The barn's brown gable, the vine by the door,—
　　Nothing changed but the hives of bees.

Before them, under the garden wall,
　　Forward and back,
Went drearily singing the chore-girl small,
　　Draping each hive with a shred of black.

Trembling, I listened: the summer sun
    Had the chill of snow;
For I knew she was telling the bees of one
    Gone on the journey we all must go!

Then I said to myself, "My Mary weeps
    For the dead to-day:
Haply her blind old grandsire sleeps
    The fret and the pain of his age away."

But her dog whined low; on the doorway sill,
    With his cane to his chin,
The old man sat; and the chore-girl still
    Sung to the bees stealing out and in.

And the song she was singing ever since
    In my ear sounds on:—
"Stay at home, pretty bees, fly not hence!
    Mistress Mary is dead and gone!"

Barbara Frietchie

Up from the meadows rich with corn,
Clear in the cool September morn,

The clustered spires of Frederick stand
Green-walled by the hills of Maryland.

Round about them orchards sweep,
Apple- and peach-tree fruited deep,

Fair as a garden of the Lord
To the eyes of the famished rebel horde,

On that pleasant morn of the early fall
When Lee marched over the mountain wall,—

Over the mountains winding down,
Horse and foot, into Frederick town.

Forty flags with their silver stars,
Forty flags with their crimson bars,

Flapped in the morning wind: the sun
Of noon looked down, and saw not one.

Up rose old Barbara Frietchie then,
Bowed with her fourscore years and ten;

Bravest of all in Frederick town,
She took up the flag the men hauled down;

In her attic-window the staff she set,
To show that one heart was loyal yet.

Up the street came the rebel tread,
Stonewall Jackson riding ahead.

Under his slouched hat left and right
He glanced: the old flag met his sight.

"Halt!"—the dust-brown ranks stood fast.
"Fire!"—out blazed the rifle-blast.

It shivered the window, pane and sash;
It rent the banner with seam and gash.

Quick, as it fell, from the broken staff
Dame Barbara snatched the silken scarf;

She leaned far out on the window-sill,
And shook it forth with a royal will.

"Shoot, if you must, this old gray head,
But spare your country's flag," she said.

A shade of sadness, a blush of shame,
Over the face of the leader came;

The nobler nature within him stirred
To life at that woman's deed and word:

"Who touches a hair of yon gray head
Dies like a dog! March on!" he said.

All day long through Frederick street
Sounded the tread of marching feet:

All day long that free flag tost
Over the heads of the rebel host.

Ever its torn folds rose and fell
On the loyal winds that loved it well;

And through the hill-gaps sunset light
Shone over it with a warm good-night.

Barbara Frietchie's work is o'er,
And the Rebel rides on his raids no more.

Honor to her! and let a tear
Fall, for her sake, on Stonewall's bier.

Over Barbara Frietchie's grave
Flag of Freedom and Union, wave!

Peace and order and beauty draw
Round thy symbol of light and law;

And ever the stars above look down
On thy stars below in Frederick town!

What the Birds Said

The birds against the April wind
    Flew northward, singing as they flew;
They sang, "The land we leave behind
    Has swords for corn-blades, blood for dew."

"O wild-birds, flying from the South,
    What saw and heard ye, gazing down?"
"We saw the mortar's upturned mouth,
    The sickened camp, the blazing town!

"Beneath the bivouac's starry lamps,
    We saw your march-worn children die;
In shrouds of moss, in cypress swamps,
    We saw your dead uncoffined lie.

"We heard the starving prisoner's sighs,
    And saw, from line and trench, your sons
Follow our flight with home-sick eyes
    Beyond the battery's smoking guns."

"And heard and saw ye only wrong
    And pain," I cried, "O wing-worn flocks?"
"We heard," they sang, "the freedman's song,
    The crash of Slavery's broken locks!

"We saw from new, uprising States
    The treason-nursing mischief spurned,
As, crowding Freedom's ample gates,
    The long-estranged and lost returned.

"O'er dusky faces, seamed and old,
    And hands horn-hard with unpaid toil,
With hope in every rustling fold,
    We saw your star-dropt flag uncoil.

"And struggling up through sounds accursed,
    A grateful murmur clomb the air;
A whisper scarcely heard at first,
    It filled the listening heavens with prayer.

"And sweet and far, as from a star,
    Replied a voice which shall not cease,
Till, drowning all the noise of war,
    It sings the blessed song of peace!"

So to me, in a doubtful day
    Of chill and slowly greening spring,
Low stooping from the cloudy gray,
    The wild-birds sang or seemed to sing.

They vanished in the misty air,
    The song went with them in their flight;
But lo! they left the sunset fair,
    And in the evening there was light.

Snow-Bound: A Winter Idyll

"As the Spirits of Darkness be stronger in the dark, so Good Spirits which be Angels of Light are augmented not only by the Divine light of the Sun, but also by our common Wood Fire: and as the celestial Fire drives away dark spirits, so also this our Fire of Wood doth the same."

—Cor. Agrippa, *Occult Philosophy*, Book I, chap v.

"Announced by all the trumpets of the sky,
Arrives the snow; and, driving o'er the fields,
Seem nowhere to alight; the whited air
Hides hills and woods, the river and the heaven,
And veils the farm-house at the garden's end.
The sled and traveller stopped, the courier's feet
Delayed, all friends shut out, the housemates sit
Around the radiant fireplace, enclosed
In a tumultuous privacy of storm."

—Emerson

The sun that brief December day
Rose cheerless over hills of gray,
And, darkly circled, gave at noon
A sadder light than waning moon.
Slow tracing down the thickening sky
Its mute and ominous prophecy,
A portent seeming less than threat,
It sank from sight before it set.
A chill no coat, however stout,
Of homespun stuff could quite shut out,
A hard, dull bitterness of cold,
    That checked, mid-vein, the circling race
    Of life-blood in the sharpened face,
The coming of the snow-storm told.
The wind blew east: we heard the roar
Of Ocean on his wintry shore,
And felt the strong pulse throbbing there
Beat with low rhythm our inland air.

Meanwhile we did our nightly chores,—
Brought in the wood from out of doors,
Littered the stalls, and from the mows

Raked down the herd's-grass for the cows;
Heard the horse whinnying for his corn;
And, sharply clashing horn on horn,
Impatient down the stanchion rows
The cattle shake their walnut bows;
While, peering from his early perch
Upon the scaffold's pole of birch,
The cock his crested helmet bent
And down his querulous challenge sent.

Unwarmed by any sunset light
The gray day darkened into night,
A night made hoary with the swarm
And whirl-dance of the blinding storm,
As zigzag wavering to and fro
Crossed and recrossed the wingéd snow:
And ere the early bed-time came
The white drift piled the window-frame,
And through the glass the clothes-line posts
Looked in like tall and sheeted ghosts.

So all night long the storm roared on:
The morning broke without a sun;
In tiny spherule traced with lines
Of Nature's geometric signs,
In starry flake, and pellicle,
All day the hoary meteor fell;
And, when the second morning shone,
We looked upon a world unknown,
On nothing we could call our own.
Around the glistening wonder bent
The blue walls of the firmament,
No cloud above, no earth below,—
A universe of sky and snow!
The old familiar sights of ours
Took marvellous shapes; strange domes and towers
Rose up where sty or corn-crib stood,
Or garden wall, or belt of wood;
A smooth white mound the brush-pile showed,

A fenceless drift what once was road;
The bridle-post an old man sat
With loose-flung coat and high cocked hat;
The well-curb had a Chinese roof;
And even the long sweep, high aloof,
In its slant splendor, seemed to tell
Of Pisa's leaning miracle.

A prompt, decisive man, no breath
Our father wasted: "Boys, a path!"
Well pleased, (for when did farmer boy
Count such a summons less than joy?)
Our buskins on our feet we drew;
    With mittened hands, and caps drawn low,
    To guard our necks and ears from snow,
We cut the solid whiteness through.
And, where the drift was deepest, made
A tunnel walled and overlaid
With dazzling crystal: we had read
Of rare Aladdin's wondrous cave,
And to our own his name we gave,
With many a wish the luck were ours
To test his lamp's supernal powers.
We reached the barn with merry din,
And roused the prisoned brutes within.
The old horse thrust his long head out,
And grave with wonder gazed about;
The cock his lusty greeting said,
And forth his speckled harem led;
The oxen lashed their tails, and hooked,
And mild reproach of hunger looked;
The hornéd patriarch of the sheep,
Like Egypt's Amun roused from sleep,
Shook his sage head with gesture mute,
And emphasized with stamp of foot.

All day the gusty north-wind bore
The loosening drift its breath before;
Low circling round its southern zone,

The sun through dazzling snow-mist shone.
No church-bell lent its Christian tone
To the savage air, no social smoke
Curled over woods of snow-hung oak.
A solitude made more intense
By dreary voicéd elements,
The shrieking of the mindless wind,
The moaning tree-boughs swaying blind,
And on the glass the unmeaning beat
Of ghostly finger-tips of sleet.
Beyond the circle of our hearth
No welcome sound of toil or mirth
Unbound the spell, and testified
Of human life and thought outside.
We minded that the sharpest ear
The buried brooklet could not hear,
The music of whose liquid lip
Had been to us companionship,
And, in our lonely life, had grown
To have an almost human tone.

As night drew on, and, from the crest
Of wooded knolls that ridged the west,
The sun, a snow-blown traveller, sank
From sight beneath the smothering bank,
We piled, with care, our nightly stack
Of wood against the chimney-back,—
The oaken log, green, huge, and thick,
And on its top the stout back-stick;
The knotty forestick laid apart,
And filled between with curious art
The ragged brush; then, hovering near,
We watched the first red blaze appear,
Heard the sharp crackle, caught the gleam
On whitewashed wall and sagging beam,
Until the old, rude-furnished room
Burst, flower-like, into rosy bloom;
While radiant with a mimic flame
Outside the sparkling drift became,

And through the bare-boughed lilac-tree
Our own warm hearth seemed blazing free.
The crane and pendent trammels showed,
The Turks' heads on the andirons glowed;
While childish fancy, prompt to tell
The meaning of the miracle,
Whispered the old rhyme: *"Under the tree,*
When fire outdoors burns merrily,
There the witches are making tea."

The moon above the eastern wood
Shone at its full; the hill-range stood
Transfigured in the silver flood,
Its blown snows flashing cold and keen,
Dead white, save where some sharp ravine
Took shadow, or the sombre green
Of hemlocks turned to pitchy black
Against the whiteness at their back.
For such a world and such a night
Most fitting that unwarming light,
Which only seemed where'er it fell
To make the coldness visible.

Shut in from all the world without,
We sat the clean-winged hearth about,
Content to let the north-wind roar
In baffled rage at pane and door,
While the red logs before us beat
The frost-line back with tropic heat;
And ever, when a louder blast
Shook beam and rafter as it passed,
The merrier up its roaring draught
The great throat of the chimney laughed.
The house-dog on his paws outspread
Laid to the fire his drowsy head,
The cat's dark silhouette on the wall
A couchant tiger's seemed to fall;
And, for the winter fireside meet,
Between the andirons' straddling feet,

The mug of cider simmered slow,
The apples sputtered in a row,
And, close at hand, the basket stood
With nuts from brown October's wood.

What matter how the night behaved?
What matter how the north-wind raved?
Blow high, blow low, not all its snow
Could quench our hearth-fire's ruddy glow.
O Time and Change!—with hair as gray
As was my sire's that winter day,
How strange it seems, with so much gone
Of life and love, to still live on!
Ah, brother! only I and thou
Are left of all that circle now,—
The dear home faces whereupon
That fitful firelight paled and shone.
Henceforward, listen as we will,
The voices of that hearth are still;
Look where we may, the wide earth o'er,
Those lighted faces smile no more.
We tread the paths their feet have worn,
    We sit beneath their orchard-trees,
    We hear, like them, the hum of bees
And rustle of the bladed corn;
We turn the pages that they read,
    Their written words we linger o'er,
But in the sun they cast no shade,
No voice is heard, no sign is made,
    No step is on the conscious floor!
Yet Love will dream, and Faith will trust,
(Since He who knows our need is just,)
That somehow, somewhere, meet we must.
Alas for him who never sees
The stars shine through his cypress-trees!
Who, hopeless, lays his dead away,
Nor looks to see the breaking day
Across the mournful marbles play!
Who hath not learned, in hours of faith,

The truth to flesh and sense unknown,
That Life is ever lord of Death,
    And Love can never lose its own!

We sped the time with stories old,
Wrought puzzles out, and riddles told,
Or stammered from our school-book lore
"The Chief of Gambia's golden shore."
How often since, when all the land
Was clay in Slavery's shaping hand,
As if a trumpet called, I've heard
Dame Mercy Warren's rousing word:
"Does not the voice of reason cry,
    Claim the first right which Nature gave,
From the red scourge of bondage fly,
    Nor deign to live a burdened slave!"
Our father rode again his ride
On Memphremagog's wooded side;
Sat down again to moose and samp
In trapper's hut and Indian camp;
Lived o'er the old idyllic ease
Beneath St. François' hemlock-trees;
Again for him the moonlight shone
On Norman cap and bodiced zone;
Again he heard the violin play
Which led the village dance away,
And mingled in its merry whirl
The grandam and the laughing girl.
Or, nearer home, our steps he led
Where Salisbury's level marshes spread
    Mile-wide as flies the laden bee;
Where merry mowers, hale and strong,
Swept, scythe on scythe, their swaths along
    The low green prairies of the sea.
We shared the fishing off Boar's Head,
    And round the rocky Isles of Shoals
    The hake-broil on the drift-wood coals;
The chowder on the sand-beach made,
Dipped by the hungry, steaming hot,

With spoons of clam-shell from the pot.
We heard the tales of witchcraft old,
And dream and sign and marvel told
To sleepy listeners as they lay
Stretched idly on the salted hay,
Adrift along the winding shores,
When favoring breezes designed to blow
The square sail of the gundalow
And idle lay the useless oars.
Our mother, while she turned her wheel
Or run the new-knit stocking-heel,
Told how the Indian hordes came down
At midnight on Cochecho town,
And how her own great-uncle bore
His cruel scalp-mark to fourscore.
Recalling, in her fitting phrase,
    So rich and picturesque and free,
    (The common unrhymed poetry
Of simple life and country ways,)
The story of her early days,—
She made us welcome to her home;
Old hearths grew wide to give us room;
We stole with her a frightened look
At the gray wizard's conjuring-book,
The fame whereof went far and wide
Through all the simple country side;
We heard the hawks at twilight play,
The boat-horn on Piscataqua,
The loon's weird laughter far away;
We fished her little trout-brook, knew
What flowers in wood and meadow grew,
What sunny hillsides autumn-brown
She climbed to shake the ripe nuts down,
Saw where in sheltered cove and bay
The ducks' black squadron anchored lay,
And heard the wild-geese calling loud
Beneath the gray November cloud.

Then, haply, with a look more grave,
And soberer tone, some tale she gave
From painful Sewell's ancient tome,
Beloved in every Quaker home,
Of faith fire-winged by martyrdom,
Or Chalkley's Journal, old and quaint,—
Gentlest of skippers, rare sea-saint!—
Who, when the dreary calms prevailed,
And water-butt and bread-cask failed,
And cruel, hungry eyes pursued
His portly presence mad for food,
With dark hints muttered under breath
Of casting lots for life or death,
Offered, if Heaven withheld supplies,
To be himself the sacrifice.
Then, suddenly, as if to save
The good man from his living grave,
A ripple on the water grew,
A school of porpoise flashed in view.
"Take, eat," he said, "and be content;
These fishes in my stead are sent
By Him who gave the tangled ram
To spare the child of Abraham."
Our uncle, innocent of books,
Was rich in lore of fields and brooks,
The ancient teachers never dumb
Of Nature's unhoused lyceum.
In moons and tides and weather wise,
He read the clouds as prophecies,
And foul or fair could well divine,
By many an occult hint and sign,
Holding the cunning-warded keys
To all the woodcraft mysteries;
Himself to Nature's heart so near
That all her voices in his ear
Of beast or bird had meanings clear,
Like Apollonius of old,
Who knew the tales the sparrows told,
Or Hermes, who interpreted

What the sage cranes of Nilus said;
A simple, guileless, childlike man,
Content to live where life began;
Strong only on his native grounds,
The little world of sights and sounds
Whose girdle was the parish bounds,
Whereof his fondly partial pride
The common features magnified,
As Surrey hills to mountains grew
In White of Selborne's loving view,—
He told how teal and loon he shot,
And how the eagle's eggs he got,
The feats on pond and river done,
The prodigies of rod and gun;
Till, warming with the tales he told,
Forgotten was the outside cold,
The bitter wind unheeded blew,
From ripening corn the pigeons flew,
The partridge drummed i' the wood, the mink
Went fishing down the river-brink.
In fields with bean or clover gay,
The woodchuck, like a hermit gray,
Peered from the doorway of his cell;
The muskrat plied the mason's trade,
And tier by tier his mud-walls laid;
And from the shagbark overhead
The grizzled squirrel dropped his shell.

Next, the dear aunt, whose smile of cheer
And voice in dreams I see and hear,—
The sweetest woman ever Fate
Perverse denied a household mate,
Who, lonely, homeless, not the less
Found peace in love's unselfishness,
And welcome wheresoe'er she went,
A calm and gracious element,
Whose presence seemed the sweet income
And womanly atmosphere of home,—
Called up her girlhood memories,

The huskings and the apple-bees,
The sleigh-rides and the summer sails,
Weaving through all the poor details
And homespun warp of circumstance
A golden woof-thread of romance.
For well she kept her genial mood
And simple faith of maidenhood;
Before her still a cloud-land lay,
The mirage loomed across her way;
The morning dew, that dries so soon
With others, glistened at her noon;
Through years of toil and soil and care
From glossy tress to thin gray hair,
All unprofaned she held apart
The virgin fancies of the heart.
Be shame to him of woman born
Who hath for such but thought of scorn.

There, too, our elder sister plied
Her evening task the stand beside;
A full, rich nature, free to trust,
Truthful and almost sternly just,
Impulsive, earnest, prompt to act,
And make her generous thought a fact,
Keeping with many a light disguise
The secret of self-sacrifice.
O heart sore-tried! thou hast the best
That Heaven itself could give thee,—rest,
Rest from all bitter thoughts and things!
    How many a poor one's blessing went
    With thee beneath the low green tent
Whose curtain never outward swings!

As one who held herself a part
Of all she saw, and let her heart
    Against the household bosom lean,
Upon the motley-braided mat
Our youngest and our dearest sat,
Lifting her large, sweet, asking eyes,
    Now bathed within the fadeless green

And holy peace of Paradise.
O, looking from some heavenly hill,
    Or from the shade of saintly palms,
    Or silver reach of river calms,
Do those large eyes behold me still?
With me one little year ago:—
The chill weight of the winter snow
    For months upon her grave has lain;
And now, when summer south-winds blow
    And brier and harebell bloom again,
I tread the pleasant paths we trod,
I see the violet-sprinkled sod
Whereon she leaned, too frail and weak
The hillside flowers she loved to seek,
Yet following me where'er I went
With dark eyes full of love's content.
The birds are glad; the brier-rose fills
The air with sweetness; all the hills
Stretch green to June's unclouded sky;
But still I wait with ear and eye
For something gone which should be nigh,
A loss in all familiar things,
In flower that blooms, and bird that sings.
And yet, dear heart! remembering thee,
    Am I not richer than of old?
Safe in thy immortality,
    What change can reach the wealth I hold?
    What chance can mar the pearl and gold
Thy love hath left in trust with me?
And while in life's late afternoon,
    Where cool and long the shadows grow,
I walk to meet the night that soon
    Shall shape and shadow overflow,
I cannot feel that thou art far,
Since near at need the angels are;
And when the sunset gates unbar,
    Shall I not see thee waiting stand,
And, white against the evening star,
    The welcome of thy beckoning hand?

Brisk wielder of the birch and rule,
The master of the district school
Held at the fire his favored place,
Its warm glow lit a laughing face
Fresh-hued and fair, where scarce appeared
The uncertain prophecy of beard.
He teased the mitten-blinded cat,
Played cross-pins on my uncle's hat,
Sang songs, and told us what befalls
In classic Dartmouth's college halls.
Born the wild Northern hills among,
From whence his yeoman father wrung
By patient toil subsistence scant,
Not competence and yet not want,
He early gained the power to pay
His cheerful, self-reliant way;
Could doff at ease his scholar's gown
To peddle wares from town to town;
Or through the long vacation's reach
In lonely lowland districts teach,
Where all the droll experience found
At stranger hearths in boarding round,
The moonlit skater's keen delight,
The sleigh-drive through the frosty night,
The rustic party, with its rough
Accompaniment of blind-man's-buff,
And whirling plate, and forfeits paid,
His winter task a pastime made.
Happy the snow-locked homes wherein
He tuned his merry violin,
Or played the athlete in the barn,
Or held the good dame's winding yarn,
Or mirth-provoking versions told
Of classic legends rare and old,
Wherein the scenes of Greece and Rome
Had all the commonplace of home,
And little seemed at best the odds
'Twixt Yankee pedlers and old gods;
Where Pindus-born Araxes took

The guise of any grist-mill brook,
And dread Olympus at his will
Became a huckleberry hill.

A careless boy that night he seemed;
    But at his desk he had the look
And air of one who wisely schemed,
    And hostage from the future took
    In trainéd thought and lore of book.
Large-brained, clear-eyed,—of such as he
Shall Freedom's young apostles be,
Who, following in War's bloody trail,
Shall every lingering wrong assail;
All chains from limb and spirit strike,
Uplift the black and white alike;
Scatter before their swift advance
The darkness and the ignorance,
The pride, the lust, the squalid sloth,
Which nurtured Treason's monstrous growth,
Made murder pastime, and the hell
Of prison-torture possible;
The cruel lie of caste refute,
Old forms remould, and substitute
For Slavery's lash the freeman's will,
For blind routine, wise-handed skill;
A school-house plant on every hill,
Stretching in radiate nerve-lines thence
The quick wires of intelligence;
Till North and South together brought
Shall own the same electric thought,
In peace a common flag salute,
And, side by side in labor's free
And unresentful rivalry,
Harvest the fields wherein they fought.

Another guest that winter night
Flashed back from lustrous eyes the light.
Unmarked by time, and yet not young,
The honeyed music of her tongue
And words of meekness scarcely told

123

A nature passionate and bold,
Strong, self-concentred, spurning guide,
Its milder features dwarfed beside
Her unbent will's majestic pride.
She sat among us, at the best,
A not unfeared, half-welcome guest,
Rebuking with her cultured phrase
Our homeliness of words and ways.
A certain pard-like, treacherous grace
 Swayed the lithe limbs and drooped the lash,
 Lent the white teeth their dazzling flash;
 And under low brows, black with night,
 Rayed out at times a dangerous light;
The sharp heat-lightnings of her face
Presaging ill to him whom Fate
Condemned to share her love or hate.
A woman tropical, intense
In thought and act, in soul and sense,
She blended in a like degree
The vixen and the devotee,
Revealing with each freak or feint
 The temper of Petruchio's Kate,
The raptures of Siena's saint.
Her tapering hand and rounded wrist
Had facile power to form a fist;
The warm, dark languish of her eyes
Was never safe from wrath's surprise.
Brows saintly calm and lips devout
Knew every change of scowl and pout;
And the sweet voice had notes more high
And shrill for social battle-cry.

Since then what old cathedral town
Has missed her pilgrim staff and gown,
What convent-gate has held its lock
Against the challenge of her knock!
Through Smyrna's plague-hushed thoroughfares,
Up sea-set Malta's rocky stairs,
Gray olive slopes of hills that hem

Thy tombs and shrines, Jerusalem,
Or startling on her desert throne
The crazy Queen of Lebanon
With claims fantastic as her own,
Her tireless feet have held their way;
And still, unrestful, bowed, and gray,
She watches under Eastern skies,
    With hope each day renewed and fresh,
    The Lord's quick coming in the flesh,
Whereof she dreams and prophesies!

Where'er her troubled path may be,
    The Lord's sweet pity with her go!
The outward wayward life we see,
    The hidden springs we may not know.
Nor is it given us to discern
    What threads the fatal sisters spun,
    Through what ancestral years has run
The sorrow with the woman born,
What forged her cruel chain of moods,
What set her feet in solitudes,
    And held the love within her mute,
What mingled madness in the blood,
    A life-long discord and annoy,
    Water of tears with oil of joy,
And hid within the folded bud
    Perversities of flower and fruit.
It is not ours to separate
The tangled skein of will and fate,
To show what metes and bounds should stand
Upon the soul's debatable land,
And between choice and Providence
Divide the circle of events;
But He who knows our frame is just,
    Merciful, and compassionate,
And full of sweet assurances
And hope for all the language is,
    That He remembereth we are dust!

At last the great logs, crumbling low,
Sent out a dull and duller glow,
The bull's-eye watch that hung in view,
Ticking its weary circuit through,
Pointed with mutely-warning sign
Its black hand to the hour of nine.
That sign the pleasant circle broke:
My uncle ceased his pipe to smoke,
Knocked from its bowl the refuse gray
And laid it tenderly away,
Then roused himself to safely cover
The dull red brands with ashes over.
And while, with care, our mother laid
The work aside, her steps she stayed
One moment, seeking to express
Her grateful sense of happiness
For food and shelter, warmth and health,
And love's contentment more than wealth,
With simple wishes (not the weak,
Vain prayers which no fulfilment seek,
But such as warm the generous heart,
O'er-prompt to do with Heaven its part)
That none might lack, that bitter night,
For bread and clothing, warmth and light.

Within our beds awhile we heard
The wind that round the gables roared,
With now and then a ruder shock,
Which made our very bedsteads rock.
We heard the loosened clapboards tost,
The board-nails snapping in the frost;
And on us, through the unplastered wall,
Felt the light sifted snow-flakes fall.
But sleep stole on, as sleep will do
When hearts are light and life is new;
Faint and more faint the murmurs grew,
Till in the summer-land of dreams

They softened to the sound of streams,
Low stir of leaves, and dip of oars,
And lapsing waves on quiet shores.

Next morn we wakened with the shout
Of merry voices high and clear;
And saw the teamsters drawing near
To break the drifted highways out.
Down the long hillside treading slow
We saw the half-buried oxen go,
Shaking the snow from heads uptost,
Their straining nostrils white with frost.
Before our door the straggling train
Drew up, an added team to gain.
The elders threshed their hands a-cold,
    Passed, with the cider-mug, their jokes
    From lip to lip; the younger folks
Down the loose snow-banks, wrestling, rolled,
Then toiled again the cavalcade
    O'er windy hill, through clogged ravine,
    And woodland paths that wound between
Low drooping pine-boughs winter-weighed.
From every barn a team afoot,
At every house a new recruit,
Where, drawn by Nature's subtlest law,
Haply the watchful young men saw
Sweet doorway pictures of the curls
And curious eyes of merry girls,
Lifting their hands in mock defence
Against the snow-ball's compliments,
And reading in each missive tost
The charm with Eden never lost.

We heard once more the sleigh-bells' sound;
    And, following where the teamsters led,
The wise old Doctor went his round,
Just pausing at our door to say,
In the brief autocratic way
Of one who, prompt at Duty's call,
Was free to urge her claim on all,

That some poor neighbor sick abed
At night our mother's aid would need.
For, one in generous thought and deed,
    What mattered in the sufferer's sight
    The Quaker matron's inward light,
The Doctor's mail of Calvin's creed?
All hearts confess the saints elect
    Who, twain in faith, in love agree,
And melt not in an acid sect
    The Christian pearl of charity!

So days went on: a week had passed
Since the great world was heard from last.
The Almanac we studied o'er,
Read and reread our little store,
Of books and pamphlets, scarce a score;
One harmless novel, mostly hid
From younger eyes, a book forbid,
And poetry, (or good or bad,
A single book was all we had,)
Where Ellwood's meek, drab-skirted Muse,
    A stranger to the heathen Nine,
    Sang, with a somewhat nasal whine,
The wars of David and the Jews.
At last the floundering carrier bore
The village paper to our door.
Lo! broadening outward as we read,
To warmer zones the horizon spread;
In panoramic length unrolled
We saw the marvels that it told.
Before us passed the painted Creeks,
    And daft McGregor on his raids
    In Costa Rica's everglades.
And up Taygetos winding slow
Rode Ypsilanti's Mainote Greeks,
A Turk's head at each saddle-bow!
Welcome to us its week-old news,
Its corner for the rustic Muse,
    Its monthly gauge of snow and rain,

128

Its record, mingling in a breath
· The wedding bell and dirge of death;
Jest, anecdote, and love-lorn tale,
The latest culprit sent to jail;
Its hue and cry of stolen and lost,
Its vendue sales and goods at cost,
    And traffic calling loud for gain.
We felt the stir of hall and street,
The pulse of life that round us beat;
The chill embargo of the snow
Was melted in the genial glow;
Wide swung again our ice-locked door,
And all the world was ours once more!

Clasp, Angel of the backward look
    And folded wings of ashen gray
    And voice of echoes far away,
The brazen covers of thy book;
The weird palimpsest old and vast,
Wherein thou hid'st the spectral past;
Where, closely mingling, pale and glow
The characters of joy and woe;
The monographs of outlived years,
Or smile-illumed or dim with tears,
    Green hills of life that slope to death,
And haunts of home, whose vistaed trees
Shade off to mournful cypresses
    With the white amaranths underneath.
Even while I look, I can but heed
    The restless sands' incessant fall,
Importunate hours that hours succeed,
Each clamorous with its own sharp need,
    And duty keeping pace with all.
Shut down and clasp the heavy lids;
I hear again the voice that bids
The dreamer leave his dream midway
For larger hopes and graver fears:
Life greatens in these later years,
The century's aloe flowers to-day!

Yet, haply, in some lull of life,
Some Truce of God which breaks its strife,
The worldling's eyes shall gather dew,
    Dreaming in throngful city ways
Of winter joys his boyhood knew;
And dear and early friends—the few
Who yet remain—shall pause to view
    These Flemish pictures of old days;
Sit with me by the homestead hearth,
And stretch the hands of memory forth
    To warm them at the wood-fire's blaze!
And thanks untraced to lips unknown
Shall greet me like the odors blown
From unseen meadow newly mown,
Or lilies floating in some pond,
Wood-fringed, the wayside gaze beyond;
The traveller owns the grateful sense
Of sweetness near, he knows not whence,
And, pausing, takes with forehead bare
The benediction of the air.

EDGAR ALLAN POE

Edgar Allan Poe (1809–1849) is one of the few American writers known equally for writing poetry and fiction. While his tales are immensely popular, few readers would fail to mention "The Raven" as one of Poe's foremost works. As he himself put it, "poetry has been not a purpose but a passion." Although he wrote few poems—only about fifty—they are among the most characteristic works of the period, with their strange romantic gothicism. As a poet Poe is perhaps most highly regarded in France, where he was a major influence on Charles Baudelaire, who translated Poe's work and claimed that, if Poe had not existed, he would have had to invent him (and to some extent he did precisely that). The development of the symbolist movement in the late nineteenth century owes something to Poe, and he remains an intriguing poet for many contemporary writers.

Born into a family of actors, Poe was orphaned by the age of three and raised by foster parents in Richmond, Virginia. John Allan, a tobacco merchant, saw to Poe's education and took him abroad to England on a business trip; but he never formally adopted Poe, and relations between the two were difficult at best. Poe was expelled from the University of Virginia for incurring gambling debts that he could not pay and that Allan refused to honor. After quarreling with Allan, Poe went to Boston, where he published his first book of verse, *Tamerlane and Other Poems* (1827). After enlisting in the U.S. Army under a false name, he was able to enroll at West Point in 1830 with the help of Allan, with whom he was briefly reconciled. Allan had inherited a fortune, and Poe hoped to become his legal heir. But after it became clear that Allan would never provide Poe with a living, Poe deliberately sought expulsion from the military academy in 1831. That same year cadets at West Point raised money to publish a volume of Poe's poetry, *Poems*.

From 1831 on, Poe worked as an editor and publisher at numerous magazines in Richmond, Baltimore, Philadelphia, and New York. During this time he published his stories and poems in magazines and brought out several volumes of poetry and fiction. He led, however, a precarious life, making enemies in the literary world with his harsh reviewing and doing his reputation harm from bouts of drunkenness. In 1835 he married his cousin, Virginia Clemm, aged thirteen, who died several years later of tuberculosis. After her death Poe courted a number of women poets, including Frances Osgood and Sarah Helen Whitman (much to the disapproval of the editor and critic Rufus Griswold, who was later Poe's literary executor and who apparently spread calumnious scandal about Poe after his death). The publication of "The Raven" in 1845 made Poe famous, and his essay about its genesis, "The Philosophy of Composition," was equally sensational. Poe, however, never achieved sufficient fame to gain financial security, and his strenuous hand-to-mouth existence took its toll on his health and disposition. He died in Baltimore after an apparent drinking binge in 1849.

Poe had very distinct ideas about the nature of poetry and the techniques proper to it. One tenet was that poems should aim for an aesthetic effect of beauty, creating an intense emotional state that could only be sustained in short poems. In his essay "The Poetic Principle" Poe writes: "I hold that a long poem does not exist. I maintain that the phrase, 'a long poem,' is simply a flat contradiction in terms." For Poe poetry is *"The Rhythmical Creation of Beauty"* and that can only be achieved in writing that is "simple, precise, terse." Though Poe is one of the most sensationally romantic of writers, he claims that the poet "must be cool, calm, unimpassioned." Whether Poe's theorizing matches his practice is a question many still ask. Regardless of what one makes of his theories, it is clear that Poe remains one of the most popular of American poets.

To Science

Science! true daughter of Old Time thou art!
    Who alterest all things with thy peering eyes.
Why preyest thou thus upon the poet's heart,
    Vulture, whose wings are dull realities?
How should he love thee? or how deem thee wise,
    Who wouldst not leave him in his wandering
To seek for treasure in the jewelled skies,
    Albeit he soared with an undaunted wing?
Hast thou not dragged Diana from her car?
    And driven the Hamadryad from the wood
To seek a shelter in some happier star?
    Hast thou not torn the Naiad from her flood,
The Elfin from the green grass, and from me
The summer dream beneath the tamarind tree?

Romance

Romance, who loves to nod and sing,
With drowsy head and folded wing,
Among the green leaves as they shake
Far down within some shadowy lake,
To me a painted paroquet
Hath been—a most familiar bird—
Taught me my alphabet to say—
To lisp my very earliest word
While in the wild wood I did lie,
A child—with a most knowing eye.

Of late, eternal Condor years
So shake the very Heaven on high
With tumult as they thunder by,
I have no time for idle cares
Through gazing on the unquiet sky.
And when an hour with calmer wings
Its down upon my spirit flings—
That little time with lyre and rhyme
To while away—forbidden things!
My heart would feel to be a crime
Unless it trembled with the strings.

"Alone"

From childhood's hour I have not been
As others were—I have not seen
As others saw—I could not bring
My passions from a common spring—
From the same source I have not taken
My sorrow—I could not awaken
My heart to joy at the same tone—
And all I lov'd—*I* lov'd alone—
Then—in my childhood—in the dawn
Of a most stormy life—was drawn
From ev'ry depth of good and ill
The mystery which binds me still—
From the torrent, or the fountain—
From the red cliff of the mountain—
From the sun that 'round me roll'd
In its autumn tint of gold—
From the lightning in the sky
As it pass'd me flying by—
From the thunder, and the storm—
And the cloud that took the form
(When the rest of Heaven was blue)
Of a demon in my view—

To Helen

Helen, thy beauty is to me
    Like those Nicéan barks of yore,
That gently, o'er a perfumed sea,
    The weary, way-worn wanderer bore
    To his own native shore.

On desperate seas long wont to roam,
    Thy hyacinth hair, thy classic face,
Thy Naiad airs have brought me home
    To the glory that was Greece,
    And the grandeur that was Rome.

Lo! in yon brilliant window-niche
    How statue-like I see thee stand,
The agate lamp within thy hand!
    Ah, Psyche, from the regions which
    Are Holy-Land!

Israfel

In Heaven a spirit doth dwell
    "Whose heart-strings are a lute;"
None sing so wildly well
As the angel Israfel,
And the giddy stars (so legends tell)
Ceasing their hymns, attend the spell
    Of his voice, all mute.

Tottering above
    In her highest noon,
    The enamoured moon
Blushes with love,
    While, to listen, the red levin
    (With the rapid Pleiads, even,
    Which were seven,)
    Pauses in Heaven.

And they say (the starry choir
    And the other listening things)
That Israfeli's fire
Is owing to that lyre
    By which he sits and sings—
The trembling living wire
Of those unusual strings.

But the skies that angel trod,
    Where deep thoughts are a duty—
Where Love's a grown-up God—
    Where the Houri glances are
Imbued with all the beauty
    Which we worship in a star.

Therefore, thou art not wrong,
    Israfeli, who despisest
An unimpassioned song;
To thee the laurels belong,
    Best bard, because the wisest!
Merrily live, and long!

The ecstasies above
    With thy burning measures suit—
Thy grief, thy joy, thy hate, thy love,
With the fervour of thy lute—
Well may the stars be mute!

Yes, Heaven is thine; but this
    Is a world of sweets and sours;
    Our flowers are merely—flowers,
And the shadow of thy perfect bliss
    Is the sunshine of ours.

If I could dwell
Where Israfel
    Hath dwelt, and he where I,
He might not sing so wildly well
    A mortal melody,
While a bolder note than this might swell
    From my lyre within the sky.

The Valley of Unrest

Once it smiled a silent dell
Where the people did not dwell;
They had gone unto the wars,
Trusting to the mild-eyed stars,
Nightly, from their azure towers,
To keep watch above the flowers,
In the midst of which all day
The red sun-light lazily lay.
Now each visitor shall confess
The sad valley's restlessness.
Nothing there is motionless—
Nothing save the airs that brood
Over the magic solitude.
Ah, by no wind are stirred those trees
That palpitate like the chill seas
Around the misty Hebrides!
Ah, by no wind those clouds are driven
That rustle through the unquiet Heaven
Uneasily, from morn till even,
Over the violets there that lie
In myriad types of the human eye—
Over the lilies there that wave
And weep above a nameless grave!
They wave: —from out their fragrant tops
Eternal dews come down in drops.
They weep: —from off their delicate stems
Perennial tears descend in gems.

The City in the Sea

Lo! Death has reared himself a throne
In a strange city lying alone
Far down within the dim West,
Where the good and the bad and the worst and the best
Have gone to their eternal rest.
There shrines and palaces and towers
(Time-eaten towers that tremble not!)
Resemble nothing that is ours.
Around, by lifting winds forgot,
Resignedly beneath the sky
The melancholy waters lie.

No rays from the holy heaven come down
On the long night-time of that town;
But light from out the lurid sea
Streams up the turrets silently—
Gleams up the pinnacles far and free—
Up domes—up spires—up kingly halls—
Up fanes—up Babylon-like walls—
Up shadowy long-forgotten bowers
Of sculptured ivy and stone flowers—
Up many and many a marvellous shrine
Whose wreathéd friezes intertwine
The viol, the violet, and the vine.

Resignedly beneath the sky
The melancholy waters lie.
So blend the turrets and shadows there
That all seem pendulous in air,
While from a proud tower in the town
Death looks gigantically down.

There open fanes and gaping graves
Yawn level with the luminous waves;
But not the riches there that lie
In each idol's diamond eye—
Not the gaily-jewelled dead
Tempt the waters from their bed;

For no ripples curl, alas!
Along that wilderness of glass—
No swellings tell that winds may be
Upon some far-off happier sea—
No heavings hint that winds have been
On seas less hideously serene.

But lo, a stir is in the air!
The wave—there is a movement there!
As if the towers had thrust aside,
In slightly sinking, the dull tide—
As if their tops had feebly given
A void within the filmy Heaven.
The waves have now a redder glow—
The hours are breathing faint and low—
And when, amid no earthly moans,
Down, down that town shall settle hence.
Hell, rising from a thousand thrones,
Shall do it reverence.

Silence

There are some qualities—some incorporate things,
    That have a double life, which thus is made
A type of that twin entity which springs
    From matter and light, evinced in solid and shade.
There is a two-fold *Silence*—sea and shore—
    Body and soul. One dwells in lonely places,
    Newly with grass o'ergrown; some solemn graces,
Some human memories and tearful lore,
Render him terrorless: his name's "No More."
He is the corporate Silence: dread him not!
    No power hath he of evil in himself;
But should some urgent fate (untimly lot!)
    Bring thee to meet his shadow (nameless elf,
That haunteth the lone regions where hath trod
No foot of man,) commend thyself to God!

The Sleeper

At midnight, in the month of June,
I stand beneath the mystic moon.
An opiate vapour, dewy, dim,
Exhales from out her golden rim,
And, softly dripping, drop by drop,
Upon the quiet mountain top,
Steals drowsily and musically
Into the universal valley.
The rosemary nods upon the grave;
The lily lolls upon the wave;
Wrapping the fog about its breast,
The ruin moulders into rest;
Looking like Lethe, see! the lake
A conscious slumber seems to take,
And would not, for the world, awake.
All Beauty sleeps!—and lo! where lies
Irene, with her Destinies!

Oh, lady bright! can it be right—
This window open to the night?
The wanton airs, from the tree-top,
Laughingly through the lattice drop—
The bodiless airs, a wizard rout,
Flit through thy chamber in and out,
And wave the curtain canopy
So fitfully—so fearfully—
Above the closed and fringed lid
'Neath which thy slumb'ring soul lies hid,
That, o'er the floor and down the wall,
Like ghosts the shadows rise and fall!
Oh, lady dear, hast thou no fear?
Why and what art thou dreaming here?
Sure thou art come o'er far-off seas,
A wonder to these garden trees!
Strange is thy pallor! strange thy dress!
Strange, above all, thy length of tress,
And this all solemn silentness!

The lady sleeps! Oh, may her sleep,
Which is enduring, so be deep!
Heaven have her in its sacred keep!
This chamber changed for one more holy,
This bed for one more melancholy,
I pray to God that she may lie
Forever with unopened eye,
While the pale sheeted ghosts go by!

My love, she sleeps! Oh, may her sleep,
As it is lasting, so be deep!
Soft may the worms about her creep!
Far in the forest, dim and old,
For her may some tall vault unfold—
Some vault that oft hath flung its black
And winged pannels fluttering back,
Triumphant, o'er the crested palls,
Of her grand family funerals—
Some sepulchre, remote, alone,
Against whose portal she hath thrown,
In childhood, many an idle stone—
Some tomb from out whose sounding door
She ne'er shall force an echo more,
Thrilling to think, poor child of sin!
It was the dead who groaned within.

Lenore

Ah, broken is the golden bowl!—the spirit flown forever!
Let the bell toll!—a saintly soul floats on the Stygian river:—
And, Guy De Vere, hast *thou* no tear?—weep now or never more!
See! on yon drear and rigid bier low lies thy love, Lenore!
Come, let the burial rite be read—the funeral song be sung!—
An anthem for the queenliest dead that ever died so young—
A dirge for her the doubly dead in that she died so young.

"Wretches! ye loved her for her wealth and ye hated her for her pride;
And, when she fell in feeble health, ye blessed her—that she died:—
How *shall* the ritual then be read—the requiem how be sung
By you—by yours, the evil eye—by yours the slanderous tongue
That did to death the innocence that died and died so young?"

Peccavimus:—yet rave not thus! but let a Sabbath song
Go up to God so solemnly the dead may feel no wrong!
The sweet Lenore hath gone before, with Hope that flew beside,
Leaving thee wild for the dear child that should have been thy bride—
For her, the fair and debonair, that now so lowly lies,
The life upon her yellow hair, but not within her eyes—
The life still there upon her hair, the death upon her eyes.

"Avaunt!—avaunt! to friends from fiends the indignant ghost is riven—
From Hell unto a high estate within the utmost Heaven—
From moan and groan to a golden throne beside the King of Heaven:—
Let *no* bell toll, then, lest her soul, amid its hallowed mirth,
Should catch the note as it doth float up from the damnéd Earth!
And I—tonight my heart is light:—no dirge will I upraise,
But waft the angel on her flight with a Paean of old days!"

Dream-Land

By a route obscure and lonely,
Haunted by ill angels only,
Where an Eidolon, named NIGHT,
On a black throne reigns upright,
I have reached these lands but newly
From an ultimate dim Thule—
From a wild weird clime that lieth, sublime,
   Out of SPACE—out of TIME.

Bottomless vales and boundless floods,
And chasms and caves, and Titan woods,
With forms that no man can discover
For the tears that drip all over;
Mountains toppling evermore
Into seas without a shore;
Seas that restlessly aspire,
Surging, unto skies of fire;
Lakes that endlessly outspread
Their lone waters—lone and dead,—
Their still waters—still and chilly
With the snows of the lolling lily.

By the lakes that thus outspread
Their lone waters, lone and dead,—
Their sad waters, sad and chilly
With the snows of the lolling lily,—
By the mountains—near the river
Murmuring lowly, murmuring ever,—
By the grey woods,—by the swamp
Where the toad and the newt encamp,—
By the dismal tarns and pools
   Where dwell the Ghouls,—
By each spot the most unholy—
In each nook most melancholy,—
There the traveller meets, aghast,
Sheeted Memories of the Past—
Shrouded forms that start and sigh
As they pass the wanderer by—

White-robed forms of friends long given,
In agony, to the Earth—and Heaven.

For the heart whose woes are legion
'Tis a peaceful, soothing region—
For the spirit that walks in shadow
'Tis—oh 'tis an Eldorado!
But the traveller, traveling through it,
May not—dare not openly view it;
Never its mysteries are exposed
To the weak human eye unclosed;
So wills its King, who hath forbid
The uplifting of the fringéd lid;
And thus the sad Soul that here passes
Beholds it but through darkened glasses.

By a route obscure and lonely,
Haunted by ill angels only,
Where an Eidolon, named NIGHT,
On a black throne reigns upright,
I have wandered home but newly
From this ultimate dim Thule.

The Raven

Once upon a midnight dreary, while I pondered, weak and weary,
Over many a quaint and curious volume of forgotten lore—
While I nodded, nearly napping, suddenly there came a tapping,
As of some one gently rapping, rapping at my chamber door.
"'Tis some visiter," I muttered, "tapping at my chamber door—
                              Only this and nothing more."

Ah, distinctly I remember it was in the bleak December;
And each separate dying ember wrought its ghost upon the floor.
Eagerly I wished the morrow;—vainly I had sought to borrow
From my books surcease of sorrow—sorrow for the lost Lenore—
For the rare and radiant maiden whom the angels name Lenore—
                              Nameless *here* for evermore.

And the silken, sad, uncertain rustling of each purple curtain
Thrilled me—filled me with fantastic terrors never felt before;
So that now, to still the beating of my heart, I stood repeating
"'Tis some visiter entreating entrance at my chamber door—
Some late visiter entreating entrance at my chamber door;—
                        This it is and nothing more."

Presently my soul grew stronger; hesitating then no longer,
"Sir," said I, "or Madam, truly your forgiveness I implore;
But the fact is I was napping, and so gently you came rapping,
And so faintly you came tapping, tapping at my chamber door,
That I scarce was sure I heard you"—here I opened wide the door;—
                        Darkness there and nothing more.

Deep into that darkness peering, long I stood there wondering, fearing,
Doubting, dreaming dreams no mortal ever dared to dream before;
But the silence was unbroken, and the stillness gave no token,
And the only word there spoken was the whispered word, "Lenore?"
This I whispered, and an echo murmured back the word, "Lenore!"
                        Merely this and nothing more.

Back into the chamber turning, all my soul within me burning,
Soon again I heard a tapping somewhat louder than before.
"Surely," said I, "surely that is something at my window lattice;
Let me see, then, what thereat is, and this mystery explore—
Let my heart be still a moment and this mystery explore;—
                        'Tis the wind and nothing more!"

Open here I flung the shutter, when, with many a flirt and flutter,
In there stepped a stately Raven of the saintly days of yore;
Not the least obeisance made he; not a minute stopped or stayed he;
But, with mien of lord or lady, perched above my chamber door—
Perched upon a bust of Pallas just above my chamber door—
                        Perched, and sat, and nothing more.

Then this ebony bird beguiling my sad fancy into smiling,
By the grave and stern decorum of the countenance it wore,
"Though thy crest be shorn and shaven, thou," I said, "art sure no craven,
Ghastly grim and ancient Raven wandering from the Nightly shore—
Tell me what thy lordly name is on the Night's Plutonian shore!"
                        Quoth the Raven "Nevermore."

Much I marvelled this ungainly fowl to hear discourse so plainly,
Though its answer little meaning—little relevancy bore;
For we cannot help agreeing that no living human being
Ever yet was blessed with seeing bird above his chamber door—
Bird or beast upon the sculptured bust above his chamber door,
                                        With such name as "Nevermore."

But the Raven, sitting lonely on the placid bust, spoke only
That one word, as if his soul in that one word he did outpour.
Nothing farther then he uttered—not a feather then he fluttered—
Till I scarcely more than muttered "Other friends have flown before—
On the morrow *he* will leave me, as my Hopes have flown before."
                                        Then the bird said "Nevermore."

Startled at the stillness broken by reply so aptly spoken,
"Doubtless," said I, "what it utters is its only stock and store
Caught from some unhappy master whom unmerciful Disaster
Followed fast and followed faster till his songs one burden bore—
Till the dirges of his Hope that melancholy burden bore
                                        Of 'Never—nevermore.'"

But the Raven still beguiling my sad fancy into smiling,
Straight I wheeled a cushioned seat in front of bird, and bust and door;
Then, upon the velvet sinking, I betook myself to linking
Fancy unto fancy, thinking what this ominous bird of yore—
What this grim, ungainly, ghastly, gaunt, and ominous bird of yore
                                        Meant in croaking "Nevermore."

This I sat engaged in guessing, but no syllable expressing
To the fowl whose fiery eyes now burned into my bosom's core;
This and more I sat divining, with my head at ease reclining
On the cushion's velvet lining that the lamp-light gloated o'er,
But whose velvet-violet lining with the lamp-light gloating o'er,
                                        She shall press, ah, nevermore!

Then, methought, the air grew denser, perfumed from an unseen censer
Swung by seraphim whose foot-falls tinkled on the tufted floor.
"Wretch," I cried, "thy God hath lent thee—by these angels he hath sent thee
Respite—respite and nepenthe from thy memories of Lenore;
Quaff, oh quaff this kind nepenthe and forget this lost Lenore!"
                                        Quoth the Raven "Nevermore."

"Prophet!" said I, "thing of evil!—prophet still, if bird or devil!—
Whether Tempter sent, or whether tempest tossed thee here ashore,
Desolate yet all undaunted, on this desert land enchanted—
On this home by Horror haunted—tell me truly, I implore—
Is there—*is* there balm in Gilead?—tell me—tell me, I implore!"
                              Quoth the Raven "Nevermore."

"Prophet!" said I, "thing of evil!—prophet still, if bird or devil!
By that Heaven that bends above us—by that God we both adore—
Tell this soul with sorrow laden if, within the distant Aidenn,
It shall clasp a sainted maiden whom the angels name Lenore—
Clasp a rare and radiant maiden whom the angels name Lenore."
                              Quoth the Raven "Nevermore."

"Be that word our sign of parting, bird or fiend!" I shrieked, upstarting—
"Get thee back into the tempest and the Night's Plutonian shore!
Leave no black plume as a token of that lie thy soul hath spoken!
Leave my loneliness unbroken!—quit the bust above my door!
Take the beak from out my heart, and take thy form from off my door!"
                              Quoth the Raven "Nevermore."

And the Raven, never flitting, still is sitting, *still* is sitting
On the pallid bust of Pallas just above my chamber door;
And his eyes have all the seeming of a demon's that is dreaming,
And the lamp-light o'er him streaming throws his shadow on the floor;
And my soul from out that shadow that lies floating on the floor
                              Shall be lifted—nevermore!

Ulalume—A Ballad

The skies they were ashen and sober;
    The leaves they were crispéd and sere—
    The leaves they were withering and sere:
It was night, in the lonesome October
    Of my most immemorial year:
It was hard by the dim lake of Auber,
    In the misty mid region of Weir:—
It was down by the dank tarn of Auber,
    In the ghoul-haunted woodland of Weir.

Here once, through an alley Titanic,
    Of cypress, I roamed with my Soul—
    Of cypress, with Psyche, my Soul.
These were days when my heart was volcanic
    As the scoriac rivers that roll—
    As the lavas that restlessly roll
Their sulphurous currents down Yaanek,
    In the ultimate climes of the Pole—
That groan as they roll down Mount Yaanek,
    In the realms of the Boreal Pole.

Our talk had been serious and sober,
    But our thoughts they were palsied and sere—
    Our memories were treacherous and sere;
For we knew not the month was October,
    And we marked not the night of the year—
    (Ah, night of all nights in the year!)
We noted not the dim lake of Auber,
    (Though once we had journeyed down here)
We remembered not the dank tarn of Auber,
    Nor the ghoul-haunted woodland of Weir.

And now, as the night was senescent,
    And star-dials pointed to morn—
    As the star-dials hinted of morn—
At the end of our path a liquescent
    And nebulous lustre was born,

Out of which a miraculous crescent
    Arose with a duplicate horn—
Astarte's bediamonded crescent,
    Distinct with its duplicate horn.

And I said—"She is warmer than Dian;
    She rolls through an ether of sighs—
    She revels in a region of sighs.
She has seen that the tears are not dry on
    These cheeks where the worm never dies,
And has come past the stars of the Lion,
    To point us the path to the skies—
    To the Lethean peace of the skies—
Come up, in despite of the Lion,
    To shine on us with her bright eyes—
Come up, through the lair of the Lion,
    With love in her luminous eyes."

But Psyche, uplifting her finger,
    Said—"Sadly this star I mistrust—
    Her pallor I strangely mistrust—
Ah, hasten!—ah, let us not linger!
    Ah, fly!—let us fly!—for we must."
In terror she spoke; letting sink her
    Wings till they trailed in the dust—
In agony sobbed; letting sink her
    Plumes till they trailed in the dust—
    Till they sorrowfully trailed in the dust.

I replied—"This is nothing but dreaming.
    Let us on, by this tremulous light!
    Let us bathe in this crystalline light!
Its Sibyllic splendor is beaming
    With Hope and in Beauty to-night—
    See!—it flickers up the sky through the night!
Ah, we safely may trust to its gleaming
    And be sure it will lead us aright—
We surely may trust to a gleaming
    That cannot but guide us aright
Since it flickers up to Heaven through the night."

Thus I pacified Psyche and kissed her,
 And tempted her out of her gloom—
 And conquered her scruples and gloom;
And we passed to the end of the vista—
 But were stopped by the door of a tomb—
 By the door of a legended tomb:—
And I said—"What is written, sweet sister,
 On the door of this legended tomb?"
 She replied—"Ulalume—Ulalume!—
 'Tis the vault of thy lost Ulalume!"

Then my heart it grew ashen and sober
 As the leaves that were crispéd and sere—
 As the leaves that were withering and sere—
And I cried—"It was surely October,
 On *this* very night of last year,
 That I journeyed—I journeyed down here!—
 That I brought a dread burden down here—
 On this night, of all nights in the year,
 Ah; what demon hath tempted me here?
Well I know, now, this dim lake of Auber—
 This misty mid region of Weir:—
Well I know, now, this dank tarn of Auber—
 This ghoul-haunted woodland of Weir."

Said we, then—the two, then—"Ah, can it
 Have been that the woodlandish ghouls—
 The pitiful, the merciful ghouls,
To bar up our way and to ban it
 From the secret that lies in these wolds—
 From the thing that lies hidden in these wolds—
Have drawn up the spectre of a planet
 From the limbo of lunary souls—
This sinfully scintillant planet
 From the Hell of the planetary souls?"

Annabel Lee

It was many and many a year ago,
    In a kingdom by the sea,
That a maiden there lived whom you may know
    By the name of Annabel Lee;—
And this maiden she lived with no other thought
    Than to love and be loved by me.

She was a child and *I* was a child,
    In this kingdom by the sea,
But we loved with a love that was more than love—
    I and my Annabel Lee—
With a love that the wingéd seraphs of Heaven
    Coveted her and me.

And this was the reason that, long ago,
    In this kingdom by the sea,
A wind blew out of a cloud by night
    Chilling my Annabel Lee;
So that her high-born kinsmen came
    And bore her away from me,
To shut her up in a sepulchre
    In this kingdom by the sea.

The angels, not half so happy in Heaven,
    Went envying her and me;
Yes! that was the reason (as all men know,
    In this kingdom by the sea)
That the wind came out of the cloud, chilling
    And killing my Annabel Lee.

But our love it was stronger by far than the love
    Of those who were older than we—
    Of many far wiser than we—
And neither the angels in Heaven above
    Nor the demons down under the sea
Can ever dissever my soul from the soul
    Of the beautiful Annabel Lee:—

For the moon never beams without bringing me dreams
 Of the beautiful Annabel Lee;
And the stars never rise but I see the bright eyes
 Of the beautiful Annabel Lee;
And so, all the night-tide, I lie down by the side
Of my darling, my darling, my life and my bride
 In her sepulchre there by the sea—
 In her tomb by the side of the sea.

OLIVER WENDELL HOLMES

Oliver Wendell Holmes (1809–1894) was a distinguished medical doctor and only secondarily a poet. Yet in his time he was among America's favorite poets and essayists and one of its wittiest public speakers. Holmes epitomized what he himself termed the Boston Brahmin caste: born into an old, established family, he attended Harvard as an undergraduate and then as a medical student; he married into another prominent Massachusetts family and was the father of the noted jurist of the same name; he maintained friendships with an impressive circle of famous men (Emerson, Hawthorne, Longfellow, Whittier, and Lowell among them). Holmes was best known for his poem "Old Ironsides" (1830), which was credited with saving the historic frigate *Constitution,* and for his humorous magazine pieces in the *Atlantic Monthly,* which were collected and published as *The Autocrat of the Breakfast Table* (1858). In addition to twelve collections of poetry he also published three novels, a biography of Emerson, and numerous volumes of articles, essays, and clinical studies.

Holmes first studied law at Harvard but then went on to medicine. He spent two years in medical school in France and completed his M.D. degree at Harvard in 1836. Among his first published works were medical texts, *Homeopathy, and Its Kindred Delusions* (1842) and an important and controversial treatise on the spread of childbed fever, *The Contagiousness of Puerperal Fever* (1843), which claimed rightly that unsanitary practices put mothers at risk. Holmes was very active in his profession: he received prizes for his work; he helped found a medical school; he was professor of anatomy at Dartmouth and later at Harvard; he became dean of the Harvard Medical School in 1847. His scientific bent carried over into his fiction, in which he portrayed his characters in a realistic and almost clinical manner, and the formal clarity of his verse owes something as well to his highly trained and sharp mind.

Old Ironsides

Ay, tear her tattered ensign down!
　　Long has it waved on high,
And many an eye has danced to see
　　That banner in the sky;
Beneath it rung the battle shout,
　　And burst the cannon's roar;—
The meteor of the ocean air
　　Shall sweep the clouds no more!

Her deck, once red with heroes' blood
　　Where knelt the vanquished foe,
When winds were hurrying o'er the flood
　　And waves were white below,
No more shall feel the victor's tread,
　　Or know the conquered knee;—
The harpies of the shore shall pluck
　　The eagle of the sea!

O better that her shattered hulk
　　Should sink beneath the wave;
Her thunders shook the mighty deep,
　　And there should be her grave;
Nail to the mast her holy flag,
　　Set every thread-bare sail,
And give her to the god of storms,—
　　The lightning and the gale!

The Chambered Nautilus

This is the ship of pearl, which, poets feign,
    Sails the unshadowed main,—
    The venturous bark that flings
On the sweet summer wind its purpled wings
In gulfs enchanted, where the siren sings,
    And coral reefs lie bare,
Where the cold sea-maids rise to sun their streaming hair.

Its webs of living gauze no more unfurl;
    Wrecked is the ship of pearl!
    And every chambered cell,
Where its dim dreaming life was wont to dwell,
As the frail tenant shaped his growing shell,
    Before thee lies revealed,—
Its irised ceiling rent, its sunless crypt unsealed!

Year after year beheld the silent toil
    That spread his lustrous coil;
    Still, as the spiral grew,
He left the past year's dwelling for the new,
Stole with soft step its shining archway through,
    Built up its idle door,
Stretched in his last-found home, and knew the old no more.

Thanks for the heavenly message brought by thee,
    Child of the wandering sea,
    Cast from her lap forlorn!
From thy dead lips a clearer note is born
Than ever Triton blew from wreathèd horn!
    While on mine ear it rings,
Through the deep caves of thought I hear a voice that sings:—

Build thee more stately mansions, O my soul,
    As the swift seasons roll!
    Leave thy low-vaulted past!
Let each new temple, nobler than the last,
Shut thee from heaven with a dome more vast,
    Till thou at length art free,
Leaving thine outgrown shell by life's unresting sea!

MARGARET FULLER

Margaret Fuller (1810–1850), one of America's foremost feminists, lived a representative transcendentalist life: she was steeped in the romantic philosophy of the period; she was a genuine enthusiast of literature and the arts; she embroiled herself in the cultural and political controversies of the time; and, as a writer and a woman, she waged a personal battle for dignity and freedom. Fuller was a formidable presence in transcendentalist circles, for with her erudition, ambition, and sheer energy she seemed to eclipse most of those around her. Fuller worked primarily in prose—in essays and articles—but her poetry reveals well the ardent nature of her intellect.

Born in Cambridge, Massachusetts, she received a thorough and stringent education from her father and various private tutors. Although a university education was unavailable to women at the time, Fuller mastered the classics and various modern languages and literatures. Her knowledge of German, in particular, opened up a lifelong interest in Goethe. In 1835 Fuller's father died, and she was constrained to set aside various projects and help attend to her siblings. She taught briefly at a progressive school run by Bronson Alcott in Boston and later at a school in Providence, Rhode Island. Fuller formed close and intense friendships with many men and women. Her famous Conversations in Boston, initially intended for the intellectual edification of women, eventually attracted a wide audience. From 1840 to 1842 Fuller edited the *Dial*, the influential transcendentalist journal that she and Emerson founded. Fuller's translation of Eckermann's *Conversations with Goethe* appeared in 1839, and *A Summer on the Lakes*, an account of a journey in the Midwest, was published in 1844. Horace Greeley, editor of the *New York Tribune*, subsequently hired her as literary critic for his newspaper, and Fuller moved to New York. She brought out her best-known work, *Women in the Nineteenth Century*, the following year. In 1846 as foreign correspondent for the *Tribune*, Fuller went abroad, where she met Wordsworth, Carlyle, George Sand, the Brownings, and the Italian revolutionary Mazzini. While in Italy she had a love affair with the Marchese Angelo Ossoli, a poor and poorly educated nobleman from Rome (it is still unclear whether they ever married). She bore him a son in 1848, during the Italian revolution in which she and Ossoli had both become active. After the fall of Rome she fled with Ossoli and her child to Florence, and in 1850 they sailed for New York. Just offshore Fire Island the ship foundered, and Fuller, Ossoli, and the child drowned. Thoreau, at Emerson's bidding, went to look for Fuller's body, but only the child's was found.

Sistrum

Triune, shaping, restless power,
Life-flow from life's natal hour,
No music chords are in thy sound;
By some thou'rt but a rattle found;
Yet, without thy ceaseless motion,
To ice would turn their dead devotion.
Life-flow of my natal hour,
I will not weary of thy power,
Till in the changes of thy sound
A chord's three parts distinct are found.
I will faithful move with thee,
God-ordered, self-fed energy,
Nature in eternity.

Flaxman

We deemed the secret lost, the spirit gone,
Which spake in Greek simplicity of thought,
And in the forms of gods and heroes wrought
Eternal beauty from the sculptured stone,—
A higher charm than modern culture won
With all the wealth of metaphysic lore,
Gifted to analyze, dissect, explore.
A many-colored light flows from one sun;
Art, 'neath its beams, a motley thread has spun;
The prism modifies the perfect day;
But thou hast known such mediums to shun,
And cast once more on life a pure, white ray.
Absorbed in the creations of thy mind,
Forgetting daily self, my truest self I find.

Freedom and Truth

To a friend

The shrine is vowed to freedom, but, my friend,
Freedom is but a means to gain an end.
Freedom should build the temple, but the shrine
Be consecrate to thought still more divine.
The human bliss which angel hopes foresaw
Is liberty to comprehend the law.
Give, then, thy book a larger scope and frame,
Comprising means and end in Truth's great name.

FRANCES SARGENT OSGOOD

Frances Sargent Osgood (1811–1850) is a complex figure: she was a popular poet whom friends represented as being shy and naive, and yet her poems suggest a wry, worldly, even coquettish personality. Osgood led an active social life in New York, where she was courted by Poe and befriended by the critic Rufus Griswold (who apparently disapproved of Poe's treatment of her). Osgood may have been the most admired woman poet in America during the mid-1840s.

Born in Boston, the daughter of Joseph Locke, a merchant, Osgood grew up in the nearby village of Higham, where she was educated at home. She showed early signs of poetic talent, and her work came to the attention of the novelist Lydia Maria Child, who was then editing the children's monthly *Juvenile Miscellany*. Under the pseudonym Florence, Osgood began publishing poems at the age of fourteen. In 1835 she married Samuel Stillman Osgood, a painter, and moved to England, where she met various painters, writers, and thinkers, including Harriet Martineau. While in England Osgood gave birth to a daughter and published two collections of poems, *A Wreath of Wild Flowers from New England* (1838) and *The Casket of Fate* (1839). Her success in England paved the way for her acceptance at home. Upon her return to America in 1839 Osgood began publishing regularly in popular journals and eventually wrote or edited eight more books in quick succession. After a second daughter was born in Boston, the Osgoods moved to New York, where a third child, Fanny Fay, was born in 1846. Osgood had been introduced to Poe in 1845, and their relationship became the cause of much gossip and speculation. (Indeed, one modern biographer claims that Poe was the father of Fanny Fay.) In any event there was difficulty in the marriage, for in 1849 Osgood and her husband separated. (Samuel Osgood left New York to join the gold rush in California.) The couple, however, was reconciled shortly before Osgood's death from tuberculosis in 1850. Osgood's final collection, *Poems* (1849), was dedicated to Rufus Griswold.

He Bade Me Be Happy

He bade me "Be happy," he whisper'd "Forget me;"
    He vow'd my affection was cherish'd in vain.
"Be happy!" "Forget me!" I would, if he'd let me—
    Why will he keep coming to say so again?

He came—it was not the first time, by a dozen—
    To take, as he said, "an eternal adieu;"
He went, and, for comfort, I turn'd to—my cousin,
    When back stalk'd the torment his vows to renew.

"You must love me no longer!" he said but this morning.
    "I love you no longer!" I meekly replied.
"Is this my reward?" he cried; "falsehood and scorning
    From her who was ever my idol, my pride!"

Forgive and Forget

"Forgive—forget! I own the wrong!"
    You fondly sigh'd when last I met you;
The task is neither hard nor long—
    I *do* forgive—I *will* forget you!

Ah! Woman Still

Ah! woman still
  Must veil the shrine,
Where feeling feeds the fire divine,
  Nor sing at will,
  Untaught by art,
The music prison'd in her heart!

Still gay the note,
  And light the lay,
The woodbird warbles on the spray,
  Afar to float;
  But homeward flown,
Within his nest, how changed the tone!

Oh! none can know,
  Who have not heard
The music-soul thrills the bird,
  The carol low
  As coo of dove
He warbles to his woodland-love!

The world would say
  'Twas vain and wild,
The impassion'd lay of Nature's child;
  And Feeling so
  Should veil the shrine
Where softly glow her fires divine!

ELLEN STURGIS HOOPER

Ellen Sturgis Hooper (1812–1848) was active in transcendentalist circles, where she was a close friend of Emerson, Fuller, and others. While few of her poems were ever published, Hooper's work was much admired by those who knew it. A year after Hooper's early death in 1848 Fuller wrote of her, "I have seen in Europe no woman more gifted by nature than she." One of her younger sisters, Caroline, was also a poet and transcendentalist.

Hooper was the second of six children born to Captain William Sturgis, founder of a successful Far East trading company and member of the state legislature, and Elizabeth Marston Davis, whose father was a prominent judge. Hooper was educated at home, where her father passed on his strong intellectual interests to all his children. A cultivated and artistic woman, Ellen Sturgis married a distinguished physician, Robert William Hooper, in 1837. They had three children. (One of them, Marian Hooper, was later the wife of Henry Adams, the writer.) In 1839 Hooper attended, with her sister Caroline, the famous Conversations in Boston run by Margaret Fuller. Hooper published a number of lyrics in the *Dial*, but most of her poems were circulated privately among her friends. Emerson, in particular, encouraged Hooper and had high expectations for her—sentiments shared by the critic Thomas Wentworth Higginson, who spoke of Hooper as "a woman of genius." With her younger sister Susan, Hooper wrote a humorous sketch of the Brook Farm community (1841–1846), an experiment in communal living that she followed with interest and not a little skepticism. For many years Hooper attended the radical Church of the Disciples, founded in Boston in 1841 by James Freeman Clarke, who published some of Hooper's poems in *The Disciples' Hymn Book*. Elizabeth Peabody—whose bookshop was a transcendentalist meeting place—also printed Hooper's work in *Aesthetic Papers* (1849). Hooper never published a book. Her early death at the age of thirty-six was felt keenly as a great loss.

"I slept and dreamed that life was Beauty"

I slept and dreamed that life was Beauty,—
I woke, and found that life was Duty.
Was thy dream then a shadowy lie?—
Toil on, poor heart, unceasingly,
And thou shalt find thy dream to be
A truth and noonday light to thee.

Heart, heart, lie still"

"Heart, heart, lie still,
Life is fleeting fast,
Strife will soon be past,"—

"I cannot lie still,
Beat strong I will"—

"Heart, heart, lie still,
Joy's but joy, and pain's but pain
Either, little loss or gain,"—

"I cannot lie still,
Beat strong, I will."

"Heart, heart, lie still,
Heaven is over all,
Rules this earthly ball,"—

"I cannot lie still,
Beat strong I will"—

"Heart, heart, lie still—"

"Heaven's sweet grace alone
Can keep in peace its own
Let that me fill
And I am still"—

"Better a sin which purposed wrong to none"

Better a sin which purposed wrong to none
Than this still wintry coldness at the heart,
A penance might be borne for evil done
And tears of grief and love might ease the smart.
But this self-satisfied and cold respect
To virtue which must be its own reward,
Heaven keep us through this danger still alive,
Lead us not into greatness, heart-abhorred—

Oh God, who framed this stern New-England land,
Its clear cold waters, and its clear, cold soul,
Thou givest tropic climes and youthful hearts
Thou weighest spirits and dost all control—
Teach me to wait for all—to bear the fault
That most I hate because it is my own,
And if I fail through foul conceit of good,
Let me sin deep so I may cast no stone.

CHRISTOPHER PEARSE CRANCH

Christopher Pearse Cranch (1813–1892), poet, painter, and musician, is as well known for his humorous caricatures of fellow transcendentalists as he is for his various writings. His ironic and mocking humor nevertheless belies his ardent belief in the romantic tenets of transcendentalism. A colorful and picturesque character—Van Wyck Brooks calls him an "all-attractive entertainer"—Cranch's reputation as a dilettante and aesthete who never fulfilled his promise has tended to obscure his real accomplishments in verse and painting.

Cranch was born in Alexandria, Virginia (then part of the District of Columbia), and attended Columbian College (later George Washington University) before entering the Harvard Divinity School in 1831. After preaching in New England and the Midwest Cranch went to Louisville, Ohio, to help James Freeman Clarke edit the *Western Messenger*, a transcendentalist journal. Deciding to pursue his artistic talents, Cranch left the ministry and became a painter (with some success). Returning to Boston, he met Emerson in 1840, attended meetings of the Transcendentalist Club, married a wealthy cousin in 1843, and published *Poems* the following year. Poe, in a review, called Cranch "one of the least intolerable of the school of Boston Transcendentalists" and later referred to him as "one of our finest poets." Cranch traveled to Europe in 1846 to study the great painters, took up residence in Rome (where he came to know the poets Robert and Elizabeth Barrett Browning), and later lived in Paris (from 1853 to 1863). Cranch eventually returned to the United States, where he spent the rest of his life, living chiefly in New York and Cambridge.

Well known as a man of talent and humor, Cranch—in addition to composing a collection of caricatures and cartoons on the "New Philosophy"—published four volumes of verse, two illustrated children's books, and a translation of Virgil's *Aeneid*.

Correspondences

All things in nature are beautiful types to the soul that can read them;
Nothing exists upon earth, but for unspeakable ends,
Every object that speaks to the senses was meant for the spirit;
Nature is but a scroll; God's handwriting thereon.
Ages ago when man was pure, ere the flood overwhelmed him,
While in the image of God every soul yet lived,
Every thing stood as a letter or word of a language familiar,
Telling of truths which now only the angels can read.
Lost to man was the key of those sacred hieroglyphics,
Stolen away by sin, till by heaven restored.
Now with infinite pains we here and there spell out a letter,
Here and there will the sense feebly shine through the dark.
When we perceive the light that breaks through the visible symbol,
What exultation is ours! *We* the discovery have made!
Yet is the meaning the same as when Adam lived sinless in Eden,
Only long hidden it slept, and now again is revealed.
Man unconsciously uses figures of speech every moment,
Little dreaming the cause why to such terms he is prone,
Little dreaming that every thing here has its own correspondence
Folded within its form, as in the body the soul.
Gleams of the mystery fall on us still, though much is forgotten,
And through our commonest speech, illumine the path of our thoughts.

Thus doth the lordly sun shine forth a type of the Godhead;
Wisdom and love the beams that stream on a darkened world.
Thus do the sparkling waters flow, giving joy to the desert,
And the fountain of life opens itself to the thirst.
Thus doth the word of God distil like the rain and the dew-drops;
Thus doth the warm wind breathe like to the Spirit of God;
And the green grass and the flowers are signs of the regeneration.

O thou Spirit of Truth, visit our minds once more,
Give us to read in letters of light the language celestial
Written all over the earth, written all over the sky—
Thus may we bring our hearts once more to know our Creator,
Seeing in all things around, types of the Infinite Mind.

Enosis

Thought is deeper than all speech,
    Feeling deeper than all thought;
Souls to souls can never teach
    What unto themselves was taught.

We are spirits clad in veils;
    Man by man was never seen;
All our deep communing fails
    To remove the shadowy screen.

Heart to heart was never known;
    Mind with mind did never meet;
We are columns left alone,
    Of a temple once complete.

Like the stars that gem the sky,
    Far apart, though seeming near,
In our light we scattered lie;
    All is thus but starlight here.

What is social company
    But a babbling summer stream?
What our wise philosophy
    But the glancing of a dream?

Only when the sun of love
    Melts the scattered stars of thought;
Only when we live above
    What the dim-eyed world hath taught;

Only when our souls are fed
    By the Fount which gave them birth,
And by inspiration led,
    Which they never drew from earth,

We like parted drops of rain
    Swelling till they meet and run,
Shall be all absorbed again,
    Melting, flowing into one.

The Ocean

"In a season of calm weather
Though inland far we be,
Our souls have sight of that immortal sea
That brought us hither,
Can in a moment travel thither,
And see the children sport upon the shore,
And hear the mighty waters rolling evermore"

—Wordsworth

Tell me, brother, what are we?—
Spirits bathing in the sea
   Of Deity!
Half afloat, and half on land,
Wishing much to leave the strand,—
Standing, gazing with devotion,
Yet afraid to trust the Ocean—
   Such are we.

Wanting love and holiness
To enjoy the wave's caress;
Wanting faith and heavenly hope,
Buoyantly to bear us up;
Yet impatient in our dwelling,
When we hear the ocean swelling,
And in every wave that rolls
We behold the happy souls
Peacefully, triumphantly
Swimming on the smiling sea,
Then we linger round the shore,
Lovers of the earth no more.

Once,—'twas in our infancy,
We were drifted by this sea
To the coast of human birth,
To this body and this earth:
Gentle were the hands that bore
Our young spirits to the shore;
Gentle lips that bade us look

Outward from our cradle nook
To the spirit-bearing ocean
With such wonder and devotion,
As each stilly Sabbath day,
We were led a little way,
Where we saw the waters swell
Far away from inland dell,
And received with grave delight
Symbols of the Infinite:—
Then our home was near the sea;
"Heaven was round our infancy:"
Night and day we heard the waves
Murmuring by us to their caves;—
Floated in unconscious life,
With no later doubts at strife,
Trustful of the upholding Power
Who sustained us hour by hour.

Now we've wandered from the shore,
Dwellers by the sea no more;
Yet at times there comes a tone
Telling of the visions flown,
Sounding from the distant sea,
Where we left our purity:
Distant glimpses of the surge
Lure us down to ocean's verge;
There we stand with vague distress,
Yearning for the measureless;
By half-wakened instincts driven,
Half loving earth, half loving heaven,
Fearing to put off and swim,
Yet impelled to turn to Him
In whose life we live and move,
And whose very name is Love.

Grant me courage, Holy One,
To become indeed thy son,
And in thee, thou Parent-Sea,
Live and love eternally.

In the Palais Royal Garden

In the Palais Royal Garden I stood listening to-day,
Just at sunset, in the crowd that flaunted up and down so gay
As the strains of "Casta Diva" rose and fell and died away.

Lonely in the crowd of French I stood and listened to the strain,
And the breath of happier hours came blowing from the past again;
But the music brought a pleasure that was near akin to pain.

Italy, dear Italy, came back, with all her orange flowers,
With her sapphire skies and ocean, with her shrines and crumbling towers,
And her dark-eyed women sitting under their vine-shaded bowers.

And the rich and brilliant concerts in my own far distant land,
Where the world-renownéd singers, circled by the orchestral band
Poured their music on the crowds like costly wine upon the sand.

All the aroma of the best and brightest hours of love and song
Mingled with the yearning music, floated to me o'er the throng.
But it died as died the sunset. Ah, it could not linger long!

Through the streets the carriages are rolling with a heavy jar,
Feebly o'er the staring gas-lamps glimmers here and there a star.
Night looks down through narrow spaces; men are near, the skies are far.

Far too are my friends, the cherished,—north and south and o'er the sea.
And to-night I pant for music and for life that cannot be,
For the foreign city's crowd is naught but solitude to me.

The Spirit of the Age

A wondrous light is filling the air,
And rimming the clouds of the old despair;
And hopeful eyes look up to see
Truth's mighty electricity,—
Auroral shimmerings swift and bright,
That wave and flash in the silent night,—
Magnetic billows travelling fast,
And flooding all the spaces vast
From dim horizon to farthest cope

Of heaven, in streams of gathering hope.
Silent they mount and spread apace,
And the watchers see old Europe's face
Lit with expression new and strange,—
The prophecy of coming change.

Meantime, while thousands, wrapt in dreams,
Sleep heedless of the electric gleams,
Or ply their wonted work and strife,
Or plot their pitiful games of life;
While the emperor bows in his formal halls,
And the clerk whirls on at the masking balls;
While the lawyer sits at his dreary files,
And the banker fingers his glittering piles,
And the priest kneels down at his lighted shrine,
And the fop flits by with his mistress fine,—
The diplomat works at his telegraph wires:
His back is turned to the heavenly fires.
Over him flows the magnetic tide,
And the candles are dimmed by the glow outside.
Mysterious forces overawe,
Absorb, suspend the usual law.
The needle stood northward an hour ago;
Now it veers like a weathercock to and fro.
The message he sends flies not as once;
The unwilling wires yield no response.
Those iron veins that pulsed but late
From a tyrant's will to a people's fate,
Flowing and ebbing with feverish strength,
Are seized by a Power whose breadth and length,
Whose height and depth, defy all gauge
Save the great spirit of the age.
The mute machine is moved by a law
That knows no accident or flaw,
And the iron thrills to a different chime
Than that which rang in the dead old time.
For Heaven is taking the matter in hand,
And baffling the tricks of the tyrant band.
The sky above and the earth beneath

Heave with a supermundane breath.
Half-truths, for centuries kept and prized,
By higher truths are polarized.
Like gamesters on a railroad train,
Careless of stoppage, sun or rain,
We juggle, plot, combine, arrange,
And are swept along by the rapid change.
And some who from their windows mark
The unwonted lights that flood the dark,
Little by little, in slow surprise
Lift into space their sleepy eyes;
Little by little are made aware
That a spirit of power is passing there,—
That a spirit is passing, strong and free,—
The soul of the nineteenth century.

Bird Language

One day in the bluest of summer weather,
    Sketching under a whispering oak,
I heard five bobolinks laughing together
    Over some ornithological joke.

What the fun was I could n't discover.
    Language of birds is a riddle on earth.
What could they find in whiteweed and clover
    To split their sides with such musical mirth?

Was it some prank of the prodigal summer,
    Face in the cloud or voice in the breeze,
Querulous catbird, woodpecker drummer,
    Cawing of crows high over the trees?

Was it some chipmunk's chatter, or weasel
    Under the stone-wall stealthy and sly?
Or was the joke about me at my easel,
    Trying to catch the tints of the sky?

Still they flew tipsily, shaking all over,
    Bubbling with jollity, brimful of glee,
While I sat listening deep in the clover,
    Wondering what their jargon could be.

'T was but the voice of a morning the brightest
    That ever dawned over yon shadowy hills;
'T was but the song of all joy that is lightest,—
    Sunshine breaking in laughter and trills.

Vain to conjecture the words they are singing;
    Only by tones can we follow the tune
In the full heart of the summer fields ringing,
    Ringing the rhythmical gladness of June!

The Pines and the Sea

Beyond the low marsh-meadows and the beach,
Seen through the hoary trunks of windy pines,
The long blue level of the ocean shines.
The distant surf, with hoarse, complaining speech,
Out from its sandy barrier seems to reach;
And while the sun behind the woods declines,
The moaning sea with sighing boughs combines,
And waves and pines make answer, each to each.
O melancholy soul, whom far and near,
In life, faith, hope, the same sad undertone
Pursues from thought to thought! thou needs must hear
An old refrain, too much, too long thine own:
'T is thy mortality infects thine ear;
The mournful strain was in thyself alone.

JONES VERY

Jones Very (1813–1880) was one of the few genuine mystics among the transcendentalists—his early poems, he said, were "communicated" to him by the Holy Ghost—and the intensity of his religious experience often caused doubt as to his sanity. However, Emerson, among others, declared him "profoundly sane," and his work earned the praise of eminent poets and critics, including William Cullen Bryant and James Freeman Clarke.

The son of a sea captain, Very was born in Salem, Massachusetts, and spent much of his childhood at sea. He attended Harvard (graduating in 1836), where he served as a tutor in Greek before entering the Divinity School. In 1837 he began experiencing intense mystical visions, which prompted his dismissal from Harvard and eventually led him to enter the MacLean Asylum for four weeks. Emerson, who admired Very's poetry, brought him to lecture at the Concord lyceum and arranged to publish his *Essays and Poems* (1839). A close friendship developed between Very and Emerson, though Very could be trying at times. Once, in a fit of exasperation over Very's rough-hewn divine inspirations, Emerson declared, "Cannot the spirit parse & spell?" Eventually, Very received a license to preach and held temporary pastorates in Maine, Massachusetts, and Rhode Island (though he never received his divinity degree). However, being too shy to preach well, he eventually retired and became a recluse, living in Salem under his sister's care for his remaining years.

Very's reputation as a poet has grown considerably in this century, though never approaching what it was among his fellow transcendentalists in the 1830s. While his poems hark back to earlier forms of Christian piety in the tradition of George Herbert and the English metaphysical poets, his verse is marked by mystical concerns that align him with the transcendentalist belief in an intuitive and spiritualized faculty of Reason.

The Columbine

Still, still my eye will gaze long-fixed on thee,
Till I forget that I am called a man,
And at thy side fast-rooted seem to be,
And the breeze comes my cheek with thine to fan;
Upon this craggy hill our life shall pass,
A life of summer days and summer joys,
Nodding our honey bells mid pliant grass
In which the bee half hid his time employs;
And here we'll drink with thirsty pores the rain,
And turn dew-sprinkled to the rising sun,
And look when in the flaming west again
His orb across the heaven its path has run;
Here left in darkness on the rocky steep,
My weary eyes shall close like folding flowers in sleep.

The New Birth

'Tis a new life—thoughts move not as they did
With slow uncertain steps across my mind,
In thronging haste fast pressing on they bid
The portals open to the viewless wind;
That comes not, save when in the dust is laid
The crown of pride that gilds each mortal brow,
And from before man's vision melting fade
The heavens and earth—Their walls are falling now—
Fast crowding on each thought claims utterance strong,
Storm-lifted waves swift rushing to the shore
On from the sea they send their shouts along,
Back through the cave-worn rocks their thunders roar,
And I a child of God by Christ made free
Start from death's slumbers to eternity.

The Garden

I saw the spot where our first parents dwelt;
And yet it wore to me no face of change,
For while amid its fields and groves I felt
As if I had not sinned, nor thought it strange;
My eye seemed but a part of every sight,
My ear heard music in each sound that rose,
Each sense forever found a new delight,
Such as the spirit's vision only knows;
Each act some new and ever-varying joy
Did by my Father's love for me prepare;
To dress the spot my ever fresh employ,
And in the glorious whole with Him to share;
No more without the flaming gate to stray,
No more for sin's dark stain the debt of death to pay.

The Dead

I see them crowd on crowd they walk the earth
Dry, leafless trees no Autumn wind laid bare;
And in their nakedness find cause for mirth,
And all unclad would winter's rudeness dare;
No sap doth through their clattering branches flow,
Whence springing leaves and blossoms bright appear;
Their hearts the living God have ceased to know,
Who gives the spring time to th'expectant year;
They mimic life, as if from him to steal
His glow of health to paint the livid cheek;
They borrow words for thoughts they cannot feel,
That with a seeming heart their tongue may speak;
And in their show of life more dead they live
Than those that to the earth with many tears they give.

The Presence

I sit within my room and joy to find
That Thou who always lov'st, art with me here,
That I am never left by Thee behind,
But by Thyself Thou keepst me ever near;
The fire burns brighter when with Thee I look,
And seems a kinder servant sent to me;
With gladder heart I read thy holy book,
Because Thou art the eyes by which I see;
This aged chair, that table, watch, and door
Around in ready service ever wait;
Nor can I ask of Thee a menial more
To fill the measure of my large estate,
For Thou Thyself, with all a Father's care,
Where'er I turn, art ever with me there.

Thy Brother's Blood

I have no Brother—they who meet me now
Offer a hand with their own wills defiled,
And while they wear a smooth unwrinkled brow
Know not that Truth can never be beguiled;
Go wash the hand that still betrays thy guilt;
Before the spirit's gaze what stain can hide?
Abel's red blood upon the earth is spilt,
And by thy tongue it cannot be denied;
I hear not with the ear—the heart doth tell
Its secret deeds to me untold before;
Go, all its hidden plunder quickly sell,
Then shalt thou cleanse thee from thy brother's gore;
Then will I take thy gift—that bloody stain
Shall not be seen upon thy hand again.

The Created

There is nought for thee by thy haste to gain;
'Tis not the swift with Me that win the race;
Through long endurance of delaying pain,
Thine opened eye shall see thy Father's face;
Nor here nor there, where now thy feet would turn,
Thou wilt find Him who ever seeks for thee;
But let obedience quench desires that burn,
And where thou art, thy Father too will be!
Behold! as day by day the spirit grows,
Thou see'st by inward light things hid before;
Till what God is, thyself, his image, shows;
And thou dost wear the robe that first thou wore,
When bright with radiance from his forming hand,
He saw thee Lord of all his creatures stand.

The New World

The night that has no star lit up by God,
The day that round men shines who still are blind,
The earth their grave-turned feet for ages trod,
And sea swept over by His mighty wind;
All these have passed away; the melting dream
That flitted o'er the sleeper's half-shut eye,
When touched by morning's golden-darting beam;
And he beholds around the earth and sky
That ever real stands; the rolling spheres,
And heaving billows of the boundless main,
That show though time is past no trace of years,
And earth restored he sees as his again;
The earth that fades not, and the heavens that stand;
Their strong foundations laid by God's right hand!

The Prayer

　　Wilt Thou not visit me?
The plant beside me feels thy gentle dew;
　　And every blade of grass I see,
From thy deep earth its quickening moisture drew.

　　Wilt Thou not visit me?
Thy morning calls on me with cheering tone;
　　And every hill and tree
Lend but one voice, the voice of Thee alone.

　　Come, for I need thy love;
More than the flower the dew, or grass the rain,
　　Come, gently as thy holy dove;
And let me in thy sight rejoice to live again.

　　I will not hide from them,
When thy storms come, though fierce may be their wrath;
　　But bow with leafy stem,
And strengthened follow on thy chosen path.

　　Yes, Thou wilt visit me:
Nor plant nor tree thy parent eye delight so well;
　　As when from sin set free
My spirit loves with thine in peace to dwell.

Autumn Leaves

The leaves though thick are falling; one by one
Decayed they drop from off their parent tree;
Their work with autumn's latest day is done,
Thou see'st them borne upon its breezes free;
They lie strown here and there, their many dyes
That yesterday so caught thy passing eye;
Soiled by the rain each leaf neglected lies,
Upon the path where now thou hurriest by;
Yet think thee not their beauteous tints less fair,
Than when they hung so gaily o'er thy head;
But rather find thee eyes, and look thee there
Where now thy feet so heedless o'er them tread;
And thou shalt see where wasting now they lie,
The unseen hues of immortality.

The Barberry-Bush

The bush that has most briers and bitter fruit,
Waits till the frost has turned its green leaves red,
Its sweetened berries will thy palate suit,
And thou may'st find, e'en there, a homely bread.
Upon the hills of Salem, scattered wide,
Their yellow blossoms gain the eye in Spring;
And straggling down upon the turnpike's side,
Their ripened bunches to your hand they bring.
I've plucked them oft in boyhood's early hour,
What then I gave such name, and thought it true;
But now I know, that other fruit, as sour,
Grows on what now thou callest *Me*, and *You*;
Yet, wilt thou wait the Autumn that I see,
'Twill sweeter taste than these red berries be.

The Hand and the Foot

The hand and foot that stir not, they shall find
Sooner than all the rightful place to go;
Now in their motion free as roving wind,
Though first no snail so limited and slow;
I mark them full of labor all the day,
Each active motion made in perfect rest;
They cannot from their path mistaken stray,
Though 'tis not theirs, yet in it they are blest;
The bird has not their hidden track found out,
Nor cunning fox though full of art he be;
It is the way unseen, the certain route,
Where ever bound, yet thou art ever free;
The path of Him, whose perfect law of love
Bids spheres and atoms in just order move.

Yourself

'Tis to yourself I speak; you cannot know
Him whom I call in speaking such an one,
For thou beneath the earth liest buried low,
Which he alone as living walks upon;
Thou mayst at times have heard him speak to you,
And often wished perchance that you were he;
And I must ever wish that it were true,
For then thou couldst hold fellowship with me;
But now thou hearst us talk as strangers, met
Above the room wherein thou liest abed;
A word perhaps loud spoken thou mayst get,
Or hear our feet when heavily they tread;
But he who speaks, or him who's spoken to,
Must both remain as strangers still to you.

The Silent

There is a sighing in the wood,
A murmur in the beating wave,
The heart has never understood
To tell in words the thoughts they gave.

Yet oft it feels an answering tone,
When wandering on the lonely shore;
And could the lips its voice make known,
'Twould sound as does the ocean's roar.

And oft beneath the windswept pine,
Some chord is struck the strain to swell;
Nor sounds nor language can define,
'Tis not for words or sounds to tell.

'Tis all unheard; that Silent Voice,
Whose goings forth, unknown to all,
Bids bending reed and bird rejoice,
And fills with music nature's hall.

And in the speechless human heart
It speaks, where'er man's feet have trod;
Beyond the lips' deceitful art,
To tell of Him, the Unseen God.

The Spheres

The brightness round the rising sun,
　　It shall be thine if thou wilt rise;
Thou too hast thine own race to run,
　　And pour thy light on waiting eyes.

The expectant millions eager turn,
　　Oft when thy coming streaks the east;
And ask when shall his glory burn,
　　Aloft to mid-day's light increased.

And star on star when thine has lit
　　The o'erhanging dome of earth's wide heaven,
Shall rise, for as by Him 'tis writ,
　　Who to each sun its path has given.

And all with thine, each wheeling sphere
　　In ways harmonious on shall move;
Tracing with golden bounds the year
　　Of the Great Parent's endless love.

The Lost

The fairest day that ever yet has shone,
Will be when thou the day within shalt see;
The fairest rose that ever yet has blown,
When thou the flower thou lookest on shalt be.
But thou art far away among Time's toys;
Thyself the day thou lookest for in them,
Thyself the flower that now thine eye enjoys,
But wilted now thou hang'st upon thy stem.
The bird thou hearest on the budding tree,
Thou hast made sing with thy forgotten voice;
But when it swells again to melody,
The song is thine in which thou wilt rejoice;
And thou new risen 'midst these wonders live,
That now to them dost all thy substance give.

The Origin of Man

I.

Man has forgot his Origin; in vain
He searches for the record of his race
In ancient books, or seeks with toil to gain
From the deep cave, or rocks some primal trace.
And some have fancied, from a higher sphere,
Forgetful of his origin he came;
To dwell awhile a wandering exile here
Subject to sense, another, yet the same.
With mind bewildered, weak how should he know
The Source Divine from whom his being springs?
The darkened spirit does its shadow throw
On written record, and on outward things;
That else might plainly to his thought reveal
The wondrous truths, which now they but conceal.

II.

Not suffering for their sins in former state,
As some have taught, their system to explain;
Nor hither sent, as by the sport of fate,
Souls that nor memory, nor love retain,
Do men into this world of nature come;
But born of God; though earthy, frail and weak;
Not all unconscious of a heavenly home,
Which they through trial, suffering, here must seek.
A heavenly Guide has come the way to show,
To lead us to the Father's house above;
From Him he came, to Him, he said, I go;
Oh may we heed the message of his love!
That we no more in darkness, doubt, may roam,
But find while here we dwell our heavenly home.

HENRY DAVID THOREAU

Henry David Thoreau (1817–1862) first came to Emerson's attention when one of the former's poems, tied to a posy of violets and thrown into the open window of Mrs. Lucy Brown of Concord, was subsequently shown to Emerson. It was not long before Emerson was calling his protégé a genius of "the purest strain, and the loftiest." Emerson went on to publish Thoreau's poems in the *Dial* but later cooled in his enthusiasm for them. In response Thoreau burnt his remaining poems, since his mentor "did not praise them." No doubt as a result we have the copious glories of Thoreau's prose—and not his poetry—for a literary legacy. Moreover, what has come down to us of the poems are mostly Thoreau's early efforts, but they are indeed "golden" accomplishments, as Emerson himself later admitted.

Thoreau, born in Concord, Massachusetts, attended Harvard, where he studied mathematics, literature, and languages, graduating in 1837. Having resigned from one teaching position (he was compelled to inflict corporal punishment on disobedient students), Thoreau ran a school in Concord with his brother from 1838 to 1841. In 1842 he went to live and work as a handyman in Emerson's house, where he stayed intermittently. At various times Thoreau also worked as a pencil maker, a surveyor, a lecturer, and a tutor, as well as a "self-appointed inspector of snow-storms and rain-storms." In 1845 he began a two-year experiment in "economic" living in a cabin on Emerson's property at Walden Pond, resulting in his best-known work, *Walden*. A member of the Transcendentalist Club and a contributor to the *Dial*, Thoreau's writings include essays, poems, sketches, scientific studies, and travel pieces. In his lifetime he published only two books (*A Week on the Concord and Merrimack Rivers* and *Walden*), but within four years of his death five others were printed posthumously (including *The Maine Woods* and *Cape Cod*). By the time of his death from tuberculosis at the age of forty-five Thoreau had become a renowned writer. Much of Thoreau's present fame rests on *Walden* and the tract *Civil Disobedience* (which influenced Tolstoy, Gandhi, and Martin Luther King, Jr.), but his greatest overall work is perhaps found in his journals, which run to over two million words in forty-seven volumes. And yet, some would agree with Emerson that Thoreau's "biography is in his verses."

"I am a parcel of vain strivings tied"

I am a parcel of vain strivings tied
    By a chance bond together,
  Dangling this way and that, their links
    Were made so loose and wide,
        Methinks,
      For milder weather.

A bunch of violets without their roots,
    And sorrel intermixed,
  Encircled by a wisp of straw
    Once coiled about their shoots,
        The law
      By which I'm fixed.

A nosegay which Time clutched from out
    Those fair Elysian fields,
  With weeds and broken stems, in haste,
    Doth make the rabble rout
        That waste
      The day he yields.

And here I bloom for a short hour unseen,
    Drinking my juices up,
  With no root in the land
    To keep my branches green,
        But stand
      In a bare cup.

Some tender buds were left upon my stem
    In mimicry of life,
  But ah! the children will not know,
    Till time has withered them,
        The woe
      With which they're rife.

But now I see I was not plucked for naught,
 And after in life's vase
Of glass set while I might survive,
 But by a kind hand brought
  Alive
 To a strange place.

That stock thus thinned will soon redeem its hours,
 And by another year,
Such as God knows, with freer air,
 More fruits and fairer flowers
  Will bear,
 While I droop here.

The Poet's Delay

In vain I see the morning rise,
 In vain observe the western blaze,
Who idly look to other skies,
 Expecting life by other ways.

Amidst such boundless wealth without,
 I only still am poor within,
The birds have sung their summer out,
 But still my spring does not begin.

Shall I then wait the autumn wind,
 Compelled to seek a milder day,
And leave no curious nest behind,
 No woods still echoing to my lay?

The Inward Morning

Packed in my mind lie all the clothes
    Which outward nature wears,
And in its fashion's hourly change
    It all things else repairs.

In vain I look for change abroad,
    And can no difference find,
Till some new ray of peace uncalled
    Illumes my inmost mind.

What is it gilds the trees and clouds,
    And paints the heavens so gay,
But yonder fast-abiding light
    With its unchanging ray?

Lo, when the sun streams through the wood,
    Upon a winter's morn,
Where'er his silent beams intrude
    The murky night is gone.

How could the patient pine have known
    The morning breeze would come,
Or humble flowers anticipate
    The insect's noonday hum,—

Till the new light with morning cheer
    From far streamed through the aisles,
And nimbly told the forest trees
    For many stretching miles?

I've heard within my inmost soul
    Such cheerful morning news,
In the horizon of my mind
    Have seen such orient hues,

As in the twilight of the dawn,
    When the first birds awake,
Are heard within some silent wood,
    Where they the small twigs break,

Or in the eastern skies are seen,
    Before the sun appears,
The harbingers of summer heats
    Which from afar he bears.

Rumors from an Aeolian Harp

There is a vale which none hath seen,
Where foot of man has never been,
Such as here lives with toil and strife,
An anxious and a sinful life.

There every virtue has its birth,
Ere it descends upon the earth,
And thither every deed returns,
Which in the generous bosom burns.

There love is warm, and youth is young,
And poetry is yet unsung,
For Virtue still adventures there,
And freely breathes her native air.

And ever, if you hearken well,
You still may hear its vesper bell,
And tread of high-souled men go by,
Their thoughts conversing with the sky.

"Light-winged Smoke, Icarian bird"

Light-winged Smoke, Icarian bird,
Melting thy pinions in thy upward flight,
Lark without song, and messenger of dawn,
Circling above the hamlets as thy nest;
Or else, departing dream, and shadowy form
Of midnight vision, gathering up thy skirts;
By night star-veiling, and by day
Darkening the light and blotting out the sun;
Go thou my incense upward from this hearth,
And ask the gods to pardon this clear flame.

"Fair Haven"

When Winter fringes every bough
    With his fantastic wreath,
And puts the seal of silence now
    Upon the leaves beneath;

When every stream in its pent-house
    Goes gurgling on its way,
And in his gallery the mouse
    Nibbleth the meadow hay;

Methinks the summer still is nigh,
    And lurketh underneath,
As that same meadow mouse doth lie
    Snug in the last year's heath.

And if perchance the chicadee
    Lisp a faint note anon,
The snow in summer's canopy,
    Which she herself put on.

Fair blossoms deck the cheerful trees,
    And dazzling fruits depend,
The north wind sighs a summer breeze,
    The nipping frosts to fend,

Bringing glad tidings unto me,
    The while I stand all ear,
Of a serene eternity,
    Which need not winter fear.

Out on the silent pond straightway
    The restless ice doth crack,
And pond sprites merry gambols play
    Amid the deafening rack.

Eager I hasten to the vale,
    As if I heard brave news,
How nature held high festival,
    Which it were hard to lose.

I gambol with my neighbor ice,
    And sympathizing quake,
As each new crack darts in a trice
    Across the gladsome lake.

One with the cricket in the ground,
    And faggot on the hearth,
Resounds the rare domestic sound
    Along the forest path.

"My life has been the poem I would have writ"

My life has been the poem I would have writ,
But I could not both live and utter it.

"On fields oer which the reaper's hand has passd"

On fields oer which the reaper's hand has passd,
Lit by the harvest moon and autumn sun,
My thoughts like stubble floating in the wind
And of such fineness as October airs,
There after harvest could I glean my life
A richer harvest reaping without toil,
And weaving gorgeous fancies at my will
In subtler webs than finest summer haze.

"Forever in my dream & in my morning thought"

Forever in my dream & in my morning thought
      Eastward a mount ascends—
But when in the sunbeam its hard outline is sought—
      It all dissolves & ends.
The woods that way are gates—the pastures too slope up
      To an unearthly ground—
But when I ask my mates, to take the staff & cup,
      It can no more be found—
Perchance I have no shoes fit for the lofty soil
      Where my thoughts graze—
No properly spun clues—nor well strained mid day oil
      Or—must I mend my ways?
It is a promised land which I have not yet earned,
      I have not made beginning
With consecrated hand—I have not even learned
      To lay the underpinning.
The mountain sinks by day—as do my lofty thoughts,
      Because I'm not highminded.
If I could think alway above these hills & warts
      I should see it, though blinded.
It is a spiral path within the pilgrim's soul
      Leads to this mountain's brow
Commencing at his hearth he reaches to this goal
      He knows not when nor how.

"What's the railroad to me?"

What's the railroad to me?
I never go to see
Where it ends.
It fills a few hollows,
And makes banks for the swallows,
It sets the sand a-blowing,
And the blackberries a-growing.

Music

Far from this atmosphere that music sounds
Bursting some azure chink in the dull clouds
Of sense that overarch my recent years
And steal his freshness from the noonday sun.
Ah, I have wandered many ways and lost
The boyant step, the whole responsive life
That stood with joy to hear what seemed then
Its echo, its own harmony borne back
Upon its ear. This tells of better space,
Far far beyond the hills the woods the clouds
That bound my low and plodding valley life,
Far from my sin, remote from my distrust,
Where first my healthy morning life perchance
Trod lightly as on clouds, and not as yet
My weary and faint hearted noon had sunk
Upon the clod while the bright day went by.
    Lately, I feared my life was empty, now
I know though a frail tenement that it still
Is worth repair, if yet its hollowness
Doth entertain so fine a guest within, and through
Its empty aisles there still doth ring
Though but the echo of so high a strain;
It shall be swept again and cleansed from sin
To be a thoroughfare for celestial airs;
Perchance the God who is proprietor
Will pity take on his poor tenant here
And countenance his efforts to improve
His property and make it worthy to revert,
At some late day Unto himself again.

WILLIAM ELLERY CHANNING

William Ellery Channing (1818–1901) was in many ways the quintessential transcendentalist poet: gifted with an idiosyncratic poetic sensibility, often spontaneous in composition, he was yet undisciplined and willful in his erratic effusions. His good friend, Thoreau, called his poetic style "sublimo-slipshod," whereas Poe attacked Channing's first book, *Poems* (1843), as being nine-tenths "utter and irredeemable nonsense." It was left to Emerson to champion Channing's verse as "more new & more charactered than anything we are likely to have" (though he too noted that Channing "defies a little too disdainfully his dictionary & logic"). Channing's reputation as a poet never quite got off the ground—and it is never likely to soar—yet his verse embodies much of the romantic temperament and conviction then afield in the heady days of transcendentalism.

Channing was born in Boston, the nephew of a famous and impressive namesake, William Ellery Channing, a Unitarian minister. The young Channing was nothing like his uncle, however, leaving Harvard in his first year out of sheer boredom with compulsory chapel. Channing was only interested in writing poetry and, later, in taking long walks with Thoreau. In a fit of impracticality he bought a farm in Illinois in 1839 but sold it two years later and moved to Cincinnati to attempt a living by writing and teaching. He married a sister of Margaret Fuller, Ellen Fuller, in 1841 and eventually moved to Concord, Massachusetts, where he included among his friends Emerson, Thoreau, Hawthorne, Fuller, and Lowell. In 1853 his wife left him, exasperated by his unwillingness to support the family. (She did return to him two years later.) After her death in 1856 the children were taken by relatives, and Channing began a long period of isolation and loneliness, despite his many illustrious acquaintances. Eventually, Franklin B. Sanborn, an old and devoted friend, took Channing in and looked after him in his last years.

Most of Channing's poetry was published in the 1840s, but he had an unexpected second period of inspiration in the 1870s and 1880s, during which he published three additional books of poems. In 1873 Channing brought out the first biography of Thoreau, *Thoreau, The Poet-Naturalist.* By the time of Channing's death, a year into the twentieth century, he was, as one critic called him, "the last dried leaf on the Transcendentalist tree."

A Poet's Hope

Flying,—flying beyond all lower regions,
Beyond the light called day, and night's repose,
Where the untrammelled soul, on her wind-pinions
Fearlessly sweeping, defies my earthly woes;—
There,—there, upon the infinitest sea,
Lady, thy hope,—so fair a hope, summons me.

Fall off, ye garments of my misty weather,
Drop from my eyes, ye scales of time's applying;
Am I not godlike? meet not here together
A past and future infinite, defying,
The cold, still, callous moment of to-day?
Am I not master of the calm alway?

Would I could summon from the deep, deep mine,
Glutted with shapely jewels, glittering bright,
One echo of that splendor, call it thine,
And weave it in the strands of living light;
For it is in me, and the sea smiles fair,
And thitherward I rage, on whirling air.

Unloose me, demons of dull care and want,
I will not stand your slave, I am your king;
Think not within your meshes vile I pant
For the wild liberty of an unclipt wing;
My empire is myself, and I defy
The external; yes! I rule the whole, or die.

All music that the fullest breeze can play
In its melodious whisperings in the wood,
All modulations which entrance the day
And deify a sunlight solitude;
All anthems that the waves sing to the ocean
Are mine for song, and yield to my devotion.

And mine the soft glaze of a loving eye,
And mine the pure shapes of the human form,
And mine the bitterest sorrow's witchery,
And spells enough to make a snow-king warm;
For an undying hope thou breathest me,—
Hope which can ride the tossing, foaming sea.

Lady, there is a hope that all men have,
Some mercy for their faults, a grassy place
To rest in, and a flower-strown, gentle grave;
Another hope which purifies our race,
That when that fearful bourne forever past,
They may find rest,—and rest *so* long to last.

I seek it not, I ask no rest for ever,
My path is onward to the farthest shores,—
Upbear me in your arms, unceasing river,
That from the soul's clear fountain swiftly pours,
Motionless not, until the end is won,
Which now I feel hath scarcely felt the sun.

To feel, to know, to soar unlimited,
Mid throngs of light-winged angels sweeping far,
And pore upon the realms unvisited,
That tesselate the unseen unthought star,
To be the thing that now I feebly dream
Flashing within my faintest, deepest gleam.

Ah! caverns of my soul! how thick your shade,
Where flows that life by which I faintly see,—
Wave your bright torches, for I need your aid,
Golden-eyed demons of my ancestry!
Your son though blinded hath a light within,
A heavenly fire which ye from suns did win.

And, lady, in thy hope my life will rise
Like the air-voyager, till I upbear
These heavy curtains of my filmy eyes,
Into a lighter, more celestial air;
A mortal's hope shall bear me safely on,
Till I the higher region shall have won.

O Time! O death! I clasp you in my arms,
For I can soothe an infinite cold sorrow,
And gaze contented on your icy charms,
And that wild snow-pile, which we call to-morrow;
Sweep on, O soft, and azure-lidded sky,
Earth's waters to your gentle gaze reply.

I am not earth-born, though I here delay;
Hope's child, I summon infiniter powers,
And laugh to see the mild and sunny day
Smile on the shrunk and thin autumnal hours;
I laugh, for hope hath happy place with me,
If my bark sinks, 't is to another sea.

Walden

It is not far beyond the Village church,
After we pass the wood that skirts the road,
A Lake,—the blue-eyed Walden, that doth smile
Most tenderly upon its neighbor Pines,
And they as if to recompense this love,
In double beauty spread their branches forth.
This Lake had tranquil loveliness and breadth,
And of late years has added to its charms,
For one attracted to its pleasant edge,
Has built himself a little Hermitage,
Where with much piety he passes life.

More fitting place I cannot fancy now,
For such a man to let the line run off
The mortal reel, such patience hath the lake,
Such gratitude and cheer is in the Pines.
But more than either lake or forest's depths,
This man has in himself; a tranquil man,
With sunny sides where well the fruit is ripe,
Good front, and resolute bearing to this life,
And some serener virtues, which control
This rich exterior prudence, virtues high,
That in the principles of Things are set,

Great by their nature and consigned to him,
Who, like a faithful Merchant, does account
To God for what he spends, and in what way.
Thrice happy art thou, Walden! in thyself,
Such purity is in thy limpid springs;
In those green shores which do reflect in thee,
And in this man who dwells upon thy edge,
A holy man within a Hermitage.
May all good showers fall gently into thee,
May thy surrounding forests long be spared,
And may the Dweller on thy tranquil shores,
There lead a life of deep tranquillity
Pure as thy Waters, handsome as thy Shores
And with those virtues which are like the Stars.

JAMES RUSSELL LOWELL

James Russell Lowell (1819–1891) was famous in his time for his barbed wit and satiric verse. *A Fable for Critics* and *The Biglow Papers*, published in 1848 (along with two other books in the same year), secured his reputation as one of America's foremost public poets. His subsequent career as founding editor of the *Atlantic Monthly*; successor to Longfellow's professorship at Harvard; and United States minister to Spain and Great Britain kept him very much in the public eye. For generations Lowell—together with Bryant, Longfellow, Whittier, and Holmes—was virtually canonized as a member of the Fireside Poets (or Schoolroom Poets, since children so often memorized their poems). But for all his many lyrics and narrative poems it is still Lowell's mordant and amusing satires that draw contemporary readers.

Lowell came from a distinguished Boston family (which also produced two important twentieth-century poets, Amy Lowell and Robert Lowell) and attended Harvard and Harvard Law School. He did not, however, pursue a legal career, deciding instead to make his living as a writer. He published poems and essays and, under the influence of his first wife, the poet Maria White, wrote for the abolitionist cause in the 1840s. Of the Lowell's four children, three died in infancy, and Maria herself died in Cambridge in 1853. Two years later Lowell was appointed to fill Longfellow's position at Harvard and subsequently went to Europe to perfect his languages. Upon Lowell's return he married his daughter's governess and settled down to teach at Harvard, edit the new *Atlantic Monthly* (and later *The North American Review*), and enjoy the social life of Boston. Lowell was a founding member of the Saturday Club, an informal gathering that included Emerson, Hawthorne, Longfellow, Holmes, and other local luminaries. As an influential editor Lowell became involved in national politics. For his support of President Hayes he was appointed minister to Spain and later Great Britain (where, though controversial, Lowell did much to soothe the testy relations still existing between the two nations). Removed from office by President Cleveland, Lowell spent his remaining years writing and dining out. Although Lowell is best known now for his satiric portraits in *A Fable for Critics*, his experimental use of dialect in *The Biglow Papers* gave impetus to the growing interest in regionalism, which after the Civil War was so evident in the work of Mark Twain, Sarah Orne Jewett, Charles W. Chestnutt, and others. Lowell is a transitional figure—looking back to the immediate past and forward to the uncertain future—but his work is always firmly rooted in the history of his own time.

from *A Fable for Critics*

There comes Emerson first, whose rich words, every one
Are like gold nails in temples to hang trophies on,
Whose prose is grand verse, while his verse, the Lord knows,
Is some of it pr——No, 'tis not even prose;
I'm speaking of metres; some poems have welled
From those rare depths of soul that have ne'er been excelled;
They're not epics, but that doesn't matter a pin,
In creating, the only hard thing's to begin;
A grass-blade's no easier to make than an oak,
If you've once found the way, you've achieved the grand stroke;
In the worst of his poems are mines of rich matter,
But thrown in a heap with a crush and a clatter;
Now it is not one thing nor another alone
Makes a poem, but rather the general tone,
The something pervading, uniting the whole,
The before unconceived, unconceivable soul,
So that just in removing this trifle or that, you
Take away, as it were, a chief limb of the statue;
Roots, wood, bark, and leaves, singly perfect may be,
But, clapt hodge-podge together, they don't make a tree.

But, to come back to Emerson, (whom, by the way,
I believe we left waiting,)—his is, we may say,
A Greek head on right Yankee shoulders, whose range
Has Olympus for one pole, for t'other the Exchange;
He seems, to my thinking, (although I'm afraid
The comparison must, long ere this, have been made,)
A Plotinus-Montaigne, where the Egyptian's gold mist
And the Gascon's shrewd wit cheek-by-jowl co-exist;
All admire, and yet scarcely six converts he's got
To I don't (nor they either) exactly know what;
For though he builds glorious temples, 'tis odd
He leaves never a doorway to get in a god.
'Tis refreshing to old-fashioned people like me,
To meet such a primitive Pagan as he,
In whose mind all creation is duly respected
As parts of himself—just a little projected;

And who's willing to worship the stars and the sun,
A convert to—nothing but Emerson.
So perfect a balance there is in his head,
That he talks of things sometimes as if they were dead;
Life, nature, love, God, and affairs of that sort,
He looks at as merely ideas; in short,
As if they were fossils stuck round in a cabinet,
Of such vast extent that our earth's a mere dab in it;
Composed just as he is inclined to conjecture her,
Namely, one part pure earth, ninety-nine parts pure lecturer;
You are filled with delight at his clear demonstration,
Each figure, word, gesture, just fits the occasion,
With the quiet precision of science he'll sort 'em,
But you can't help suspecting the whole a *post mortem*.

There are persons, mole-blind to the soul's make and style,
Who insist on a likeness 'twixt him and Carlyle;
To compare him with Plato would be vastly fairer,
Carlyle's the more burly, but E. is the rarer;
He sees fewer objects, but clearlier, truelier,
If C.'s as original, E.'s more peculiar;
That he's more of a man you might say of the one,
Of the other he's more of an Emerson;
C.'s the Titan, as shaggy of mind as of limb,—
E. the clear-eyed Olympian, rapid and slim;
The one's two-thirds Norseman, the other half Greek,
Where the one's most abounding, the other 's to seek;
C.'s generals require to be seen in the mass,—
E.'s specialties gain if enlarged by the glass;
C. gives nature and God his own fits of the blues,
And rims common-sense things with mystical hues,—
E. sits in a mystery calm and intense,
And looks coolly around him with sharp common-sense;
C. shows you how every-day matters unite
With the dim transdiurnal recesses of night,—
While E., in a plain, preternatural way,
Makes mysteries matters of mere every day;
C. draws all his characters quite *à la* Fuseli,—
He don't sketch their bundles of muscles and thews illy,

But he paints with a brush so untamed and profuse,
They seem nothing but bundles of muscles and thews;
E. is rather like Flaxman, lines strait and severe,
And a colorless outline, but full, round, and clear;—
To the men he thinks worthy he frankly accords
The design of a white marble statue in words.
C. labors to get at the centre, and then
Take a reckoning from there of his actions and men;
E. calmly assumes the said centre as granted,
And, given himself, has whatever is wanted.

He has imitators in scores, who omit
No part of the man but his wisdom and wit,—
Who go carefully o'er the sky-blue of his brain,
And when he has skimmed it once, skim it again;
If at all they resemble him, you may be sure it is
Because their shoals mirror his mists and obscurities,
As a mud-puddle seems deep as heaven for a minute,
While a cloud that floats o'er is reflected within it.

There comes———, for instance; to see him's rare sport,
Tread in Emerson's tracks with legs painfully short;
How he jumps, how he strains, and gets red in the face,
To keep step with the mystagogue's natural pace!
He follows as close as a stick to a rocket,
His fingers exploring the prophet's each pocket.
Fie, for shame, brother bard; with good fruit of your own,
Can't you let neighbor Emerson's orchards alone?
Besides, 'tis no use, you'll not find e'en a core,—
———has picked up all the windfalls before.
They might strip every tree, and E. never would catch 'em,
His Hesperides have no rude dragon to watch 'em;
When they send him a dishfull, and ask him to try 'em,
He never suspects how the sly rogues came by 'em;
He wonders why 'tis there are none such his trees on,
And thinks 'em the best he has tasted this season.

. . .

There is Hawthorne, with genius so shrinking and rare
That you hardly at first see the strength that is there;
A frame so robust, with a nature so sweet,
So earnest, so graceful, so solid, so fleet,
Is worth a descent from Olympus to meet;
'Tis as if a rough oak that for ages had stood,
With his gnarled bony branches like ribs of the wood,
Should bloom, after cycles of struggle and scathe,
With a single anemone trembly and rathe;
His strength is so tender, his wildness so meek,
That a suitable parallel sets one to seek,—
He's a John Bunyan Fouqué, a Puritan Tieck;
When Nature was shaping him, clay was not granted
For making so full-sized a man as she wanted,
So, to fill out her model, a little she spared
From some finer-grained stuff for a woman prepared,
And she could not have hit a more excellent plan
For making him fully and perfectly man.
The success of her scheme gave her so much delight,
That she tried it again, shortly after, in Dwight;
Only, while she was kneading and shaping the clay,
She sang to her work in her sweet childish way,
And found, when she'd put the last touch to his soul,
That the music had somehow got mixed with the whole.

. . .

There comes Poe with his raven, like Barnaby Rudge,
Three-fifths of him genius and two-fifths sheer fudge,
Who talks like a book of iambs and pentameters,
In a way to make people of common-sense damn metres,
Who has written some things quite the best of their kind,
But the heart somehow seems all squeezed out by the mind,
Who—but hey-day! What's this? Messieurs Mathews and Poe,
You mustn't fling mud-balls at Longfellow so,
Does it make a man worse that his character's such
As to make his friends love him (as you think) too much?
Why, there is not a bard at this moment alive
More willing than he that his fellows should thrive;
While you are abusing him thus, even now

He would help either one of you out of a slough;
You may say that he's smooth and all that till you're hoarse,
But remember that elegance also is force;
After polishing granite as much as you will,
The heart keeps its tough old persistency still;
Deduct all you can that still keeps you at bay,—
Why, he'll live till men weary of Collins and Gray;
I'm not over-fond of Greek metres in English,
To me rhyme's a gain, so it be not too jinglish,
And your modern hexameter verses are no more
Like Greek ones than sleek Mr. Pope is like Homer;
As the roar of the sea to the coo of a pigeon is,
So, compared to your moderns, sounds old Melesigenes;
I may be too partial, the reason, perhaps, o't is
That I've heard the old blind man recite his own rhapsodies,
And my ear with that music impregnate may be,
Like the poor exiled shell with the soul of the sea,
Or as one can't bear Strauss when his nature is cloven
To its deeps within deeps by the stroke of Beethoven;
But, set that aside, and 'tis truth that I speak,
Had Theocritus written in English, not Greek,
I believe that his exquisite sense would scarce change a line
In that rare, tender, virgin-like pastoral Evangeline.
That's not ancient nor modern, its place is apart
Where time has no sway, in the realm of pure Art,
'Tis a shrine of retreat from Earth's hubbub and strife
As quiet and chaste as the author's own life.

JULIA WARD HOWE

Julia Ward Howe (1819–1910) is best known today as the author of the "Battle-Hymn of the Republic," but during the course of her long life she was a prolific writer of poems, articles, lectures, even sermons. Howe was an active feminist and author of such works as *Margaret Fuller* (a biography), *Sex and Education*, and *Is Polite Society Polite?* By the turn of the century she was known as America's Grand Old Lady.

Howe was born in New York but moved to Boston upon marrying Samuel Gridley Howe, a humanitarian reformer much older than she and more traditional in his thinking. He opposed Howe's career as a writer, but she refused to give it up, even while laboring under the heavy responsibilities of raising six children. Both, however, were active in antislavery causes and together edited the abolitionist paper *The Commonwealth*. The "Battle-Hymn of the Republic" (written after hearing Union soldiers singing their favorite song, "John Brown's Body") appeared in the *Atlantic Monthly* in 1862; it eventually became the unofficial anthem of the North. Although Howe was a popular poet in the 1850s and 1860s, her readership began to decline. By 1868 she had turned her energies in a new direction: the campaign for women's rights. Howe was a founder and first president of the New England Woman Suffrage Association and later president of the National Association for the Advancement of Women. She was also president of the Women's International Peace Association and became somewhat of a custodian for the social conscience and morals of America. Most of her writings went unpublished by the commercial press.

Battle-Hymn of the Republic

Mine eyes have seen the glory of the coming of the Lord:
He is trampling out the vintage where the grapes of wrath are stored;
He hath loosed the fateful lightning of his terrible swift sword:
  His truth is marching on.

I have seen Him in the watch-fires of a hundred circling camps;
They have builded Him an altar in the evening dews and damps;
I can read His righteous sentence by the dim and flaring lamps.
  His day is marching on.

I have read a fiery gospel, writ in burnished rows of steel:
"As ye deal with my contemners, so with you my grace shall deal;
Let the Hero, born of woman, crush the serpent with his heel,
  Since God is marching on."

He has sounded forth the trumpet that shall never call retreat;
He is sifting out the hearts of men before his judgment-seat:
Oh! be swift, my soul, to answer Him! be jubilant, my feet!
  Our God is marching on.

In the beauty of the lilies Christ was born across the sea,
With a glory in his bosom that transfigures you and me:
As he died to make men holy, let us die to make men free,
  While God is marching on.

The Soul-Hunter

Who hunts so late 'neath evening skies,
A smouldering love-brand in his eyes?
His locks outshame the black of night,
Its stars are duller than his sight
  Who hunts so late, so dark.

A drooping mantle shrouds his form,
To shield him from the winter's storm?
Or is there something at his side,
That, with himself, he strives to hide,
  Who hunts so late, so dark?

He hath such promise, silver sweet,
Such silken hands, such fiery feet,
That, where his look has charmed the prey,
His swift-winged passion forces way,
    Who hunts so late, so dark.

Sure no one underneath the moon
Can whisper to so soft a tune:
The hours would flit from dusk to dawn
Lighter than dews upon the lawn
    With him, so late, so dark.

But, should there break a day of need,
Those hands will try no valorous deed:
No help is in that sable crest,
Nor manhood is that hollow breast
    That sighed so late, so dark.

O maiden of the salt waves make
Thy sinless shroud, for God's dear sake;
Or to the flame commit thy bloom;
Or lock thee, living, in the tomb
    So desolate and dark,—

Before thou list one stolen word
Of him who lures thee like a bird.
He wanders with the Devil's bait,
For human souls he lies in wait,
    Who hunts so late, so dark.

WALT WHITMAN

Walt Whitman (1819–1892) published *Leaves of Grass* in 1855 and in so doing altered the course of American poetry. Although it took years for Whitman to find his readership, once his genius was recognized and accepted he became America's representative poet. Particularly in the twentieth century Whitman's work has been a watershed for many poets, seeming to open up possibilities of expression and expansiveness of form. But Whitman's influence is both pervasive and subtle, and few poets—both here and abroad—have been untouched by his prodigious spirit.

The son of a farmer and carpenter from Long Island, Whitman's family moved to Brooklyn when he was four. Whitman left school at eleven and began working in a variety of occupations, primarily in printing and journalism. After a five-year stint of teaching on Long Island, Whitman, at the age of twenty-one, moved to Manhattan, where he worked as a compositor and then as an editor of a daily newspaper, the *Aurora*. Taking up the persona of a New York dandy, he frequented the theater, opera, lecture hall, and museum, immersing himself in both high and popular culture of the time. After being fired from his position at the *Aurora* (apparently for laziness), he wrote a temperance novel, *Franklin Evans, or the Inebriate*, in 1842. During this period he contributed journalistic pieces to various newspapers and magazines and became involved in politics. Returning to Brooklyn in 1845, he eventually became editor of the *Daily Eagle*, a Democratic party organ, where he also wrote book reviews. In 1848, however, he was dismissed for his strong Free-Soil views (opposing the westward expansion of slavery) and subsequently traveled to New Orleans, where he worked briefly for a newspaper. This trip appears to have been momentous as a catalyst, for soon after his return to Brooklyn he began writing and publishing poems in earnest. In 1855, after working as a journalist, editor, bookseller, and carpenter, Whitman self-published *Leaves of Grass*.

Whitman energetically promoted his new book, sending out numerous copies and even writing anonymous reviews for the papers. One critical response came from Emerson, who immediately hailed *Leaves of Grass* as "the most extraordinary piece of wit and wisdom that America has yet produced." Whitman shamelessly circulated the letter and later printed it in the back of the enlarged second edition, along with his own open letter to Emerson in reply. Thereafter, Whitman continually revised *Leaves of Grass*, expanding it and reshaping it right up to his death. In 1860 Whitman went to Boston to oversee a new edition and was welcomed by Emerson (though not by others of the Saturday Club, who thought Whitman bumptious and scandalous). Emerson himself cautioned Whitman about printing the new erotic "Children of Adam" poems, but Whitman stood firm.

With the advent of the Civil War, Whitman began visiting convalescing soldiers, first in New York and then in Washington, where he had gone upon receiving news that his brother, George, had been wounded. From 1862 until 1873 Whitman lived in Washington. During the war he worked as a volunteer nurse tending wounded soldiers, and afterward he was employed in various government jobs. In 1865 he was fired from his position at the Department of the Interior when the secretary deemed his poetry immoral. Whitman was championed by several admirers, most notably his friend William O'Connor, who published an extravagant defense, *The Good Gray Poet*, in 1866, the same year Whitman published his Civil War poems, *Drum-Taps*. In 1868 *Poems of Walt Whitman* was published in London, and as a result of his growing reputation there Whitman began to be taken more seriously by American critics. During this period Whitman published two collections of prose, *Democratic Vistas* (1871) and *Memoranda During the War* (1875). In 1873 Whitman was paralyzed by a stroke and moved to Camden, New Jersey, to live in his brother's household, where he remained for the rest of his life. He did, however, lecture and travel, and he continued to write. The "Centennial" edition of *Leaves of Grass* came out in 1876, while the 1881 edition was withdrawn by his publishers in Boston when a legal suit over obscenity was threatened. *Specimen Days* and *Collect* appeared in 1882; *November Boughs* and *Complete Poems and Prose*, in 1888, the year of Whitman's second stroke. The "deathbed" edition of *Leaves of Grass* was published in 1891; Whitman died in March 1892.

from Song of Myself (1855)

[1]
I celebrate myself,
And what I assume you shall assume,
For every atom belonging to me as good belongs to you.

I loafe and invite my soul,
I lean and loafe at my ease . . . . observing a spear of summer grass.

[2]
Houses and rooms are full of perfumes . . . . the shelves are crowded with
    perfumes,
I breathe the fragrance myself, and know it and like it,
The distillation would intoxicate me also, but I shall not let it.

The atmosphere is not a perfume . . . . it has no taste of the distillation . . . .
it is odorless,
It is for my mouth forever . . . . I am in love with it,
I will go to the bank by the wood and become undisguised and naked,
I am mad for it to be in contact with me.

The smoke of my own breath,
Echos, ripples, and buzzed whispers . . . . loveroot, silkthread, crotch and
    vine,
My respiration and inspiration . . . . the beating of my heart . . . . the
    passing of blood and air through my lungs,
The sniff of green leaves and dry leaves, and of the shore and darkcolored
    sea-rocks, and of hay in the barn,
The sound of the belched words of my voice . . . . words loosed to the
    eddies of the wind,
A few light kisses . . . . a few embraces . . . . a reaching around of arms,
The play of shine and shade on the trees as the supple boughs wag,
The delight alone or in the rush of the streets, or along the fields and
    hillsides,
The feeling of health . . . . the full-noon trill . . . . the song of me rising
    from bed and meeting the sun.

Have you reckoned a thousand acres much? Have you reckoned the earth
    much?
Have you practiced so long to learn to read?
Have you felt so proud to get at the meaning of poems?

Stop this day and night with me and you shall possess the origin of all
    poems,
You shall possess the good of the earth and sun . . . . there are millions of
    suns left,
You shall no longer take things at second or third hand . . . . nor look
    through the eyes of the dead . . . . nor feed on the spectres in books,
You shall not look through my eyes either, nor take things from me,
You shall listen to all sides and filter them from yourself.

[3]
I have heard what the talkers were talking . . . . the talk of the beginning
    and the end,
But I do not talk of the beginning or the end.

There was never any more inception than there is now,
Nor any more youth or age than there is now;
And will never be any more perfection than there is now,
Nor any more heaven or hell than there is now.

Urge and urge and urge,
Always the procreant urge of the world.

Out of the dimness opposite equals advance . . . . Always substance and
    increase,
Always a knit of identity . . . . always distinction . . . . always a breed of life.

To elaborate is no avail . . . . Learned and unlearned feel that it is so.

Sure as the most certain sure . . . . plumb in the uprights, well entretied,
    braced in the beams,
Stout as a horse, affectionate, haughty, electrical,
I and this mystery here we stand.

Clear and sweet is my soul . . . . and clear and sweet is all that is not my soul.

Lack one lacks both . . . . and the unseen is proved by the seen,
Till that becomes unseen and receives proof in its turn.

Showing the best and dividing it from the worst, age vexes age,
Knowing the perfect fitness and equanimity of things, while they discuss I
    am silent, and go bathe and admire myself.

Welcome is every organ and attribute of me, and of any man hearty and
    clean,
Not an inch nor a particle of an inch is vile, and none shall be less familiar

    than the rest.

I am satisfied . . . . I see, dance, laugh, sing;
As God comes a loving bedfellow and sleeps at my side all night and close
    on the peep of the day,
And leaves for me baskets covered with white towels bulging the house
    with their plenty,
Shall I postpone my acceptation and realization and scream at my eyes,
That they turn from gazing after and down the road,
And forthwith cipher and show me to a cent,
Exactly the contents of one, and exactly the contents of two, and which is
    ahead?

[4]
Trippers and askers surround me,
People I meet . . . . the effect upon me of my early life . . . . of the ward and
    city I live in . . . . of the nation,
The latest news . . . . discoveries, inventions, societies . . . . authors old and
    new,
My dinner, dress, associates, looks, business, compliments, dues,
The real or fancied indifference of some man or woman I love,
The sickness of one of my folks—or of myself . . . . or ill-doing . . . . or
    loss or lack of money . . . . or depressions or exaltations,
They come to me days and nights and go from me again,
But they are not the Me myself.

Apart from the pulling and hauling stands what I am,
Stands amused, complacent, compassionating, idle, unitary,
Looks down, is erect, bends an arm on an impalpable certain rest,
Looks with its sidecurved head curious what will come next,
Both in and out of the game, and watching and wondering at it.

Backward I see in my own days where I sweated through fog with linguists
and contenders,
I have no mockings or arguments . . . . I witness and wait.

[5]
I believe in you my soul . . . . the other I am must not abase itself to you,
And you must not be abased to the other.

Loafe with me on the grass . . . . loose the stop from your throat,
Not words, not music or rhyme I want . . . . not custom or lecture, not
even the best,
Only the lull I like, the hum of your valved voice.

I mind how we lay in June, such a transparent summer morning;
You settled your head athwart my hips and gently turned over upon me,
And parted the shirt from my bosom-bone, and plunged your tongue to
my barestript heart,
And reached till you felt my beard, and reached till you held my feet.

Swiftly arose and spread around me the peace and joy and knowledge that
pass all the art and argument of the earth;
And I know that the hand of God is the elderhand of my own,
And I know that the spirit of God is the eldest brother of my own,
And that all the men ever born are also my brothers . . . . and the women
my sisters and lovers,
And that a kelson of the creation is love;
And limitless are leaves stiff or drooping in the fields,
And brown ants in the little wells beneath them,
And mossy scabs of the wormfence, and heaped stones, and elder and
mullen and pokeweed.

[6]
A child said, What is the grass? fetching it to me with full hands;
How could I answer the child? . . . . I do not know what it is any more
than he.

I guess it must be the flag of my disposition, out of hopeful green stuff
woven.

Or I guess it is the handkerchief of the Lord,

A scented gift and remembrancer designedly dropped,

Bearing the owner's name someway in the corners, that we may see and
remark, and say Whose?

Or I guess the grass is itself a child . . . . the produced babe of the
vegetation.

Or I guess it is a uniform hieroglyphic,

And it means, Sprouting alike in broad zones and narrow zones,

Growing among black folks as among white,

Kanuck, Tuckahoe, Congressman, Cuff, I give them the same, I receive
them the same.

And now it seems to me the beautiful uncut hair of graves.

Tenderly will I use you curling grass,

It may be you transpire from the breasts of young men,

It may be if I had known them I would have loved them;

It may be you are from old people and from women, and from offspring
taken soon out of their mothers' laps,

And here you are the mothers' laps.

This grass is very dark to be from the white heads of old mothers,

Darker than the colorless beards of old men,

Dark to come from under the faint red roofs of mouths.

O I perceive after all so many uttering tongues!

And I perceive they do not come from the roofs of mouths for nothing.

I wish I could translate the hints about the dead young men and women,

And the hints about old men and mothers, and the offspring taken soon
out of their laps.

What do you think has become of the young and old men?

And what do you think has become of the women and children?

They are alive and well somewhere;

The smallest sprout shows there is really no death,

And if ever there was it led forward life, and does not wait at the end to
arrest it,

And ceased the moment life appeared.

All goes onward and outward . . . . and nothing collapses,
And to die is different from what any one supposed, and luckier.

[11]
Twenty-eight young men bathe by the shore,
Twenty-eight young men, and all so friendly,
Twenty-eight years of womanly life, and all so lonesome.

She owns the fine house by the rise of the bank,
She hides handsome and richly drest aft the blinds of the window.

Which of the young men does she like the best?
Ah the homeliest of them is beautiful to her.

Where are you off to, lady? for I see you,
You splash in the water there, yet stay stock still in your room.

Dancing and laughing along the beach came the twenty-ninth bather,
The rest did not see her, but she saw them and loved them.

The beards of the young men glistened with wet, it ran from their long
    hair,
Little streams passed all over their bodies.

An unseen hand also passed over their bodies,
It descended tremblingly from their temples and ribs.

The young men float on their backs, their white bellies swell to the sun . . . .
    they do not ask who seizes fast to them,
They do not know who puffs and declines with pendant and bending arch,
They do not think whom they souse with spray.

[20]
Who goes there! hankering, gross, mystical, nude?
How is it I extract strength from the beef I eat?

What is a man anyhow? What am I? and what are you?
All I mark as my own you shall offset it with your own,
Else it were time lost listening to me.

I do not snivel that snivel the world over,
That months are vacuums and the ground but wallow and filth,
That life is a suck and a sell, and nothing remains at the end but threadbare
    crape and tears.

Whimpering and truckling fold with powders for invalids . . . . conformity
    goes to the fourth-removed,
I cock my hat as I please indoors or out.

Shall I pray? Shall I venerate and be ceremonious?
I have pried through the strata and analyzed to a hair,
And counselled with doctors and calculated close and found no sweeter fat
    than sticks to my own bones.

In all people I see myself, none more and not one a barleycorn less,
And the good or bad I say of myself I say of them.

And I know I am solid and sound,
To me the converging objects of the universe perpetually flow,
All are written to me, and I must get what the writing means.

And I know I am deathless,
I know this orbit of mine cannot be swept by a carpenter's compass,
I know I shall not pass like a child's carlacue cut with a burnt stick at night.

I know I am august,
I do not trouble my spirit to vindicate itself or be understood,
I see that the elementary laws never apologize,
I reckon I behave no prouder than the level I plant my house by after all.

I exist as I am, that is enough,
If no other in the world be aware I sit content,
And if each and all be aware I sit content.

One world is aware, and by far the largest to me, and that is myself,
And whether I come to my own today or in ten thousand or ten million
    years,
I can cheerfully take it now, or with equal cheerfulness I can wait.

My foothold is tenoned and mortised in granite,
I laugh at what you call dissolution,
And I know the amplitude of time.

[24]
Walt Whitman, an American, one of the roughs, a kosmos,
Disorderly fleshy and sensual . . . . eating drinking and breeding,
No sentimentalist . . . . no stander above men and women or apart from
    them . . . . no more modest than immodest.

Unscrew the locks from the doors!
Unscrew the doors themselves from their jambs!

Whoever degrades another degrades me . . . . and whatever is done or said
    returns at last to me,
And whatever I do or say I also return.

Through me the afflatus surging and surging . . . . through me the current
    and index.

I speak the password primeval . . . . I give the sign of democracy;
By God! I will accept nothing which all cannot have their counterpart of
    on the same terms.

Through me many long dumb voices,
Voices of the interminable generations of slaves,
Voices of prostitutes and of deformed persons,
Voices of the diseased and despairing, and of thieves and dwarfs,
Voices of cycles of preparation and accretion,
And of the threads that connect the stars—and of wombs, and of the
    fatherstuff,
And of the rights of them the others are down upon,
Of the trivial and flat and foolish and despised,
Of fog in the air and beetles rolling balls of dung.

Through me forbidden voices,
Voices of sexes and lusts . . . . voices veiled, and I remove the veil,
Voices indecent by me clarified and transfigured.

I do not press my finger across my mouth,
I keep as delicate around the bowels as around the head and heart,
Copulation is no more rank to me than death is.

I believe in the flesh and the appetites,
Seeing hearing and feeling are miracles, and each part and tag of me is a
    miracle.

Divine am I inside and out, and I make holy whatever I touch or am
    touched from;
The scent of these arm-pits is aroma finer than prayer,
This head is more than churches or bibles or creeds.

. . . .

[31]

I believe a leaf of grass is no less than the journeywork of the stars,
And the pismire is equally perfect, and a grain of sand, and the egg of the
    wren,
And the tree-toad is a chef-d'ouvre for the highest,
And the running blackberry would adorn the parlors of heaven,
And the narrowest hinge in my hand puts to scorn all machinery,
And the cow crunching with depressed head surpasses any statue,
And a mouse is miracle enough to stagger sextillions of infidels,
And I could come every afternoon of my life to look at the farmer's girl
    boiling her iron tea-kettle and baking shortcake.

. . . .

[33]

Swift wind! Space! My Soul! Now I know it is true what I guessed at;
What I guessed when I loafed on the grass,
What I guessed while I lay alone in my bed . . . . and again as I walked the
    beach under the paling stars of the morning.

My ties and ballasts leave me . . . . I travel . . . . I sail . . . . my elbows rest in
    the sea-gaps,
I skirt the sierras . . . . my palms cover continents,
I am afoot with my vision.

. . . .

[35]

Did you read in the seabooks of the oldfashioned frigate-fight?
Did you learn who won by the light of the moon and stars?

Our foe was no skulk in his ship, I tell you,
His was the English pluck, and there is no tougher or truer, and never was,
    and never will be;
Along the lowered eve he came, horribly raking us.

We closed with him . . . . the yards entangled . . . . the cannon touched,
My captain lashed fast with his own hands.

We had received some eighteen-pound shots under the water,
On our lower-gun-deck two large pieces had burst at the first fire, killing
    all around and blowing up overhead.

Ten o'clock at night, and the full moon shining and the leaks on the gain,
and five feet of water reported,
The master-at-arms loosing the prisoners confined in the after-hold to
give them a chance for themselves.

The transit to and from the magazine was now stopped by the sentinels,
They saw so many strange faces they did not know whom to trust.

Our frigate was afire . . . . the other asked if we demanded quarters? if our
colors were struck and the fighting done?

I laughed content when I heard the voice of my little captain,
We have not struck, he composedly cried, We have just begun our part of
the fighting.

Only three guns were in use,
One was directed by the captain himself against the enemy's mainmast,
Two well-served with grape and canister silenced his musketry and cleared
his decks.

The tops alone seconded the fire of this little battery, especially the maintop,
They all held out bravely during the whole of the action.

Not a moment's cease,
The leaks gained fast on the pumps . . . . the fire eat toward the powder-
magazine,
One of the pumps was shot away . . . . it was generally thought we were
sinking.

Serene stood the little captain,
He was not hurried . . . . his voice was neither high nor low,
His eyes gave more light to us than our battle-lanterns.

Toward twelve at night, there in the beams of the moon they surrendered
to us.

[50]
There is that in me . . . . I do not know what it is . . . . but I know it is in me.

Wrenched and sweaty . . . . calm and cool then my body becomes;
I sleep . . . . I sleep long.

I do not know it . . . . it is without name . . . . it is a word unsaid,
It is not in any dictionary or utterance or symbol.

Something it swings on more than the earth I swing on,
To it the creation is the friend whose embracing awakes me.

Perhaps I might tell more . . . . Outlines! I plead for my brothers and sisters.

Do you see O my brothers and sisters?
It is not chaos or death . . . . it is form and union and plan . . . . it is eternal
   life . . . . it is happiness.

[51]
The past and present wilt . . . . I have filled them and emptied them,
And proceed to fill my next fold of the future.

Listener up there! Here you . . . . what have you to confide to me?
Look in my face while I snuff the sidle of evening,
Talk honestly, for no one else hears you, and I stay only a minute longer.

Do I contradict myself?
Very well then . . . . I contradict myself;
I am large . . . . I contain multitudes.

I concentrate toward them that are nigh . . . . I wait on the door-slab.

Who has done his day's work and will soonest be through with his supper?
Who wishes to walk with me?

Will you speak before I am gone? Will you prove already too late?

[52]
The spotted hawk swoops by and accuses me . . . . he complains of my gab
   and my loitering.

I too am not a bit tamed . . . . I too am untranslatable,
I sound my barbaric yawp over the roofs of the world.

The last scud of day holds back for me,
It flings my likeness after the rest and true as any on the shadowed wilds,
It coaxes me to the vapor and the dusk.

I depart as air . . . . I shake my white locks at the runaway sun,
I effuse my flesh in eddies and drift it in lacy jags.

I bequeath myself to the dirt to grow from the grass I love,
If you want me again look for me under your bootsoles.

You will hardly know who I am or what I mean,
But I shall be good health to you nevertheless,
And filter and fibre your blood.

Failing to fetch me at first keep encouraged,
Missing me one place search another,
I stop some where waiting for you

The Sleepers (1855)

[1]
I wander all night in my vision,
Stepping with light feet . . . . swiftly and noiselessly stepping and stopping,
Bending with open eyes over the shut eyes of sleepers;
Wandering and confused . . . . lost to myself . . . . ill-assorted . . . .
    contradictory,
Pausing and gazing and bending and stopping.

How solemn they look there, stretched and still;
How quiet they breathe, the little children in their cradles.

The wretched features of ennuyees, the white features of corpses, the livid
    faces of drunkards, the sick-gray faces of onanists,
The gashed bodies on battlefields, the insane in their strong-doored
    rooms, the sacred idiots,
The newborn emerging from gates and dying emerging from gates,
The night pervades them and enfolds them.

The married couple sleep calmly in their bed, he with his palm on the hip
    of the wife, and she with her palm on the hip of the husband,
The sisters sleep lovingly side by side in their bed,
The men sleep lovingly side by side in theirs,
And the mother sleeps with her little child carefully wrapped.

The blind sleep, and the deaf and dumb sleep,
The prisoner sleeps well in the prison . . . . the runaway son sleeps,
The murderer that is to be hung next day . . . . how does he sleep?
And the murdered person . . . . how does he sleep?

221

The female that loves unrequited sleeps,
And the male that loves unrequited sleeps;
The head of the moneymaker that plotted all day sleeps,
And the enraged and treacherous dispositions sleep.

I stand with drooping eyes by the worstsuffering and restless,
I pass my hands soothingly to and fro a few inches from them;
The restless sink in their beds . . . . they fitfully sleep.

The earth recedes from me into the night,
I saw that it was beautiful . . . . and I see that what is not the earth is
    beautiful.

I go from bedside to bedside . . . . I sleep close with the other sleepers,
    each in turn;
I dream in my dream all the dreams of the other dreamers,
And I become the other dreamers.

I am a dance . . . . Play up there! the fit is whirling me fast.

I am the everlaughing . . . . it is new moon and twilight,
I see the hiding of douceurs . . . . I see nimble ghosts whichever way I look,
Cache and cache again deep in the ground and sea, and where it is neither
    ground or sea.

Well do they do their jobs, those journeymen divine,
Only from me can they hide nothing and would not if they could;
I reckon I am their boss, and they make me a pet besides,
And surround me, and lead me and run ahead when I walk,
And lift their cunning covers and signify me with stretched arms, and
    resume the way;
Onward we move, a gay gang of blackguards with mirthshouting music and
    wildflapping pennants of joy.

I am the actor and the actress . . . . the voter . . the politician,
The emigrant and the exile . . the criminal that stood in the box,
He who has been famous, and he who shall be famous after today,
The stammerer . . . . the wellformed person . . the wasted or feeble person.

I am she who adorned herself and folded her hair expectantly,
My truant lover has come and it is dark.

Double yourself and receive me darkness,
Receive me and my lover too . . . . he will not let me go without him.

I roll myself upon you as upon a bed . . . . I resign myself to the dusk.

He whom I call answers me and takes the place of my lover,
He rises with me silently from the bed.

Darkness you are gentler than my lover . . . . his flesh was sweaty and
    panting,
I feel the hot moisture yet that he left me.

My hands are spread forth . . I pass them in all directions,
I would sound up the shadowy shore to which you are journeying.

Be careful, darkness . . . . already, what was it touched me?
I thought my lover had gone . . . . else darkness and he are one,
I hear the heart-beat . . . . I follow . . I fade away.

O hotcheeked and blushing! O foolish hectic!
O for pity's sake, no one must see me now! . . . . my clothes were stolen
    while I was abed,
Now I am thrust forth, where shall I run?

Pier that I saw dimly last night when I looked from the windows,
Pier out from the main, let me catch myself with you and stay . . . . I will
    not chafe you;
I feel ashamed to go naked about the world,
And am curious to know where my feet stand . . . . and what is this flooding
    me, childhood or manhood . . . . and the hunger that crosses the bridge
    between.

The cloth laps a first sweet eating and drinking,
Laps life-swelling yolks . . . . laps ear of rose-corn, milky and just ripened:
The white teeth stay, and the boss-tooth advances in darkness,
And liquor is spilled on lips and bosoms by touching glasses, and the best
    liquor afterward.

[2]
I descend my western course . . . . my sinews are flaccid,
Perfume and youth course through me, and I am their wake.

It is my face yellow and wrinkled instead of the old woman's,
I sit low in a strawbottom chair and carefully darn my grandson's stockings.

223

It is I too . . . . the sleepless widow looking out on the winter midnight,
I see the sparkles of starshine on the icy and pallid earth.

A shroud I see—and I am the shroud . . . . I wrap a body and lie in the coffin;
It is dark here underground . . . . it is not evil or pain here . . . . it is blank
here, for reasons.

It seems to me that everything in the light and air ought to be happy;
Whoever is not in his coffin and the dark grave, let him know he has
enough.

[3]
I see a beautiful gigantic swimmer swimming naked through the eddies of
the sea,
His brown hair lies close and even to his head . . . . he strikes out with
courageous arms . . . . he urges himself with his legs.

I see his white body . . . . I see his undaunted eyes;
I hate the swift-running eddies that would dash him headforemost on the
rocks.

What are you doing you ruffianly red-trickled waves?
Will you kill the courageous giant? Will you kill him in the prime of his
middle age?

Steady and long he struggles;
He is baffled and banged and bruised . . . . he holds out while his strength
holds out,
The slapping eddies are spotted with his blood . . . . they bear him away
. . . . they roll him and swing him and turn him:
His beautiful body is borne in the circling eddies . . . . it is continually
bruised on rocks,
Swiftly and out of sight is borne the brave corpse.

[4]
I turn but do not extricate myself;
Confused . . . . a pastreading . . . . another, but with darkness yet.

The beach is cut by the razory ice-wind . . . . the wreck-guns sound,
The tempest lulls and the moon comes floundering through the drifts.

I look where the ship helplessly heads end on . . . . I hear the burst as she
strikes . . I hear the howls of dismay . . . . they grow fainter and fainter.

I cannot aid with my wringing fingers;
I can but rush to the surf and let it drench me and freeze upon me.

I search with the crowd . . . . not one of the company is washed to us alive;
In the morning I help pick up the dead and lay them in rows in a barn.

[5]
Now of the old war-days . . the defeat at Brooklyn;
Washington stands inside the lines . . he stands on the entrenched hills
    amid a crowd of officers,
His face is cold and damp . . . . he cannot repress the weeping drops . . . .
    he lifts the glass perpetually to his eyes . . . . the color is blanched from
    his cheeks,
He sees the slaughter of the southern braves confided to him by their
    parents.

The same at last and at last when peace is declared,
He stands in the room of the old tavern . . . . the wellbeloved soldiers all
    pass through,
The officers speechless and slow draw near in their turns,
The chief encircles their necks with his arm and kisses them on the cheek,
He kisses lightly the wet cheeks one after another . . . . he shakes hands and
    bids goodbye to the army.

[6]
Now I tell what my mother told me today as we sat at dinner together,
Of when she was a nearly grown girl living home with her parents on the
    old homestead.

A red squaw came out breakfasttime to the old homestead,
On her back she carried a bundle of rushes for rushbottoming chairs;
Her hair straight shiny coarse black and profuse halfenveloped her face,
Her step was free and elastic . . . . her voice sounded exquisitely as she
    spoke.

My mother looked in delight and amazement at the stranger,
She looked at the beauty of her tallborne face and full and pliant limbs,
The more she looked upon her she loved her,
Never before had she seen such wonderful beauty and purity;
She made her sit on a bench by the jamb of the fireplace . . . . she cooked
    food for her,
She had no work to give her but she gave her remembrance and fondness.

The red squaw staid all the forenoon, and toward the middle of the
    afternoon she went away;
O my mother was loth to have her go away,
All the week she thought of her . . . . she watched for her many a month,
She remembered her many a winter and many a summer,
But the red squaw never came nor was heard of there again.

Now Lucifer was not dead . . . . or if he was I am his sorrowful terrible heir;
I have been wronged . . . . I am oppressed . . . . I hate him that oppresses me,
    I will either destroy him, or he shall release me.

Damn him! how he does defile me,
How he informs against my brother and sister and takes pay for their blood,
How he laughs when I look down the bend after the steamboat that carries
    away my woman.

Now the vast dusk bulk that is the whale's bulk . . . . it seems mine,
Warily, sportsman! though I lie so sleepy and sluggish, my tap is death.

[7]
A show of the summer softness . . . . a contact of something unseen . . . . an
    amour of the light and air;
I am jealous and overwhelmed with friendliness,
And will go gallivant with the light and the air myself,
And have an unseen something to be in contact with them also.

O love and summer! you are in the dreams and in me,
Autumn and winter are in the dreams . . . . the farmer goes with his thrift,
The droves and crops increase . . . . the barns are wellfilled.

Elements merge in the night . . . . ships make tacks in the dreams . . . . the
    sailor sails . . . . the exile returns home,
The fugitive returns unharmed . . . . the immigrant is back beyond months
    and years;
The poor Irishman lives in the simple house of his childhood, with the
    wellknown neighbors and faces,
They warmly welcome him . . . . he is barefoot again . . . . he forgets he is
    welloff;
The Dutchman voyages home, and the Scotchman and Welchman voyage
    home . . and the native of the Mediterranean voyages home;
To every port of England and France and Spain enter wellfilled ships;

The Swiss foots it toward his hills . . . . the Prussian goes his way, and the
    Hungarian his way, and the Pole goes his way,
The Swede returns, and the Dane and Norwegian return.

The homeward bound and the outward bound,
The beautiful lost swimmer, the ennuyee, the onanist, the female that loves
    unrequited, the moneymaker,
The actor and actress . . those through with their parts and those waiting
    to commence,
The affectionate boy, the husband and wife, the voter, the nominee that is
    chosen and the nominee that has failed,
The great already known, and the great anytime after to day,
The stammerer, the sick, the perfectformed, the homely,
The criminal that stood in the box, the judge that sat and sentenced him,
    the fluent lawyers, the jury, the audience,
The laugher and weeper, the dancer, the midnight widow, the red squaw,
The consumptive, the erysipalite, the idiot, he that is wronged,
The antipodes, and every one between this and them in the dark,
I swear they are averaged now . . . . one is no better than the other,
The night and sleep have likened them and restored them.

I swear they are all beautiful,
Every one that sleeps is beautiful . . . . every thing in the dim night is
    beautiful,
The wildest and bloodiest is over and all is peace.

Peace is always beautiful,
The myth of heaven indicates peace and night.

The myth of heaven indicates the soul;
The soul is always beautiful . . . . it appears more or it appears less . . . . it
    comes or lags behind,
It comes from its embowered garden and looks pleasantly on itself and
    encloses the world;
Perfect and clean the genitals previously jetting, and perfect and clean the
    womb cohering,
The head wellgrown and proportioned and plumb, and the bowels and
    joints proportioned and plumb.

The soul is always beautiful,
The universe is duly in order . . . . every thing is in its place,

What is arrived is in its place, and what waits is in its place;

The twisted skull waits . . . . the watery or rotten blood waits,

The child of the glutton or venerealee waits long, and the child of the
drunkard waits long, and the drunkard himself waits long,

The sleepers that lived and died wait . . . . the far advanced are to go on in
their turns, and the far behind are to go on in their turns,

The diverse shall be no less diverse, but they shall flow and unite . . . . they
unite now.

[8]

The sleepers are very beautiful as they lie unclothed,

They flow hand in hand over the whole earth from east to west as they lie
unclothed;

The Asiatic and African are hand in hand . . . . the European and American
are hand in hand,

Learned and unlearned are hand in hand . . . and male and female are hand
in hand;

The bare arm of the girl crosses the bare breast of her lover . . . . they press
close without lust . . . . his lips press her neck,

The father holds his grown or ungrown son in his arms with
measureless love . . . . and the son holds the father in his arms with
measureless love,

The white hair of the mother shines on the white wrist of the daughter,

The breath of the boy goes with the breath of the man . . . . friend is
inarmed by friend,

The scholar kisses the teacher and the teacher kisses the scholar . . . . the
wronged is made right,

The call of the slave is one with the master's call . . and the master salutes
the slave,

The felon steps forth from the prison . . . . the insane becomes sane . . . .
the suffering of sick persons is relieved,

The sweatings and fevers stop . . the throat that was unsound is sound . . the
lungs of the consumptive are resumed . . the poor distressed head is free,

The joints of the rheumatic move as smoothly as ever, and smoother than
ever,

Stiflings and passages open . . . . the paralysed become supple,

The swelled and convulsed and congested awake to themselves in condition,

They pass the invigoration of the night and the chemistry of the night and
awake.

I too pass from the night;
I stay awhile away O night, but I return to you again and love you;
Why should I be afraid to trust myself to you?
I am not afraid . . . . I have been well brought forward by you;
I love the rich running day, but I do not desert her in whom I lay so long;
I know not how I came of you, and I know not where I go with you . . . .
  but I know I came well and shall go well.

I will stop only a time with the night . . . . and rise betimes.

I will duly pass the day O my mother and duly return to you;
Not you will yield forth the dawn again more surely than you will yield
  forth me again,
Not the womb yields the babe in its time more surely than I shall be
  yielded from you in my time.

I Sing the Body Electric (1855)

[1]
The bodies of men and women engirth me, and I engirth them,
They will not let me off nor I them till I go with them and respond to
  them and love them.

Was it dreamed whether those who corrupted their own live bodies could
  conceal themselves?
And whether those who defiled the living were as bad as they who defiled
  the dead?

[2]
The expression of the body of man or woman balks account,
The male is perfect and that of the female is perfect.

The expression of a wellmade man appears not only in his face,
It is in his limbs and joints also . . . . it is curiously in the joints of his hips
  and wrists,
It is in his walk . . the carriage of his neck . . the flex of his waist and knees
  . . . . dress does not hide him,
The strong sweet supple quality he has strikes through the cotton and
  flannel;
To see him pass conveys as much as the best poem . . perhaps more,
You linger to see his back and the back of his neck and shoulderside.

The sprawl and fulness of babes . . . . the bosoms and heads of women. . . . the folds of their dress . . . . their style as we pass in the street . . . . the contour of their shape downwards;

The swimmer naked in the swimmingbath . . seen as he swims through the salt transparent greenshine, or lies on his back and rolls silently with the heave of the water;

Framers bare-armed framing a house . . hoisting the beams in their places . . or using the mallet and mortising-chisel,

The bending forward and backward of rowers in rowboats . . . . the horseman in his saddle;

Girls and mothers and housekeepers in all their exquisite offices,

The group of laborers seated at noontime with their open dinnerkettles, and their wives waiting,

The female soothing a child . . . . the farmer's daughter in the garden or cowyard,

The woodman rapidly swinging his axe in the woods . . . . the young fellow hoeing corn . . . . the sleighdriver guiding his six horses through the crowd,

The wrestle of wrestlers . . two apprentice-boys, quite grown, lusty, goodnatured, nativeborn, out on the vacant lot at sundown after work,

The coats vests and caps thrown down . . the embrace of love and resistance,

The upperhold and underhold—the hair rumpled over and blinding the eyes;

The march of firemen in their own costumes—the play of the masculine muscle through cleansetting trowsers and waistbands,

The slow return from the fire . . . . the pause when the bell strikes suddenly again—the listening on the alert,

The natural perfect and varied attitudes . . . . the bent head, the curved neck, the counting:

Suchlike I love . . . . I loosen myself and pass freely . . . . and am at the mother's breast with the little child,

And swim with the swimmer, and wrestle with wrestlers, and march in line with the firemen, and pause and listen and count.

[3]

I knew a man . . . . he was a common farmer . . . . he was the father of five sons . . . . and in them were the fathers of sons . . . and in them were the fathers of sons.

This man was of wonderful vigor and calmness and beauty of person;

The shape of his head, the richness and breadth of his manners, the pale
     yellow and white of his hair and beard, the immeasurable meaning of
     his black eyes,

These I used to go and visit him to see . . . . He was wise also,

He was six feet tall . . . . he was over eighty years old . . . . his sons were
     massive clean bearded tanfaced and handsome,

They and his daughters loved him . . . all who saw him loved him . . . they
     did not love him by allowance . . . they loved him with personal love;

He drank water only . . . . the blood showed like scarlet through the clear
     brown skin of his face;

He was a frequent gunner and fisher . . . . he sailed his boat himself . . . he
     had a fine one presented to him by a shipjoiner . . . . he had fowling-
     pieces, presented to him by men that loved him;

When he went with his five sons and many grandsons to hunt or fish you
     would pick him out as the most beautiful and vigorous of the gang,

You would wish long and long to be with him . . . . you would wish to sit by
     him in the boat that you and he might touch each other.

[4]
I have perceived that to be with those I like is enough,

To stop in company with the rest at evening is enough,

To be surrounded by beautiful curious breathing laughing flesh is enough,

To pass among them . . to touch any one . . . . to rest my arm ever so
     lightly round his or her neck for a moment . . . . what is this then?

I do not ask any more delight . . . . I swim in it as in a sea.

There is something in staying close to men and women and looking on
     them and in the contact and odor of them that pleases the soul well,

All things please the soul, but these please the soul well.

[5]
This is the female form,

A divine nimbus exhales from it from head to foot,

It attracts with fierce undeniable attraction,

I am drawn by its breath as if I were no more than a helpless vapor . . . . all
     falls aside but myself and it,

Books, art, religion, time . . the visible and solid earth . . the atmosphere
     and the fringed clouds . . what was expected of heaven or feared of
     hell are now consumed,

Mad filaments, ungovernable shoots play out of it . . the response likewise
ungovernable,

Hair, bosom, hips, bend of legs, negligent falling hands—all diffused . . . .
mine too diffused,

Ebb stung by the flow, and flow stung by the ebb . . . . loveflesh swelling
and deliciously aching,

Limitless limpid jets of love hot and enormous . . . . quivering jelly of love
. . . white-blow and delirious juice,

Bridegroom-night of love working surely and softly into the prostrate
dawn,

Undulating into the willing and yielding day,

Lost in the cleave of the clasping and sweetfleshed day.

This is the nucleus . . . after the child is born of woman the man is born of
woman,

This is the bath of birth . . . this is the merge of small and large and the
outlet again.

Be not ashamed women . . your privilege encloses the rest . . it is the exit of
the rest,

You are the gates of the body and you are the gates of the soul.

The female contains all qualities and tempers them . . . . she is in her place
. . . . she moves with perfect balance,

She is all things duly veiled . . . . she is both passive and active . . . . she is to
conceive daughters as well as sons, and sons as well as daughters.

As I see my soul reflected in nature . . . . as I see through a mist one with
inexpressible completeness and beauty . . . . see the bent head and arms
folded over the breast . . . . the female I see,

I see the bearer of the great fruit which is immortality . . . . the good
thereof is not tasted by roues, and never can be.

[6]

The male is not less the soul, nor more . . . . he too is in his place,

He too is all qualities . . . . he is action and power . . . . the flush of the
known universe is in him,

Scorn becomes him well and appetite and defiance become him well,

The fiercest largest passions . . bliss that is utmost and sorrow that is
utmost become him well . . . . pride is for him,

The fullspread pride of man is calming and excellent to the soul;
Knowledge becomes him . . . . he likes it always . . . . he brings everything
    to the test of himself,
Whatever the survey . . whatever the sea and the sail, he strikes soundings
    at last only here,
Where else does he strike soundings except here?

The man's body is sacred and the woman's body is sacred . . . . it is no
    matter who,
Is it a slave? Is it one of the dullfaced immigrants just landed on the wharf?

Each belongs here or anywhere just as much as the welloff . . . . just as
    much as you,
Each has his or her place in the procession.

All is a procession,
The universe is a procession with measured and beautiful motion.

Do you know so much that you call the slave or the dullface ignorant?
Do you suppose you have a right to a good sight . . . and he or she has no
    right to a sight?
Do you think matter has cohered together from its diffused float, and the
    soil is on the surface and water runs and vegetation sprouts for you . .
    and not for him and her?

[7]
A slave at auction!
I help the auctioneer . . . . the sloven does not half know his business.

Gentlemen look on this curious creature,
Whatever the bids of the bidders they cannot be high enough for him,
For him the globe lay preparing quintillions of years without one animal or
    plant,
For him the revolving cycles truly and steadily rolled.

In that head the allbaffling brain,
In it and below it the making of the attributes of heroes.

Examine these limbs, red black or white . . . . they are very cunning in
    tendon and nerve;
They shall be stript that you may see them.

Exquisite senses, lifelit eyes, pluck, volition,
Flakes of breastmuscle, pliant backbone and neck, flesh not flabby,
    goodsized arms and legs,
And wonders within there yet.

Within there runs his blood . . . . the same old blood . . the same red
    running blood;
There swells and jets his heart . . . . There all passions and desires . . all
    reachings and aspirations:
Do you think they are not there because they are not expressed in parlors
    and lecture-rooms?

This is not only one man . . . . he is the father of those who shall be fathers
    in their turns,
In him the start of populous states and rich republics,
Of him countless immortal lives with countless embodiments and
    enjoyments.

How do you know who shall come from the offspring of his offspring
    through the centuries?
Who might you find you have come from yourself if you could trace back
    through the centuries?

[8]
A woman at auction,
She too is not only herself . . . . she is the teeming mother of mothers,
She is the bearer of them that shall grow and be mates to the mothers.

Her daughters or their daughters' daughters . . who knows who shall mate
    with them?
Who knows through the centuries what heroes may come from them?

In them and of them natal love . . . . in them the divine mystery . . . . the
    same old beautiful mystery.

Have you ever loved a woman?
Your mother . . . . is she living? . . . . Have you been much with her? and
    has she been much with you?
Do you not see that these are exactly the same to all in all nations and
    times all over the earth?

If life and soul are sacred the human body is sacred;
And the glory and sweet of a man is the token of manhood untainted,
And in man or woman a clean strong firmfibred body is beautiful as the
    most beautiful face.

Have you seen the fool that corrupted his own live body? or the fool that
    corrupted her own live body?
For they do not conceal themselves, and cannot conceal themselves.

Who degrades or defiles the living human body is cursed,
Who degrades or defiles the body of the dead is not more cursed.

There Was a Child Went Forth (1855)

There was a child went forth every day,
And the first object he looked upon and received with wonder or pity or
    love or dread, that object he became,
And that object became part of him for the day or a certain part of the day
    . . . . or for many years or stretching cycles of years.

The early lilacs became part of this child,
And grass, and white and red morningglories, and white and red clover,
    and the song of the phœbe-bird,
And the March-born lambs, and the sow's pink-faint litter, and the mare's
    foal, and the cow's calf, and the noisy brood of the barnyard or by the
    mire of the pond-side . . and the fish suspending themselves so
    curiously below there . . and the beautiful curious liquid . . and the
    water-plants with their graceful flat heads . . all became part of him.

And the field-sprouts of April and May became part of him . . . . wintergrain
    sprouts, and those of the light-yellow corn, and of the esculent
    roots of the garden,
And the appletrees covered with blossoms, and the fruit afterward . . . . and
    woodberries . . and the commonest weeds by the road;
And the old drunkard staggering home from the outhouse of the tavern
    whence he had lately risen,
And the schoolmistress that passed on her way to the school . . and the
    friendly boys that passed . . and the quarrelsome boys . . and the tidy
    and freshcheeked girls . . and the barefoot negro boy and girl,
And all the changes of city and country wherever he went.

His own parents . . he that had propelled the fatherstuff at night, and
  fathered him . . and she that conceived him in her womb and birthed
  him . . . . they gave this child more of themselves than that,
They gave him afterward every day . . . . they and of them became part of
  him.

The mother at home quietly placing the dishes on the suppertable,
The mother with mild words . . . . clean her cap and gown . . . . a
  wholesome odor falling off her person and clothes as she walks by:
The father, strong, selfsufficient, manly, mean, angered, unjust,
The blow, the quick loud word, the tight bargain, the crafty lure,
The family usages, the language, the company, the furniture . . . . the
  yearning and swelling heart,
Affection that will not be gainsayed . . . . The sense of what is real . . . . the
  thought if after all it should prove unreal,
The doubts of daytime and the doubts of nighttime . . . the curious
  whether and how,
Whether that which appears so is so . . . . Or is it all flashes and specks?
Men and women crowding fast in the streets . . if they are not flashes and
  specks what are they?
The streets themselves, and the facades of houses . . . . the goods in the
  windows,
Vehicles . . teams . . the tiered wharves, and the huge crossing at the ferries;
The village on the highland seen from afar at sunset . . . . the river
  between,
Shadows . . aureola and mist . . light falling on roofs and gables of white or
  brown, three miles off,
The schooner near by sleepily dropping down the tide . . the little boat
  slacktowed astern,
The hurrying tumbling waves and quickbroken crests and slapping;
The strata of colored clouds . . . . the long bar of maroontint away solitary
  by itself . . . . the spread of purity it lies motionless in,
The horizon's edge, the flying seacrow, the fragrance of saltmarsh and
  shoremud;
These became part of that child who went forth every day,
  and who now goes and will always go forth every day,
And these become of him or her that peruses them now.

A Woman Waits for Me

A woman waits for me, she contains all, nothing is lacking,
Yet all were lacking if sex were lacking, or if the moisture of the right man
    were lacking.

Sex contains all, bodies, souls,
Meanings, proofs, purities, delicacies, results, promulgations,
Songs, commands, health, pride, the maternal mystery, the seminal milk,
All hopes, benefactions, bestowals, all the passions, loves, beauties, delights
    of the earth,
All the governments, judges, gods, follow'd persons of the earth,
These are contain'd in sex as parts of itself and justifications of itself.

Without shame the man I like knows and avows the deliciousness of his sex,
Without shame the woman I like knows and avows hers.

Now I will dismiss myself from impassive women,
I will go stay with her who waits for me, and with those women that are
    warm-blooded and sufficient for me,
I see that they understand me and do not deny me,
I see that they are worthy of me, I will be the robust husband of those
    women.

They are not one jot less than I am,
They are tann'd in the face by shining suns and blowing winds,
Their flesh has the old divine suppleness and strength,
They know how to swim, row, ride, wrestle, shoot, run, strike, retreat,
    advance, resist, defend themselves,
They are ultimate in their own right—they are calm, clear, well-possess'd
    of themselves.

I draw you close to me, you women,
I cannot let you go, I would do you good,
I am for you, and you are for me, not only for our own sake, but for others'
    sakes,
Envelop'd in you sleep greater heroes and bards,
They refuse to awake at the touch of any man but me.

It is I, you women, I make my way,
I am stern, acrid, large, undissuadable, but I love you,
I do not hurt you any more than is necessary for you,

I pour the stuff to start sons and daughters fit for these
    States, I press with slow rude muscle,
I brace myself effectually, I listen to no entreaties,
I dare not withdraw till I deposit what has so long accumulated within me.

Through you I drain the pent-up rivers of myself,
In you I wrap a thousand onward years,
On you I graft the grafts of the best-beloved of me and America,
The drops I distil upon you shall grow fierce and athletic girls, new artists,
    musicians, and singers,
The babes I beget upon you are to beget babes in their turn,
I shall demand perfect men and women out of my love-spendings,
I shall expect them to interpenetrate with others, as I and you
    interpenetrate now,
I shall count on the fruits of the gushing showers of them, as
    I count on the fruits of the gushing showers I give now,
I shall look for loving crops from the birth, life, death, immortality, I plant
    so lovingly now.

Spontaneous Me

Spontaneous me, Nature,
The loving day, the mounting sun, the friend I am happy with,
The arm of my friend hanging idly over my shoulder,
The hillside whiten'd with blossoms of the mountain ash,
The same late in autumn, the hues of red, yellow, drab, purple, and light
    and dark green,
The rich coverlet of the grass, animals and birds, the private untrimm'd
    bank, the primitive apples, the pebble-stones,
Beautiful dripping fragments, the negligent list of one after another as I
    happen to call them to me or think of them,
The real poems, (what we call poems being merely pictures,)
The poems of the privacy of the night, and of men like me,
This poem drooping shy and unseen that I always carry, and that all men
    carry,
(Know once for all, avow'd on purpose, wherever are men like me, are our
    lusty lurking masculine poems,)
Love-thoughts, love-juice, love-odor, love-yielding, love-climbers, and the
    climbing sap,

Arms and hands of love, lips of love, phallic thumb of love, breasts of love,
  bellies press'd and glued together with love,
Earth of chaste love, life that is only life after love,
The body of my love, the body of the woman I love, the body of the man,
  the body of the earth,
Soft forenoon airs that blow from the south-west,
The hairy wild-bee that murmurs and hankers up and down, that gripes
  the full-grown lady-flower, curves upon her with amorous firm legs,
  takes his will of her, and holds himself tremulous and tight till he is
  satisfied;
The wet of woods through the early hours,
Two sleepers at night lying close together as they sleep, one with an arm
  slanting down across and below the waist of the other,
The smell of apples, aromas from crush'd sage-plant, mint, birch-bark,
The boy's longings, the glow and pressure as he confides to me what he
  was dreaming,
The dead leaf whirling its spiral whirl and falling still and content to the
  ground,
The no-form'd stings that sights, people, objects, sting me with,
The hubb'd sting of myself, stinging me as much as it ever can any one,
The sensitive, orbic, underlapp'd brothers, that only privileged feelers may
  be intimate where they are,
The curious roamer the hand roaming all over the body, the bashful
  withdrawing of flesh where the fingers soothingly pause and edge
  themselves,
The limpid liquid within the young man,
The vex'd corrosion so pensive and so painful,
The torment, the irritable tide that will not be at rest,
The like of the same I feel, the like of the same in others,
The young man that flushes and flushes, and the young woman that flushes
  and flushes,
The young man that wakes deep at night, the hot hand seeking to repress
  what would master him,
The mystic amorous night, the strange half-welcome pangs, visions,
  sweats,
The pulse pounding through palms and trembling encircling
  fingers, the young man all color'd, red, ashamed, angry;
The souse upon me of my lover the sea, as I lie willing and naked,
The merriment of the twin babes that crawl over the grass in the sun, the

mother never turning her vigilant eyes from them,
The walnut-trunk, the walnut-husks, and the ripening or ripen'd
long-round walnuts,
The continence of vegetables, birds, animals,
The consequent meanness of me should I skulk or find myself indecent,
while birds and animals never once skulk or find themselves indecent,
The great chastity of paternity, to match the great chastity of maternity,
The oath of procreation I have sworn, my Adamic and fresh daughters,
The greed that eats me day and night with hungry gnaw, till I saturate
what shall produce boys to fill my place when I am through,
The wholesome relief, repose, content,
And this bunch pluck'd at random from myself,
It has done its work—I toss it carelessly to fall where it may.

Trickle Drops

Trickle drops! my blue veins leaving!
O drops of me! trickle, slow drops,
Candid from me falling, drip, bleeding drops,
From wounds made to free you whence you were prison'd,
From my face, from my forehead and lips,
From my breast, from within where I was conceal'd, press forth red drops,
confession drops,
Stain every page, stain every song I sing, every word I say, bloody drops,
Let them know your scarlet heat, let them glisten,
Saturate them with yourself all ashamed and wet,
Glow upon all I have written or shall write, bleeding drops,
Let it all be seen in your light, blushing drops.

I Saw in Louisiana a Live-Oak Growing

I saw in Louisiana a live-oak growing,
All alone stood it and the moss hung down from the branches,
Without any companion it grew there uttering joyous leaves of dark green,
And its look, rude, unbending, lusty, made me think of myself,
But I wonder'd how it could utter joyous leaves standing alone there
without its friend near, for I knew I could not,
And I broke off a twig with a certain number of leaves upon it, and twined
around it a little moss,

And brought it away, and I have placed it in sight in my room,
It is not needed to remind me as of my own dear friends,
(For I believe lately I think of little else than of them,)
Yet it remains to me a curious token, it makes me think of manly love;
For all that, and though the live-oak glistens there in Louisiana solitary in
    a wide flat space,
Uttering joyous leaves all its life without a friend a lover near,
I know very well I could not.

Here the Frailest Leaves of Me

Here the frailest leaves of me and yet my strongest lasting,
Here I shade and hide my thoughts, I myself do not expose them,
And yet they expose me more than all my other poems.

Crossing Brooklyn Ferry

1
Flood-tide below me! I see you face to face!
Cloud of the west—sun there half an hour high—I see you also face to face.

Crowds of men and women attired in the usual costumes, how curious you
    are to me!
On the ferry-boats the hundreds and hundreds that cross, returning home,
    are more curious to me than you suppose,
And you that shall cross from shore to shore years hence are more to me,
    and more in my meditations, than you might suppose.

2
The impalpable sustenance of me from all things at all hours of the day,
The simple, compact, well-join'd scheme, myself disintegrated, every one
    disintegrated yet part of the scheme,
The similitudes of the past and those of the future,
The glories strung like beads on my smallest sights and hearings, on the
    walk in the street and the passage over the river,
The current rushing so swiftly and swimming with me far away,
The others that are to follow me, the ties between me and them,
The certainty of others, the life, love, sight, hearing of others.

Others will enter the gates of the ferry and cross from shore to shore,
Others will watch the run of the flood-tide,
Others will see the shipping of Manhattan north and west, and the heights
    of Brooklyn to the south and east,
Others will see the islands large and small;
Fifty years hence, others will see them as they cross, the sun half an hour high,
A hundred years hence, or ever so many hundred years hence, others will
    see them,
Will enjoy the sunset, the pouring-in of the flood-tide, the falling-back to
    the sea of the ebb-tide.

3

It avails not, time nor place—distance avails not,
I am with you, you men and women of a generation, or ever so many
    generations hence,
Just as you feel when you look on the river and sky, so I felt,
Just as any of you is one of a living crowd, I was one of a crowd,
Just as you are refresh'd by the gladness of the river and the bright flow, I
    was refresh'd,
Just as you stand and lean on the rail, yet hurry with the swift current, I
    stood yet was hurried,
Just as you look on the numberless masts of ships and the thick-stemm'd
    pipes of steamboats, I look'd.

I too many and many a time cross'd the river of old,
Watched the Twelfth-month sea-gulls, saw them high in the air floating
    with motionless wings, oscillating their bodies,
Saw how the glistening yellow lit up parts of their bodies and left the rest
    in strong shadow,
Saw the slow-wheeling circles and the gradual edging toward the south,
Saw the reflection of the summer sky in the water,
Had my eyes dazzled by the shimmering track of beams,
Look'd at the fine centrifugal spokes of light round the shape of my head
    in the sunlit water,
Look'd on the haze on the hills southward and south-westward,
Look'd on the vapor as it flew in fleeces tinged with violet,
Look'd toward the lower bay to notice the vessels arriving,
Saw their approach, saw aboard those that were near me,
Saw the white sails of schooners and sloops, saw the ships at anchor,
The sailors at work in the rigging or out astride the spars,

The round masts, the swinging motion of the hulls, the slender serpentine
    pennants,
The large and small steamers in motion, the pilots in their pilot-houses,
The white wake left by the passage, the quick tremulous whirl of the
    wheels,
The flags of all nations, the falling of them at sunset,
The scallop-edged waves in the twilight, the ladled cups, the frolicsome
    crests and glistening,
The stretch afar growing dimmer and dimmer, the gray walls of the granite
    storehouses by the docks,
On the river the shadowy group, the big steam-tug closely flank'd on
    each side by the barges, the hay-boat, the belated lighter,
On the neighboring shore the fires from the foundry chimneys burning
    high and glaringly into the night,
Casting their flicker of black contrasted with wild red and yellow light over
    the tops of houses, and down into the clefts of streets.

4
These and all else were to me the same as they are to you,
I loved well those cities, loved well the stately and rapid river,
The men and women I saw were all near to me,
Others the same—others who look back on me because I look'd forward
    to them,
(The time will come, though I stop here to-day and to-night.)

5
What is it then between us?
What is the count of the scores or hundreds of years between us?

Whatever it is, it avails not—distance avails not, and place avails not,
I too lived, Brooklyn of ample hills was mine,
I too walk'd the streets of Manhattan island, and bathed in the waters
    around it,
I too felt the curious abrupt questionings stir within me,
In the day among crowds of people sometimes they came upon me,
In my walks home late at night or as I lay in my bed they came upon me,
I too had been struck from the float forever held in solution,
I too had receiv'd identity by my body,
That I was I knew was of my body, and what I should be I knew I should
    be of my body.

6

It is not upon you alone the dark patches fall,
The dark threw its patches down upon me also,
The best I had done seem'd to me blank and suspicious,
My great thoughts as I supposed them, were they not in reality meagre?
Nor is it you alone who know what it is to be evil,
I am he who knew what it was to be evil,
I too knotted the old knot of contrariety,
Blabb'd, blush'd, resented, lied, stole, grudg'd,
Had guile, anger, lust, hot wishes I dared not speak,
Was wayward, vain, greedy, shallow, sly, cowardly, malignant,
The wolf, the snake, the hog, not wanting in me,
The cheating look, the frivolous word, the adulterous wish, not wanting,
Refusals, hates, postponements, meanness, laziness, none of these wanting,
Was one with the rest, the days and haps of the rest,
Was call'd by my nighest name by clear loud voices of young men as they
     saw me approaching or passing,
Felt their arms on my neck as I stood, or the negligent leaning of their
     flesh against me as I sat,
Saw many I loved in the street or ferry-boat or public assembly, yet never
     told them a word,
Lived the same life with the rest, the same old laughing, gnawing, sleeping,
Play'd the part that still looks back on the actor or actress,
The same old role, the role that is what we make it, as great as we like,
Or as small as we like, or both great and small.

7

Closer yet I approach you,
What thought you have of me now, I had as much of you—I laid in my
     stores in advance,
I consider'd long and seriously of you before you were born.

Who was to know what should come home to me?
Who knows but I am enjoying this?
Who knows, for all the distance, but I am as good as looking at you now,
     for all you cannot see me?

8

Ah, what can ever be more stately and admirable to me than mast-hemm'd
     Manhattan?

River and sunset and scallop-edg'd waves of flood-tide?
The sea-gulls oscillating their bodies, the hay-boat in the twilight, and the
    belated lighter?
What gods can exceed these that clasp me by the hand, and with voices I
    love call me promptly and loudly by my nighest name as I approach?
What is more subtle than this which ties me to the woman or man that
    looks in my face?
Which fuses me into you now, and pours my meaning into you?

We understand then do we not?
What I promis'd without mentioning it, have you not accepted?
What the study could not teach—what the preaching could not
    accomplish is accomplish'd, is it not?

9

Flow on, river! flow with the flood-tide, and ebb with the ebb-tide!
Frolic on, crested and scallop-edg'd waves!
Gorgeous clouds of the sunset! drench with your splendor me, or the men
    and women generations after me!
Cross from shore to shore, countless crowds of passengers!
Stand up, tall masts of Mannahatta! stand up, beautiful hills of Brooklyn!
Throb, baffled and curious brain! throw out questions and answers!
Suspend here and everywhere, eternal float of solution!
Gaze, loving and thirsting eyes, in the house or street or public assembly!
Sound out, voices of young men! loudly and musically call me by my
    nighest name!
Live, old life! play the part that looks back on the actor or actress!
Play the old role, the role that is great or small according as one makes it!
Consider, you who peruse me, whether I may not in unknown ways be
    looking upon you;
Be firm, rail over the river, to support those who lean idly, yet haste with
    the hasting current;
Fly on, sea-birds! fly sideways, or wheel in large circles high in the air;
Receive the summer sky, you water, and faithfully hold it till all downcast
    eyes have time to take it from you!
Diverge, fine spokes of light, from the shape of my head, or any one's
    head, in the sunlit water!
Come on, ships from the lower bay! pass up or down, white-sail'd
    schooners, sloops, lighters!
Flaunt away, flags of all nations! be duly lower'd at sunset!

Burn high your fires, foundry chimneys! cast black shadows at nightfall!
    cast red and yellow light over the tops of the houses!
Appearances, now or henceforth, indicate what you are,
You necessary film, continue to envelop the soul,
About my body for me, and your body for you, be hung our divinest
    aromas,
Thrive, cities—bring your freight, bring your shows, ample and sufficient
    rivers,
Expand, being than which none else is perhaps more spiritual,
Keep your places, objects than which none else is more lasting.

You have waited, you always wait, you dumb, beautiful ministers,
We receive you with free sense at last, and are insatiate henceforward,
Not you any more shall be able to foil us, or withhold yourselves from us,
We use you, and do not cast you aside—we plant you permanently within us,
We fathom you not—we love you—there is perfection in you also,
You furnish your parts toward eternity,
Great or small, you furnish your parts toward the soul.

Out of the Cradle Endlessly Rocking

Out of the cradle endlessly rocking,
Out of the mocking-bird's throat, the musical shuttle,
Out of the Ninth-month midnight,
Over the sterile sands and the fields beyond, where the child leaving his
    bed wander'd alone, bareheaded, barefoot,
Down from the shower'd halo,
Up from the mystic play of shadows twining and twisting as if they were
    alive,
Out from the patches of briers and blackberries,
From the memories of the bird that chanted to me,
From your memories sad brother, from the fitful risings and fallings I heard,
From under that yellow half-moon late-risen and swollen as if with tears,
From those beginning notes of yearning and love there in the mist,
From the thousand responses of my heart never to cease,
From the myriad thence-arous'd words,
From the word stronger and more delicious than any,
From such as now they start the scene revisiting,
As a flock, twittering, rising, or overhead passing,

Borne hither, ere all eludes me, hurriedly,
A man, yet by these tears a little boy again,
Throwing myself on the sand, confronting the waves,
I, chanter of pains and joys, uniter of here and hereafter,
Taking all hints to use them, but swiftly leaping beyond them,
A reminiscence sing.

Once Paumanok,
When the lilac-scent was in the air and Fifth-month grass was growing,
Up this seashore in some briers,
Two feather'd guests from Alabama, two together,
And their nest, and four light-green eggs spotted with brown,
And every day the he-bird to and fro near at hand,
And every day the she-bird crouch'd on her nest, silent, with bright eyes,
And every day I, a curious boy, never too close, never disturbing them,
Cautiously peering, absorbing, translating.

Shine! shine! shine!
Pour down your warmth, great sun!
While we bask, we two together.

Two together!
Winds blow south, or winds blow north,
Day come white, or night come black,
Home, or rivers and mountains from home,
Singing all time, minding no time,
While we two keep together.

Till of a sudden,
May-be kill'd, unknown to her mate,
One forenoon the she-bird crouch'd not on the nest,
Nor return'd that afternoon, nor the next,
Nor ever appear'd again.

And thenceforward all summer in the sound of the sea,
And at night under the full of the moon in calmer weather,
Over the hoarse surging of the sea,
Or flitting from brier to brier by day,
I saw, I heard at intervals the remaining one, the he-bird,
The solitary guest from Alabama.

Blow! blow! blow!
Blow up sea-winds along Paumanok's shore;
I wait and I wait till you blow my mate to me.

Yes, when the stars glisten'd,
All night long on the prong of a moss-scallop'd stake,
Down almost amid the slapping waves,
Sat the lone singer wonderful causing tears.

He call'd on his mate,
He pour'd forth the meanings which I of all men know.

Yes my brother I know,
The rest might not, but I have treasur'd every note,
For more than once dimly down to the beach gliding,
Silent, avoiding the moonbeams, blending myself with the shadows,
Recalling now the obscure shapes, the echoes, the sounds and sights after
     their sorts,
The white arms out in the breakers tirelessly tossing,
I, with bare feet, a child, the wind wafting my hair,
Listen'd long and long.

Listen'd to keep, to sing, now translating the notes,
Following you my brother.

Soothe! soothe! soothe!
Close on its wave soothes the wave behind,
And again another behind embracing and lapping, every one close,
But my love soothes not me, not me.

Low hangs the moon, it rose late,
It is lagging—O I think it is heavy with love, with love.

O madly the sea pushes upon the land,
With love, with love.

O night! do I not see my love fluttering out among the breakers?
What is that little black thing I see there in the white? Loud! loud! loud!
Loud I call to you, my love!
High and clear I shoot my voice over the waves,
Surely you must know who is here, is here,
You must know who I am, my love.

Low-hanging moon!
What is that dusky spot in your brown yellow?
O it is the shape, the shape of my mate!
O moon do not keep her from me any longer.

Land! land! O land!
Whichever way I turn, O I think you could give me my mate back again if you
    only would,
For I am almost sure I see her dimly whichever way I look.

O rising stars!
Perhaps the one I want so much will rise, will rise with some of you.

O throat! O trembling throat!
Sound clearer through the atmosphere!
Pierce the woods, the earth,
Somewhere listening to catch you must be the one I want.

Shake out carols!
Solitary here, the night's carols!
Carols of lonesome love! death's carols!
Carols under that lagging, yellow, waning moon!
O under that moon where she droops almost down into the sea!
O reckless despairing carols.

But soft! sink low!
Soft! let me just murmur,
And do you wait a moment you husky-nois'd sea,
For somewhere I believe I heard my mate responding to me,
So faint, I must be still, be still to listen,
But not altogether still, for then she might not come immediately to me.

Hither my love!
Here I am! here!
With this just-sustain'd note I announce myself to you,
This gentle call is for you my love, for you.

Do not be decoy'd elsewhere,
That is the whistle of the wind, it is not my voice,
That is the fluttering, the fluttering of the spray,
Those are the shadows of leaves.

O darkness! O in vain!
O I am very sick and sorrowful.

O brown halo in the sky near the moon, drooping upon the sea!
O troubled reflection in the sea!
O throat! O throbbing heart!
And I singing uselessly, uselessly all the night.

O past! O happy life! O songs of joy!
In the air, in the woods, over fields,
Loved! loved! loved! loved! loved!
But my mate no more, no more with me!
We two together no more.

The aria sinking,
All else continuing, the stars shining,
The winds blowing, the notes of the bird continuous echoing,
With angry moans the fierce old mother incessantly moaning,
On the sands of Paumanok's shore gray and rustling,
The yellow half-moon enlarged, sagging down, drooping, the face of the
  sea almost touching,
The boy ecstatic, with his bare feet the waves, with his hair the atmosphere
  dallying,
The love in the heart long pent, now loose, now at last tumultuously
  bursting,
The aria's meaning, the ears, the soul, swiftly depositing,
The strange tears down the cheeks coursing,
The colloquy there, the trio, each uttering,
The undertone, the savage old mother incessantly crying
To the boy's soul's questions sullenly timing, some drown'd secret hissing,
To the outsetting bard.

Demon or bird! (said the boy's soul,)
Is it indeed toward your mate you sing? or is it really to me?
For I, that was a child, my tongue's use sleeping, now I have heard you,
Now in a moment I know what I am for, I awake,
And already a thousand singers, a thousand songs, clearer, louder and more
  sorrowful than yours,
A thousand warbling echoes have started to life within me, never to die.

O you singer solitary, singing by yourself, projecting me,
O solitary me listening, never more shall I cease perpetuating you,
Never more shall I escape, never more the reverberations,
Never more the cries of unsatisfied love be absent from me,
Never again leave me to be the peaceful child I was before what there in
    the night,
By the sea under the yellow and sagging moon,
The messenger there arous'd, the fire, the sweet hell within,
The unknown want, the destiny of me.

O give me the clew! (it lurks in the night here somewhere,)
O if I am to have so much, let me have more!

A word then, (for I will conquer it,)
The word final, superior to all,
Subtle, sent up—what is it?—I listen;
Are you whispering it, and have been all the time, you sea-waves?
Is that it from your liquid rims and wet sands?

Whereto answering, the sea,
Delaying not, hurrying not,
Whisper'd me through the night, and very plainly before daybreak,
Lisp'd to me the low and delicious word death,
And again death, death, death, death,
Hissing melodious, neither like the bird nor like my arous'd child's heart,
But edging near as privately for me rustling at my feet,
Creeping thence steadily up to my ears and laving me softly all over,
Death, death, death, death, death.

Which I do not forget,
But fuse the song of my dusky demon and brother,
That he sang to me in the moonlight on Paumanok's gray beach,
With the thousand responsive songs at random,
My own songs awaked from that hour,
And with them the key, the word up from the waves,
The word of the sweetest song and all songs,
That strong and delicious word which, creeping to my feet,
(Or like some old crone rocking the cradle, swathed in sweet
    garments, bending aside,)
The sea whisper'd me.

As I Ebb'd with the Ocean of Life

1

As I ebb'd with the ocean of life,
As I wended the shores I know,
As I walk'd where the ripples continually wash you Paumanok,
Where they rustle up hoarse and sibilant,
Where the fierce old mother endlessly cries for her castaways,
I musing late in the autumn day, gazing off southward,
Held by this electric self out of the pride of which I utter poems,
Was seiz'd by the spirit that trails in the lines underfoot,
The rim, the sediment that stands for all the water and all the land of the
    globe.

Fascinated, my eyes reverting from the south, dropt, to follow those
    slender windrows,
Chaff, straw, splinters of wood, weeds, and the sea-gluten,
Scum, scales from shining rocks, leaves of salt-lettuce, left by the tide,
Miles walking, the sound of breaking waves the other side of me,
Paumanok there and then as I thought the old thought of likenesses,
These you presented to me you fish-shaped island,
As I wended the shores I know,
As I walk'd with that electric self seeking types.

2

As I wend to the shores I know not,
As I list to the dirge, the voices of men and women wreck'd,
As I inhale the impalpable breezes that set in upon me,
As the ocean so mysterious rolls toward me closer and closer,
I too but signify at the utmost a little wash'd-up drift,
A few sands and dead leaves to gather,
Gather, and merge myself as part of the sands and drift.

O baffled, balk'd, bent to the very earth,
Oppress'd with myself that I have dared to open my mouth,
Aware now that amid all that blab whose echoes recoil upon me I have not
    once had the least idea who or what I am,
But that before all my arrogant poems the real Me stands yet
    untouch'd, untold, altogether unreach'd,
Withdrawn far, mocking me with mock-congratulatory signs and bows,

With peals of distant ironical laughter at every word I have written,
Pointing in silence to these songs, and then to the sand beneath.

I perceive I have not really understood any thing, not a single object, and
    that no man ever can,
Nature here in sight of the sea taking advantage of me to dart upon me and
    sting me,
Because I have dared to open my mouth to sing at all.

3
You oceans both, I close with you,
We murmur alike reproachfully rolling sands and drift, knowing not why,
These little shreds indeed standing for you and me and all.

You friable shore with trails of debris,
You fish-shaped island, I take what is underfoot,
What is yours is mine my father.

I too Paumanok,
I too have bubbled up, floated the measureless float, and been wash'd on
    your shores,
I too am but a trail of drift and debris,
I too leave little wrecks upon you, you fish-shaped island.

I throw myself upon your breast my father,
I cling to you so that you cannot unloose me,
I hold you so firm till you answer me something.

Kiss me my father,
Touch me with your lips as I touch those I love,
Breathe to me while I hold you close the secret of the murmuring I envy.

4
Ebb, ocean of life, (the flow will return,)
Cease not your moaning you fierce old mother,
Endlessly cry for your castaways, but fear not, deny not me,
Rustle not up so hoarse and angry against my feet as I touch you or gather
    from you.

I mean tenderly by you and all,
I gather for myself and for this phantom looking down where we lead, and
    following me and mine.

Me and mine, loose windrows, little corpses,
Froth, snowy white, and bubbles,
(See, from my dead lips the ooze exuding at last,
See, the prismatic colors glistening and rolling,)
Tufts of straw, sands, fragments,
Buoy'd hither from many moods, one contradicting another,
From the storm, the long calm, the darkness, the swell,
Musing, pondering, a breath, a briny tear, a dab of liquid or soil,
Up just as much out of fathomless workings fermented and thrown,
A limp blossom or two, torn, just as much over waves floating, drifted at
  random,
Just as much for us that sobbing dirge of Nature,
Just as much whence we come that blare of the cloud-trumpets,
We, capricious, brought hither we know not whence, spread out before you,
You up there walking or sitting,
Whoever you are, we too lie in drifts at your feet.

When I Heard the Learn'd Astronomer

When I heard the learn'd astronomer,
When the proofs, the figures, were ranged in columns before me,
When I was shown the charts and diagrams, to add, divide, and measure
  them,
When I sitting heard the astronomer where he lectured with much
  applause in the lecture-room,
How soon unaccountable I became tired and sick,
Till rising and gliding out I wander'd off by myself,
In the mystical moist night-air, and from time to time,
Look'd up in perfect silence at the stars.

Cavalry Crossing a Ford

A line in long array where they wind betwixt green islands,
They take a serpentine course, their arms flash in the sun—hark to the
  musical clank,
Behold the silvery river, in it the splashing horses loitering stop to drink,
Behold the brown-faced men, each group, each person a picture, the
  negligent rest on the saddles,

Some emerge on the opposite bank, others are just entering the ford—while,
Scarlet and blue and snowy white,
The guidon flags flutter gayly in the wind.

When Lilacs Last in the Dooryard Bloom'd

1

When lilacs last in the dooryard bloom'd,
And the great star early droop'd in the western sky in the night,
I mourn'd, and yet shall mourn with ever-returning spring.

Ever-returning spring, trinity sure to me you bring,
Lilac blooming perennial and drooping star in the west,
And thought of him I love.

2

O powerful western fallen star!
O shades of night—O moody, tearful night!
O great star disappear'd—O the black murk that hides the star!
O cruel hands that hold me powerless—O helpless soul of me!
O harsh surrounding cloud that will not free my soul.

3

In the dooryard fronting an old farm-house near the white-wash'd palings,
Stands the lilac-bush tall-growing with heart-shaped leaves of rich green,
With many a pointed blossom rising delicate, with the perfume strong I love,
With every leaf a miracle—and from this bush in the dooryard,
With delicate-color'd blossoms and heart-shaped leaves of rich green,
A sprig with its flower I break.

4

In the swamp in secluded recesses,
A shy and hidden bird is warbling a song.

Solitary the thrush,
The hermit withdrawn to himself, avoiding the settlements,
Sings by himself a song.

Song of the bleeding throat,
Death's outlet song of life, (for well dear brother I know,
If thou wast not granted to sing thou would'st surely die.)

5

Over the breast of the spring, the land, amid cities,
Amid lanes and through old woods, where lately the violets peep'd from
the ground, spotting the gray debris,
Amid the grass in the fields each side of the lanes, passing the endless grass,
Passing the yellow-spear'd wheat, every grain from its shroud in the dark-
brown fields uprisen,
Passing the apple-tree blows of white and pink in the orchards,
Carrying a corpse to where it shall rest in the grave,
Night and day journeys a coffin.

6

Coffin that passes through lanes and streets,
Through day and night with the great cloud darkening the land,
With the pomp of the inloop'd flags with the cities draped in black,
With the show of the States themselves as of crape-veil'd women standing,
With processions long and winding and the flambeaus of the night,
With the countless torches lit, with the silent sea of faces and the unbared
heads,
With the waiting depot, the arriving coffin, and the sombre faces,
With dirges through the night, with the thousand voices rising strong and
solemn,
With all the mournful voices of the dirges pour'd around the coffin,
The dim-lit churches and the shuddering organs—where amid these you
journey,
With the tolling tolling bells' perpetual clang,
Here, coffin that slowly passes,
I give you my sprig of lilac.

7

(Nor for you, for one alone,
Blossoms and branches green to coffins all I bring,
For fresh as the morning, thus would I chant a song for you
O sane and sacred death.
All over bouquets of roses,
O death, I cover you over with roses and early lilies,
But mostly and now the lilac that blooms the first,
Copious I break, I break the sprigs from the bushes,
With loaded arms I come, pouring for you,
For you and the coffins all of you O death.)

8

O western orb sailing the heaven,
Now I know what you must have meant as a month since I walk'd,
As I walk'd in silence the transparent shadowy night,
As I saw you had something to tell as you bent to me night after night,
As you droop'd from the sky low down as if to my side, (while the other
    stars all look'd on,)
As we wander'd together the solemn night, (for something I know not
    what kept me from sleep,)
As the night advanced, and I saw on the rim of the west how full you were
    of woe,
As I stood on the rising ground in the breeze in the cool transparent night,
As I watch'd where you pass'd and was lost in the netherward black of the
    night,
As my soul in its trouble dissatisfied sank, as where you sad orb,
Concluded, dropt in the night, and was gone.

9

Sing on there in the swamp,
O singer bashful and tender, I hear your notes, I hear your call,
I hear, I come presently, I understand you,
But a moment I linger, for the lustrous star has detain'd me,
The star my departing comrade holds and detains me.

10

O how shall I warble myself for the dead one there I loved?
And how shall I deck my song for the large sweet soul that has gone?
And what shall my perfume be for the grave of him I love?

Sea-winds blown from east and west,
Blown from the Eastern sea and blown from the Western sea, till there on
    the prairies meeting,
These and with these and the breath of my chant,
I'll perfume the grave of him I love.

11

O what shall I hang on the chamber walls?
And what shall the pictures be that I hang on the walls,
To adorn the burial-house of him I love?

Pictures of growing spring and farms and homes,

With the Fourth-month eve at sundown, and the gray smoke lucid and
bright,

With floods of the yellow gold of the gorgeous, indolent, sinking sun,
burning, expanding the air,

With the fresh sweet herbage under foot, and the pale green leaves of the
trees prolific,

In the distance the flowing glaze, the breast of the river, with a
wind-dapple here and there,

With ranging hills on the banks, with many a line against the sky, and
shadows,

And the city at hand with dwellings so dense, and stacks of chimneys,

And all the scenes of life and the workshops, and the workmen homeward
returning.

12

Lo, body and soul—this land,

My own Manhattan with spires, and the sparkling and hurrying tides, and
the ships,

The varied and ample land, the South and the North in the light, Ohio's
shores and flashing Missouri,

And ever the far-spreading prairies cover'd with grass and corn.

Lo, the most excellent sun so calm and haughty,

The violet and purple morn with just-felt breezes,

The gentle soft-born measureless light,

The miracle spreading bathing all, the fulfill'd noon,

The coming eve delicious, the welcome night and the stars,

Over my cities shining all, enveloping man and land.

13

Sing on, sing on you gray-brown bird,

Sing from the swamps, the recesses, pour your chant from the bushes,

Limitless out of the dusk, out of the cedars and pines.

Sing on dearest brother, warble your reedy song,

Loud human song, with voice of uttermost woe.

O liquid and free and tender!

O wild and loose to my soul—O wondrous singer!

You only I hear—yet the star holds me, (but will soon depart,)

Yet the lilac with mastering odor holds me.

14

Now while I sat in the day and look'd forth,
In the close of the day with its light and the fields of spring, and the
    farmers preparing their crops,
In the large unconscious scenery of my land with its lakes and forests,
In the heavenly aerial beauty, (after the perturb'd winds and the storms,)
Under the arching heavens of the afternoon swift passing, and the voices of
    children and women,
The many-moving sea-tides, and I saw the ships how they sail'd,
And the summer approaching with richness, and the fields all busy with
    labor,
And the infinite separate houses, how they all went on, each with its meals
    and minutia of daily usages,
And the streets how their throbbings throbb'd, and the cities pent—lo,
    then and there,
Falling upon them all and among them all, enveloping me with the rest,
Appear'd the cloud, appear'd the long black trail,
And I knew death, its thought, and the sacred knowledge of death.

Then with the knowledge of death as walking one side of me,
And the thought of death close-walking the other side of me,
And I in the middle as with companions, and as holding the hands of
    companions,
I fled forth to the hiding receiving night that talks not,
Down to the shores of the water, the path by the swamp in the dimness,
To the solemn shadowy cedars and ghostly pines so still.

And the singer so shy to the rest receiv'd me,
The gray-brown bird I know receiv'd us comrades three,
And he sang the carol of death, and a verse for him I love.

From deep secluded recesses,
From the fragrant cedars and the ghostly pines so still,
Came the carol of the bird.

And the charm of the carol rapt me,
As I held as if by their hands my comrades in the night,
And the voice of my spirit tallied the song of the bird.

Come lovely and soothing death,
Undulate round the world, serenely arriving, arriving,
In the day, in the night, to all, to each,
Sooner or later delicate death.

Prais'd be the fathomless universe,
For life and joy, and for objects and knowledge curious,
And for love, sweet love—but praise! praise! praise!
For the sure-enwinding arms of cool-enfolding death.

Dark mother always gliding near with soft feet,
Have none chanted for thee a chant of fullest welcome?
Then I chant it for thee, I glorify thee above all,
I bring thee a song that when thou must indeed come, come unfalteringly.

Approach strong deliveress,
When it is so, when thou hast taken them I joyously sing the dead,
Lost in the loving floating ocean of thee,
Laved in the flood of thy bliss O death.

From me to thee glad serenades,
Dances for thee I propose saluting thee, adornments and feastings for thee,
And the sights of the open landscape and the high-spread sky are fitting,
And life and the fields, and the huge and thoughtful night.

The night in silence under many a star,
The ocean shore and the husky whispering wave whose voice I know,
And the soul turning to thee O vast and well-veil'd death,
And the body gratefully nestling close to thee.

Over the tree-tops I float thee a song,
Over the rising and sinking waves, over the myriad fields and the prairies wide,
Over the dense-pack'd cities all and the teeming wharves and ways,
I float this carol with joy, with joy to thee O death.

15

To the tally of my soul,
Loud and strong kept up the gray-brown bird,
With pure deliberate notes spreading filling the night.

Loud in the pines and cedars dim,
Clear in the freshness moist and the swamp-perfume,
And I with my comrades there in the night.

While my sight that was bound in my eyes unclosed,
As to long panoramas of visions.

And I saw askant the armies,
I saw as in noiseless dreams hundreds of battle-flags,
Borne through the smoke of the battles and pierc'd with missiles I saw them,
And carried hither and yon through the smoke, and torn and bloody,
And at last but a few shreds left on the staffs, (and all in silence,)
And the staffs all splinter'd and broken.

I saw battle-corpses, myriads of them,
And the white skeletons of young men, I saw them,
I saw the debris and debris of all the slain soldiers of the war,
But I saw they were not as was thought,
They themselves were fully at rest, they suffer'd not,
The living remain'd and suffer'd, the mother suffer'd,
And the wife and the child and the musing comrade suffer'd,
And the armies that remain'd suffer'd.

16

Passing the visions, passing the night,
Passing, unloosing the hold of my comrades' hands,
Passing the song of the hermit bird and the tallying song of my soul,
Victorious song, death's outlet song, yet varying ever-altering song,
As low and wailing, yet clear the notes, rising and falling, flooding the
    night,
Sadly sinking and fainting, as warning and warning, and yet again bursting
    with joy,
Covering the earth and filling the spread of the heaven,
As that powerful psalm in the night I heard from recesses,
Passing, I leave thee lilac with heart-shaped leaves,
I leave thee there in the door-yard, blooming, returning with spring.

I cease from my song for thee,
From my gaze on thee in the west, fronting the west, communing with
thee,
O comrade lustrous with silver face in the night.

Yet each to keep and all, retrievements out of the night,
The song, the wondrous chant of the gray-brown bird,
And the tallying chant, the echo arous'd in my soul,
With the lustrous and drooping star with the countenance full of woe,
With the holders holding my hand nearing the call of the bird,
Comrades mine and I in the midst, and their memory ever to keep, for the
    dead I loved so well,
For the sweetest, wisest soul of all my days and lands—and this for his dear
    sake,
Lilac and star and bird twined with the chant of my soul,
There in the fragrant pines and the cedars dusk and dim.

The Last Invocation

At the last, tenderly,
From the walls of the powerful fortress'd house,
From the clasp of the knitted locks, from the keep of the well-closed doors,
Let me be wafted.

Let me glide noiselessly forth;
With the key of softness unlock the locks—with a whisper,
Set ope the doors O soul.

Tenderly—be not impatient,
(Strong is your hold O mortal flesh,
Strong is your hold O love.)

A Clear Midnight

This is thy hour O Soul, thy free flight into the wordless,
Away from books, away from art, the day erased, the lesson done,
Thee fully forth emerging, silent, gazing, pondering the themes thou
    lovest best,
Night, sleep, death and the stars.

A Noiseless Patient Spider

A noiseless patient spider,
I mark'd where on a little promontory it stood isolated,
Mark'd how to explore the vacant vast surrounding,
It launch'd forth filament, filament, filament, out of itself,
Ever unreeling them, ever tirelessly speeding them.

And you O my soul where you stand,
Surrounded, detached, in measureless oceans of space,
Ceaselessly musing, venturing, throwing, seeking the spheres to connect
  them,
Till the bridge you will need be form'd, till the ductile anchor hold,
Till the gossamer thread you fling catch somewhere, O my soul.

So Long!

To conclude, I announce what comes after me.

I remember I said before my leaves sprang at all,
I would raise my voice jocund and strong with reference to consummations.

When America does what was promis'd,
When through these States walk a hundred millions of superb persons,
When the rest part away for superb persons and contribute to them,
When breeds of the most perfect mothers denote America,
Then to me and mine our due fruition.

I have press'd through in my own right,
I have sung the body and the soul, war and peace have I sung, and the
  songs of life and death,
And the songs of birth, and shown that there are many births.

I have offer'd my style to every one, I have journey'd with confident step;
While my pleasure is yet at the full I whisper *So long*!
And take the young woman's hand and the young man's hand for the last
  time.

I announce natural persons to arise,
I announce justice triumphant,
I announce the uncompromising liberty and equality,
I announce the justification of candor and the justification of pride.

I announce that the identity of these States is a single identity only,
I announce the Union more and more compact, indissoluble,
I announce splendors and majesties to make all the previous politics of the
     earth insignificant.

I announce adhesiveness, I say it shall be limitless, unloosen'd,
I say you shall yet find the friend you were looking for.

I announce a man or woman coming, perhaps you are the one, (*So long!*)
I announce the great individual, fluid as Nature, chaste, affectionate,
     compassionate, fully arm'd.

I announce a life that shall be copious, vehement, spiritual, bold,
I announce an end that shall lightly and joyfully meet its translation.

I announce myriads of youths, beautiful, gigantic, sweet-blooded,
I announce a race of splendid and savage old men.

O thicker and faster—(*So long!*)
O crowding too close upon me,
I foresee too much, it means more than I thought,
It appears to me I am dying.

Hasten throat and sound your last,
Salute me—salute the days once more. Peal the old cry once more.

Screaming electric, the atmosphere using,
At random glancing, each as I notice absorbing,
Swiftly on, but a little while alighting,
Curious envelop'd messages delivering,
Sparkles hot, seed ethereal down in the dirt dropping,
Myself unknowing, my commission obeying, to question it never daring,
To ages and ages yet the growth of the seed leaving,
To troops out of the war arising, they the tasks I have set promulging,
To women certain whispers of myself bequeathing, their affection me
     more clearly explaining,

To young men my problems offering—no dallier I—I the muscle of their
    brains trying,
So I pass, a little time vocal, visible, contrary,
Afterward a melodious echo, passionately bent for, (death making me really
    undying,)
The best of me then when no longer visible, for toward that I have been
    incessantly preparing.

What is there more, that I lag and pause and crouch extended with unshut
    mouth?
Is there a single final farewell?

My songs cease, I abandon them,
From behind the screen where I hid I advance personally solely to you.

Camerado, this is no book,
Who touches this touches a man,
(Is it night? are we here together alone?)
It is I you hold and who holds you,
I spring from the pages into your arms—decease calls me forth.

O how your fingers drowse me,
Your breath falls around me like dew, your pulse lulls the tympans of my
    ears,
I feel immerged from head to foot,
Delicious, enough.

Enough O deed impromptu and secret,
Enough O gliding present—enough O summ'd-up past.

Dear friend whoever you are take this kiss,
I give it especially to you, do not forget me,
I feel like one who has done work for the day to retire awhile,
I receive now again of my many translations, from my avataras ascending,
    while others doubtless await me,
An unknown sphere more real than I dream'd, more direct, darts
    awakening rays about me, *So long!*
Remember my words, I may again return,
I love you, I depart from materials,
I am as one disembodied, triumphant, dead.

Hours Continuing Long

Hours continuing long, sore and heavy-hearted,

Hours of the dusk, when I withdraw to a lonesome and unfrequented spot,
  seating myself, leaning my face in my hands;

Hours sleepless, deep in the night, when I go forth, speeding swiftly the
  country roads, or through the city streets, or pacing miles and miles,
  stifling plaintive cries;

Hours discouraged, distracted—for the one I cannot content myself
  without, soon I saw him content himself without me;

Hours when I am forgotten, (O weeks and months are passing, but I
  believe I am never to forget!)

Sullen and suffering hours! (I am ashamed—but it is useless—I am what I
  am;)

Hours of my torment—I wonder if other men ever have the like, out of the
  like feelings?

Is there even one other like me—distracted—his friend, his lover, lost to
  him?

Is he too as I am now? Does he still rise in the morning, dejected, thinking
  who is lost to him? and at night, awaking, think who is lost?

Does he too harbor his friendship silent and endless? harbor his anguish
  and passion?

Does some stray reminder, or the casual mention of a name, bring the fit
  back upon him, taciturn and deprest?

Does he see himself reflected in me? In these hours, does he see the face of
  his hours reflected?

HERMAN MELVILLE

Herman Melville (1819–1891) is to prose what Whitman is to poetry: a great capacious talent who forcibly marked American literature. Melville's novels, especially *Moby-Dick*, stand as remarkable instances of the literary energy of the period, but then so do his poems. Melville published four collections of poetry, including a book-length poem, *Clarel: A Poem and a Pilgrimage* (set in the Holy Land), and the same intensity and mastery of language found in the prose is evident in the poetry. Perhaps it is better to say that Melville is to poetry what Melville is to prose.

Melville was born in New York City into an old and wealthy family, but after the financial panic of 1830, in which his father's business failed, the Melvilles moved to Albany. In 1832 the father died—deeply in debt—and the family was thereafter cared for by relatives. Melville left school at the age of twelve and worked at a variety of occupations, including bank clerk, farmhand, store clerk, bookkeeper, and eventually teacher (at a school near Pittsfield, Massachusetts). In 1839 he worked as a crew member on a ship bound for Liverpool and, after returning and failing to find work (even as far afield as the Midwest), shipped aboard a South Seas whaler, the *Acushnet*, in 1841. On that voyage Melville jumped ship in the Marquesas in the South Pacific and lived briefly with a native tribe. He later joined an Australian whaler but was soon discharged in Tahiti as a mutineer and imprisoned by the British. Escaping from prison, Melville sailed on a Nantucket whaler to Honolulu, where he enlisted in the U. S. Navy. In 1843 he returned to Boston as an ordinary seaman on the frigate *United States*. Discharged in 1844, he began to work on his first novel, *Typee*, which was published in 1846 to much acclaim and controversy. *Omoo* followed in 1847 with equal success. In that year Melville married the daughter of Lemuel Shaw, chief justice of Massachusetts, who helped Melville buy a house in New York. Melville's next novel, *Mardi*, was a commercial failure, owing mostly to its confounding style, and Melville (now with a family to support) was forced to retrench and turn out more marketable books. *Redburn* (1849) and *White-Jacket* (1850) followed. After a trip to Europe, Melville bought a farm near Pittsfield, where he met Hawthorne in 1850. The two became close friends.

Melville was already working on *Moby-Dick* when he met Hawthorne, and in 1851 he published it with high hopes. The book, however, did not sell well. Many saw it as morally suspect and not a little mad. Melville's next novel, *Pierre, or The Ambiguities* (1852), fared even worse. Depressed—indeed tortured—by these failures and subject to alarming physical ailments, Melville nonetheless turned out magazine stories (collected in *The Piazza Tales* [1856]) and a historical novel, *Israel Potter* (1855). In 1856 Melville's father-in-law sent him abroad to Europe and the Near East. *The Confidence-Man* was published in 1857, but it too sank out of sight. Melville, desperate for money, gave some lectures and sought appropriate employment, but to no avail. In 1863 he moved his family back to New York. After visits to the war front in 1864 he brought out a book of poems, *Battle-Pieces and Aspects of the War* (1866). During what was a very difficult period for Melville, his family began to fear for his sanity and their own well-being. He was, however, finally offered a post at the customs office in New York, which brought more stability. Tragically, in 1867 Melville's oldest son killed himself. By then Melville's literary reputation had all but vanished; he was unread and unknown. *Clarel*, Melville's long, philosophic poem, was published privately in 1876, paid for from a bequest of a dying uncle. In the 1880s Melville's financial situation improved, and in 1885 he resigned his custom post. The following year his second son died in California. Two later books of poems were also published privately, *John Marr and Other Sailors* (1888) and *Timeoleon* (1891). His last prose work, *Billy Budd, Sailor*, was left unpublished until 1924.

Toward the end of his life Melville's works were being rediscovered, particularly in England, and he lived long enough to be gratified by a new generation of appreciative readers. It was not, however, until the 1920s that the true Melville revival began. From an obscure nineteenth-century adventure writer ("the man who lived among the cannibals") he came to be seen quite suddenly as one of our most distinctive writers.

The Portent

(1859)

Hanging from the beam,
    Slowly swaying (such the law),
Gaunt the shadow on your green,
    Shenandoah!
The cut is on the crown
(Lo, John Brown,)
And the stabs shall heal no more.

Hidden in the cap
    Is the anguish none can draw;
So your future veils its face,
    Shenandoah!
But the streaming beard is shown
(Weird John Brown),
The meteor of the war.

A Utilitarian View of the Monitor's Fight

Plain be the phrase, yet apt the verse,
    More ponderous than nimble;
For since grimed War here laid aside
His Orient pomp, 'twould ill befit
      Overmuch to ply
    The rhyme's barbaric cymbal.

Hail to victory without the gaud
    Of glory; zeal that needs no fans
Of banners; plain mechanic power
Plied cogently in War now placed—
    Where War belongs—
    Among the trades and artisans.

Yet this was battle, and intense—
    Beyond the strife of fleets heroic;
Deadlier, closer, calm 'mid storm;
No passion; all went on by crank,
      Pivot, and screw,
    And calculations of caloric.

Needless to dwell; the story's known.
    The ringing of those plates on plates
Still ringeth round the world—
The clangor of that blacksmiths' fray.
     The anvil-din
    Resounds this message from the Fates:

War yet shall be, and to the end;
    But war-paint shows the streaks of weather;
War yet shall be, but warriors
Are now but operatives; War's made
     Less grand than Peace,
    And a singe runs through lace and feather.

Malvern Hill

(July, 1862)

Ye elms that wave on Malvern Hill
    In prime of morn and May,
Recall ye how McClellan's men
     Here stood at bay?
While deep within yon forest dim
    Our rigid comrades lay—
Some with the cartridge in their mouth,
Others with fixed arms lifted South—
     Invoking so
The cypress glades? Ah wilds of woe!

The spires of Richmond, late beheld
    Through rifts in musket-haze,
Were closed from view in clouds of dust
     On leaf-walled ways,
Where streamed our wagons in caravan;

And the Seven Nights and Days
Of march and fast, retreat and fight,
Pinched our grimed faces to ghastly plight—
    Does the elm wood
Recall the haggard beards of blood?

The battle-smoked flag, with stars eclipsed,
    We followed (it never fell!)—
In silence husbanded our strength—
    Received their yell;
Till on this slope we patient turned
    With cannon ordered well;
Reverse we proved was not defeat;
But ah, the sod what thousands meet!—
    Does Malvern Wood
Bethink itself, and muse and brood?

    We elms of Malvern Hill
      Remember every thing;
    But sap the twig will fill:
    Wag the world how it will,
      Leaves must be green in Spring.

The Maldive Shark

    About the Shark, phlegmatical one,
Pale sot of the Maldive sea,
The sleek little pilot-fish, azure and slim,
How alert in attendance be.
From his saw-pit of mouth, from his charnel of maw
They have nothing of harm to dread,
But liquidly glide on his ghastly flank
Or before his Gorgonian head;
Or lurk in the port of serrated teeth
In white triple tiers of glittering gates,
And there find a haven when peril's abroad,
An asylum in jaws of the Fates!

They are friends; and friendly they guide him to prey,
Yet never partake of the treat—
Eyes and brains to the dotard lethargic and dull,
Pale ravener of horrible meat.

To Ned

Where is the world we roved, Ned Bunn?
    Hollows thereof lay rich in shade
By voyagers old inviolate thrown
    Ere Paul Pry cruised with Pelf and Trade.
To us old lads some thoughts come home
Who roamed a world young lads no more shall roam.

Nor less the satiate year impends
    When, wearying of routine-resorts,
The pleasure-hunter shall break loose,
    Ned, for our Pantheistic ports:—
Marquesas and glenned isles that be
Authentic Edens in a Pagan sea.

The charm of scenes untried shall lure,
    And, Ned, a legend urge the flight—
The Typee-truants under stars
    Unknown to Shakespere's *Midsummer-Night*;
And man, if lost to Saturn's Age,
Yet feeling life no Syrian pilgrimage.

But, tell, shall he the tourist find
    Our isles the same in violet-glow
Enamoring us what years and years—
    Ah, Ned, what years and years ago!
Well, Adam advances, smart in pace,
But scarce by violets that advance you trace.

But we, in anchor-watches calm,
    The Indian Psyche's languor won,
And, musing, breathed primeval balm
    From Edens ere yet over-run;
Marvelling mild if mortal twice,
Here and hereafter, touch a Paradise.

After the Pleasure Party

Lines Traced Under an Image of Amor Threatening

Fear me, virgin whosoever
Taking pride from love exempt,
    Fear me, slighted. Never, never
Brave me, nor my fury tempt:
Downy wings, but wroth they beat
Tempest even in reason's seat.

    Behind the house the upland falls
With many an odorous tree—
White marbles gleaming through green halls—
Terrace by terrace, down and down,
And meets the star-lit Mediterranean Sea.

    'Tis Paradise. In such an hour
Some pangs that rend might take release.
Nor less perturbed who keeps this bower
Of balm, nor finds balsamic peace?
From whom the passionate words in vent
After long revery's discontent?

    "Tired of the homeless deep,
Look how their flight yon hurrying billows urge
    Hitherward but to reap
Passive repulse from the iron-bound verge!
Insensate, can they never know
'Tis mad to wreck the impulsion so?

    "An art of memory is, they tell:
But to forget! forget the glade
Wherein Fate sprung Love's ambuscade,
To flout pale years of cloistral life
And flush me in this sensuous strife.
'Tis Vesta struck with Sappho's smart.
No fable her delirious leap:
With more of cause in desperate heart,
Myself could take it—but to sleep!

"Now first I feel, what all may ween,
That soon or late, if faded e'en,
One's sex asserts itself. Desire,
The dear desire through love to sway,
Is like the Geysers that aspire—
Through cold obstruction win their fervid way.
But baffled here—to take disdain,
To feel rule's instinct, yet not reign;
To dote, to come to this drear shame—
Hence the winged blaze that sweeps my soul
Like prairie-fires that spurn control,
Where withering weeds incense the flame.

"And kept I long heaven's watch for this,
Contemning love, for this, even this?
O terrace chill in Northern air,
O reaching ranging tube I placed
Against yon skies, and fable chased
Till, fool, I hailed for sister there
Starred Cassiopea in Golden Chair.
In dream I throned me, nor I saw
In cell the idiot crowned with straw.

"And yet, ah yet, scarce ill I reigned,
Through self-illusion self-sustained,
When now—enlightened, undeceived—
What gain I, barrenly bereaved!
Than this can be yet lower decline—
Envy and spleen, can these be mine?

"The peasant-girl demure that trod
Beside our wheels that climbed the way,
And bore along a blossoming rod
That looked the sceptre of May-Day—
On her—to fire this petty hell,
His softened glance how moistly fell!
The cheat! on briers her buds were strung;
And wiles peeped forth from mien how meek.

The innocent bare-foot! young, so young!
To girls, strong man's a novice weak.
To tell such beads! And more remain,
Sad rosary of belittling pain.

"When after lunch and sallies gay
Like the Decameron folk we lay
In sylvan groups; and I——let be!
O, dreams he, can he dream that one
Because not roseate feels no sun?
The plain lone bramble thrills with Spring
As much as vines that grapes shall bring.

"Me now fair studies charm no more.
Shall great thoughts writ, or high themes sung
Damask wan checks—unlock his arm
About some radiant ninny flung?
How glad, with all my starry lore,
I'd buy the veriest wanton's rose
Would but my bee therein repose.

"Could I remake me! or set free
This sexless bound in sex, then plunge
Deeper than Sappho, in a lunge
Piercing Pan's paramount mystery!
For, Nature, in no shallow surge
Against thee either sex may urge,
Why hast thou made us but in halves—
Co-relatives? This makes us slaves.
If these co-relatives never meet
Self-hood itself seems incomplete.
And such the dicing of blind fate
Few matching halves here meet and mate.
What Cosmic jest or Anarch blunder
The human integral clove asunder
And shied the fractions through life's gate?

"Ye stars that long your votary knew
Rapt in her vigil, see me here!
Whither is gone the spell ye threw
When rose before me Cassiopea?
Usurped on by love's stronger reign—
But, lo, your very selves do wane:
Light breaks—truth breaks! Silvered no more,
But chilled by dawn that brings the gale
Shivers yon bramble above the vale,
And disillusion opens all the shore."

One knows not if Urania yet
The pleasure-party may forget;
Or whether she lived down the strain
Of turbulent heart and rebel brain;
For Amor so resents a slight,
And hers had been such haught disdain,
He long may wreak his boyish spite,
And boy-like, little reck the pain.

One knows not, no. But late in Rome
(For queens discrowned a congruous home)
Entering Albani's porch she stood
Fixed by an antique pagan stone
Colossal carved. No anchorite seer,
Not Thomas à Kempis, monk austere,
Religious more are in their tone;
Yet far, how far from Christian heart
That form august of heathen Art.
Swayed by its influence, long she stood,
Till surged emotion seething down,
She rallied and this mood she won:

"Languid in frame for me,
To-day by Mary's convent-shrine,
Touched by her picture's moving plea
In that poor nerveless hour of mine,
I mused—A wanderer still must grieve.
Half I resolved to kneel and believe,
Believe and submit, the veil take on.

But thee, arm'd Virgin! less benign,
Thee now I invoke, thou mightier one.
Helmeted woman—if such term
Befit thee, far from strife
Of that which makes the sexual feud
And clogs the aspirant life—
O self-reliant, strong and free,
Thou in whom power and peace unite,
Transcender! raise me up to thee,
Raise me and arm me!"

        Fond appeal.
For never passion peace shall bring,
Nor Art inanimate for long
Inspire. Nothing may help or heal
While Amor incensed remembers wrong.
Vindictive, not himself he'll spare;
For scope to give his vengeance play
Himself he'll blaspheme and betray.

    Then for Urania, virgins everywhere,
O pray! Example take too, and have care.

Monody

To have known him, to have loved him,
    After loneness long;
And then to be estranged in life,
    And neither in the wrong;
And now for death to set his seal—
    Ease me, a little ease, my song!

By wintry hills his hermit-mound
    The sheeted snow-drifts drape,
And houseless there the snow-bird flits
    Beneath the fir-tree's crape:
Glazed now with ice the cloistral vine
    That hid the shyest grape.

Art

In placid hours well-pleased we dream
Of many a brave unbodied scheme.
But form to lend, pulsed life create,
What unlike things must meet and mate:
A flame to melt—a wind to freeze;
Sad patience—joyous energies;
Humility—yet pride and scorn;
Instinct and study; love and hate;
Audacity—reverence. These must mate,
And fuse with Jacob's mystic heart,
To wrestle with the angel—Art.

Fragments of a Lost Gnostic Poem of the 12th Century

. . . .

Found a family, build a state,
The pledged event is still the same:
Matter in end will never abate
His ancient brutal claim.

. . . .

Indolence is heaven's ally here,
And energy the child of hell:
The Good Man pouring from his pitcher clear
But brims the poisoned well.

HENRY HOWARD BROWNELL

Henry Howard Brownell (1820–1872) was one of the few poets of any literary distinction to see action in the Civil War and survive to write of it. Most Civil War poetry was patriotic or didactic in nature and rarely survived the conflict. Brownell, however, wrote descriptive accounts of naval battles that he witnessed—often composing under fire—and the vividness and immediacy of the circumstances seem to carry over into the verse itself.

Brownell was born in Providence, Rhode Island, and educated at Trinity College (then Washington College) in Hartford. After a brief period of teaching school in Mobile, Alabama (where, ironically, he would return for the battle of Mobile Bay), he went back to East Hartford and began practicing law in 1844. However, Brownell soon left the law to earn his living as a writer. His early volumes of poetry were unremarkable: *Poems* was published in 1847 and *Ephemerson* in 1855. Between those two collections he also published *The People's Book of Ancient and Modern History* (1851) and *The Discovery, Pioneers, and Settlers of North and South America* (1853). When war broke out, Brownell was a loyal supporter of the Union cause. In 1862 he published in the Hartford *Evening Press* a rhymed version of Admiral David G. Farragut's "General Orders" to his fleet poised for battle at New Orleans. The poem was subsequently reprinted in various papers and eventually came to the attention of Farragut himself, who liked the poem and wrote to Brownell. When Farragut learned that Brownell wished to see a naval battle, he apparently arranged to have Brownell given a rank and assigned to him personally as a secretary on board the *Hartford*. Brownell witnessed the battles of Mobile Bay and Vicksburg, calmly taking detailed notes of the action—occasionally in verse—while the fighting went on around him. In 1864 he published his war poems in *Lyrics of a Day, or Newspaper-Poetry by a Volunteer in the U.S. Service.* These were Brownell's best poems, and they were immensely popular. Oliver Wendell Holmes deemed him "Our Battle Laureate" and thought him one of the "most highly endowed persons" he knew. After the war Brownell traveled for three years as a secretary to Farragut on European cruises. In 1866 he brought out an expanded edition of his poems, *War Lyrics.* Brownell remained a bachelor during his short life. He died from skin cancer at the age of fifty-two.

Night-Quarters

Tang! tang! went the gong's wild roar
    Through the hundred cells of our great Sea-Hive!
    Five seconds—it couldn't be more—
And the whole Swarm was humming and alive—
    (We were on an enemy's shore).

    With savage haste, in the dark,
    (Our steerage hadn't a spark,)
    Into boot and hose they blundered—
From for'ard came a strange, low roar,
    The dull and smothered racket
    Of lower rig and jacket
    Hurried on, by the hundred—
How the berth deck buzzed and swore!

The third of minutes ten,
And half a thousand men,
From the dream-gulf, dead and deep,
Of the seaman's measured sleep,
In the taking of a lunar,
    In the serving of a ration,
    Every man at his station!—
Three and a quarter, or sooner!
    Never a skulk to be seen—
From the look-out aloft to the gunner
    Lurking in his black magazine.

There they stand, still as death,
And, (a trifle out of breath,
    It may be,) we of the Staff,
All on the poop, to a minute,
Wonder if there's anything in it—
    Doubting if to growl or laugh.

But, somehow, every hand
Feels for hilt and brand,
Tries if buckle and frog be tight—
So, in the chilly breeze, we stand
Peering through the dimness of the night—
The men, by twos and ones,
Grim and silent at the guns,
Ready, if a Foe heave in sight!

But, as we looked aloft,
There, all white and soft,
Floated on the fleecy clouds,
(Stray flocks in heaven's blue croft)—
How they shone, the eternal stars,
'Mid the black masts and spars
And the great maze of lifts and shrouds!

The Burial of the Dane

Blue Gulf all around us,
Blue sky overhead—
Muster all on the quarter,
We must bury the dead!

It is but a Danish sailor,
Rugged of front and form;
A common son of the forecastle,
Grizzled with sun and storm.

His name, and the strand he hailed from
We know—and there's nothing more!
But perhaps his mother is waiting
In the lonely Island of Fohr.

Still, as he lay there dying,
Reason drifting awreck,
"'Tis my watch," he would mutter,
"I must go upon deck!"

Aye, on deck—by the foremast!—
    But watch and look-out are done;
The Union-Jack laid o'er him,
    How quiet he lies in the sun!

Slow the ponderous engine,
    Stay the hurrying shaft!
Let the roll of the ocean
    Cradle our giant craft—
Gather around the grating,
    Carry your messmate aft!

Stand in order, and listen
    To the holiest page of prayer!
Let every foot be quiet,
    Every head be bare—
The soft trade-wind is lifting
    A hundred locks of hair.

Our captain reads the service,
    (A little spray on his cheeks,)
The grand old words of burial,
    And the trust a true heart seeks—
"We therefore commit his body
To the deep"—and, as he speaks,

Launched from the weather railing,
    Swift as the eye can mark,
The ghastly, shotted hammock
    Plunges, away from the shark,
Down, a thousand fathoms,
    Down into the dark!

A thousand summers and winters
    The stormy Gulf shall roll
High o'er his canvas coffin,
    But, silence to doubt and dole!
There's a quiet harbor somewhere,
    For the poor a-weary soul.

Free the fettered engine,
   Speed the tireless shaft!
Loose to'gallant and topsail,
   The breeze is fair abaft!

Blue sea all around us,
   Blue sky bright o'erhead—
Every man to his duty!
   We have buried our dead.

Steamship Cahawba, at Sea, Jan. 20th, 1858.

FREDERICK GODDARD TUCKERMAN

Frederick Goddard Tuckerman (1821–1873) was an obscure poet in his own time, though his admirers included Emerson, Hawthorne, Longfellow, and probably his friend Alfred, Lord Tennyson. He published only one volume of poetry, *Poems* (1860); though that book was reprinted three times, he soon vanished from the literary scene. Tuckerman was rediscovered in the early twentieth century by Louis How, an anthologist, and by Walter Prichard Eaton, a drama critic, who wrote an article on Tuckerman that appeared in 1909. The poet Witter Bynner read the article and, upon finding many unpublished poems still in manuscript, brought out an edition of Tuckerman's sonnets in 1931. "The Cricket," now Tuckerman's most famous poem, was unpublished until 1950, and an edition of collected poems only appeared in 1965, almost a century after the poet's death. Tuckerman, like Emily Dickinson, was a reclusive poet whose reputation is a twentieth-century phenomenon.

Tuckerman was a native of Boston and attended Harvard in 1837. (His tutors included Jones Very.) He left for a year because of eye trouble but returned in 1839 and graduated from Harvard Law School in 1842. He practiced law for several years but disliked it and, having an independent income, decided to give up his practice to pursue his real interests: literature, botany, astronomy, and meteorology. Tuckerman moved to Greenfield, in western Massachusetts, in 1847, after marrying a local woman, Hannah Lucinda Jones. The couple had three children, but Hannah died in 1857 within a week of giving birth to their third child. As the critic Edmund Wilson points out, "she haunts the whole series of his sonnets." From that point on Tuckerman lived in seclusion at Greenfield. His only extended travel had occurred earlier in 1851 and 1854, when he went to Europe and eventually became good friends with Tennyson. Even the publication of his *Poems* in 1860 seems hardly to have disturbed the solitude of his retirement from society.

Tuckerman was perhaps better known as an authority on local flora than as a poet, and he may have published more astronomical observations than poems, but in this century he has come to be considered a poet of rare and exquisite originality.

from *Sonnets, First Series*

VII

Dank fens of cedar; hemlock-branches gray
With tress and trail of mosses wringing-wet;
Beds of the black pitch-pine in dead leaves set
Whose wasted red has wasted to white away;
Remnants of rain, and droppings of decay,—
Why hold ye so my heart, nor dimly let
Through your deep leaves the light of yesterday,
The faded glimmer of a sunshine set?
Is it that in your darkness, shut from strife,
The bread of tears becomes the bread of life?
Far from the roar of day, beneath your boughs
Fresh griefs beat tranquilly, and loves and vows
Grow green in your gray shadows, dearer far
Even than all lovely lights, and roses, are?

X

An upper chamber in a darkened house,
Where, ere his footsteps reached ripe manhood's brink,
Terror and anguish were his cup to drink,—
I cannot rid the thought, nor hold it close;
But dimly dream upon that man alone;—
Now though the autumn clouds most softly pass;
The cricket chides beneath the doorstep stone,
And greener than the season grows the grass.
Nor can I drop my lids, nor shade my brows,
But there he stands beside the lifted sash;
And, with a swooning of the heart, I think
Where the black shingles slope to meet the boughs,
And—shattered on the roof like smallest snows—
The tiny petals of the mountain-ash.

from *Sonnets, Third Series*

X

Sometimes I walk where the deep water dips
Against the land. Or on where fancy drives
I walk and muse aloud, like one who strives
To tell his half-shaped thought with stumbling lips,
And view the ocean sea, the ocean ships,
With joyless heart: still but myself I find
And restless phantoms of my restless mind:
Only the moaning of my wandering words,
Only the wailing of the wheeling plover,
And this high rock beneath whose base the sea
Has wormed long caverns, like my tears in me:
And hard like this I stand, and beaten and blind,
This desolate rock with lichens rusted over,
Hoar with salt-sleet and chalkings of the birds.

The Cricket

I

The humming bee purrs softly o'er his flower;
    From lawn and thicket
The dogday locust singeth in the sun
    From hour to hour:
Each has his bard, and thou, ere day be done,
    Shalt have no wrong.
So bright that murmur mid the insect crowd,
Muffled and lost in bottom-grass, or loud
    By pale and picket:
Shall I not take to help me in my song
    A little cooing cricket?

II

The afternoon is sleepy; let us lie
Beneath these branches whilst the burdened brook,
Muttering and moaning to himself, goes by;
And mark our minstrel's carol whilst we look
Toward the faint horizon swooning blue.
  Or in a garden bower,
Trellised and trammeled with deep drapery
   Of hanging green,
   Light glimmering through—
There let the dull hop be,
Let bloom, with poppy's dark refreshing flower:
Let the dead fragrance round our temples beat,
Stunning the sense to slumber, whilst between
The falling water and fluttering wind
   Mingle and meet,
   Murmur and mix,
No few faint pipings from the glades behind,
   Or alder-thicks:
But louder as the day declines,
From tingling tassel, blade, and sheath,
Rising from nets of river vines,
   Winrows and ricks,
   Above, beneath,
   At every breath,
At hand, around, illimitably
Rising and falling like the sea,
   Acres of cricks!

III

Dear to the child who hears thy rustling voice
Cease at his footstep, though he hears thee still,
Cease and resume with vibrance crisp and shrill,
Thou sittest in the sunshine to rejoice.
Night lover too; bringer of all things dark
And rest and silence; yet thou bringest to me
Always that burthen of the unresting Sea,
The moaning cliffs, the low rocks blackly stark;
These upland inland fields no more I view,

But the long flat seaside beach, the wild seamew,
    And the overturning wave!
Thou bringest too, dim accents from the grave
To him who walketh when the day is dim,
Dreaming of those who dream no more of him,
With edged remembrances of joy and pain;
And heydey looks and laughter come again:
Forms that in happy sunshine lie and leap,
With faces where but now a gap must be,
Renunciations, and partitions deep
And perfect tears, and crowning vacancy!
And to thy poet at the twilight's hush,
No chirping touch of lips with laugh and blush,
But wringing arms, hearts wild with love and woe,
Closed eyes, and kisses that would not let go!

IV

So wert thou loved in that old graceful time
    When Greece was fair,
While god and hero hearkened to thy chime;
    Softly astir
Where the long grasses fringed Caÿster's lip;
Long-drawn, with glimmering sails of swan and ship,
    And ship and swan;
    Or where
    Reedy Eurotas ran.
Did that low warble teach thy tender flute
    Xenaphyle?
Its breathings mild? say! did the grasshopper
Sit golden in thy purple hair
    O Psammathe?
    Or wert thou mute,
Grieving for Pan amid the alders there?
And by the water and along the hill
That thirsty tinkle in the herbage still,
Though the lost forest wailed to horns of Arcady?

V

Like the Enchanter old—
Who sought mid the dead water's weeds and scum
For evil growths beneath the moonbeam cold,
    Or mandrake or dorcynium;
And touched the leaf that opened both his ears,
So that articulate voices now he hears
In cry of beast, or bird, or insect's hum,—
Might I but find thy knowledge in thy song!
    That twittering tongue,
Ancient as light, returning like the years.
    So might I be,
Unwise to sing, thy true interpreter
Through denser stillness and in sounder dark,
Than ere thy notes have pierced to harrow me.
    So might I stir
    The world to hark
    To thee my lord and lawgiver,
    And cease my quest:
Content to bring thy wisdom to the world;
Content to gain at last some low applause,
    Now low, now lost
Like thine from mossy stone, amid the stems and straws,
    Or garden gravemound tricked and dressed—
    Powdered and pearled
    By stealing frost—
In dusky rainbow beauty of euphorbias!
For larger would be less indeed, and like
The ceaseless simmer in the summer grass
To him who toileth in the windy field,
    Or where the sunbeams strike,
Naught in innumerable numerousness.
    So might I much possess,
    So much must yield;
But failing this, the dell and grassy dike,
The water and the waste shall still be dear,
And all the pleasant plots and places
    Where thou hast sung, and I have hung
    To ignorantly hear.

Then Cricket, sing thy song! or answer mine!
Thine whispers blame, but mine has naught but praises.
It matters not. Behold! the autumn goes,
    The shadow grows,
The moments take hold of eternity;
Even while we stop to wrangle or repine
    Our lives are gone—
    Like thinnest mist,
Like yon escaping color in the tree;
Rejoice! rejoice! whilst yet the hours exist—
Rejoice or mourn, and let the world swing on
Unmoved by cricket song of thee or me.

JAMES MONROE WHITFIELD

James Monroe Whitfield (1822–1871) was an African–American poet who, as an activist, wrote to further the causes of black emancipation and emigration. He was an oratorical poet who read his verses in churches and public forums, but he also published poems in various periodicals and brought out a volume of his poetry, *America and Other Poems*, in 1853. His is a clear, strong voice, edged with anger and urgency.

Whitfield was the child of free blacks who lived in New Hampshire. He was educated in public schools in Exeter and early on became involved in the movement to resettle blacks in colonies in California and Central America. In 1839 he moved from Boston to Buffalo, New York, where he worked as a barber. He began publishing poems in *Frederick Douglass' Paper* and elsewhere, collecting them in *America and Other Poems*, published in Buffalo. In 1854 and 1856 he traveled to Cleveland to attend the National Emigration Conventions organized by Martin Delany. Whitfield and Frederick Douglass entered into a friendly but lively debate in print over the question of black separatism and emigration, and in 1858 Whitfield began editing the procolonizationist *African-American Repository*. He may have journeyed to Central America in 1859 to look into the possibilities of black colonization, but by 1861 he was in San Francisco and soon after no longer supported the emigrationist movement. He traveled throughout the West, working primarily as a barber. During this period he also became involved in the Masonic movement, becoming a grand master in California in 1864 and later setting up a lodge in Nevada. He continued to write poems, publishing them in the San Francisco papers, including his long verse oration, "Poem Written for the Celebration of President Lincoln's Emancipation Proclamation," which appeared in 1867. He died in San Francisco in 1871.

America

America, it is to thee,
Thou boasted land of liberty,—
It is to thee I raise my song,
Thou land of blood, and crime, and wrong.
It is to thee, my native land,
From whence has issued many a band
To tear the black man from his soil,
And force him here to delve and toil;
Chained on your blood-bemoistened sod,
Cringing beneath a tyrant's rod,
Stripped of those rights which Nature's God
    Bequeathed to all the human race,
Bound to a petty tyrant's nod,
    Because he wears a paler face.
Was it for this, that freedom's fires
Were kindled by your patriot sires?
Was it for this, they shed their blood,
On hill and plain, on field and flood?
Was it for this, that wealth and life
Were staked upon that desperate strife,
Which drenched this land for seven long years
With blood of men, and women's tears?
When black and white fought side by side,
    Upon the well-contested field,—
Turned back the fierce opposing tide,
    And made the proud invader yield—
When, wounded, side by side they lay,
    And heard with joy the proud hurrah
From their victorious comrades say
    That they had waged successful war,
The thought ne'er entered in their brains
That they endured those toils and pains,
To forge fresh fetters, heavier chains
For their own children, in whose veins
Should flow that patriotic blood,
So freely shed on field and flood.
Oh no; they fought, as they believed,

For the inherent rights of man;
But mark, how they have been deceived
    By slavery's accursed plan.
They never thought, when thus they shed
    Their heart's best blood, in freedom's cause,
That their own sons would live in dread,
    Under unjust, oppressive laws:
That those who quietly enjoyed
    The rights for which they fought and fell,
Could be the framers of a code,
    That would disgrace the fiends of hell!
Could they have looked, with prophet's ken,
    Down to the present evil time,
    Seen free-born men, uncharged with crime,
Consigned unto a slaver's pen,—
Or thrust into a prison cell,
With thieves and murderers to dwell—
While that same flag whose stripes and stars
Had been their guide through freedom's wars
As proudly waved above the pen
Of dealers in the souls of men!
Or could the shades of all the dead,
    Who fell beneath that starry flag,
Visit the scenes where they once bled,
    On hill and plain, on vale and crag,
By peaceful brook, or ocean's strand,
    By inland lake, or dark green wood,
Where'er the soil of this wide land
    Was moistened by their patriot blood,—
And then survey the country o'er,
    From north to south, from east to west,
And hear the agonizing cry
Ascending up to God on high,
From western wilds to ocean's shore,
    The fervent prayer of the oppressed;
The cry of helpless infancy
    Torn from the parent's fond caress
By some base tool of tyranny,
    And doomed to woe and wretchedness;

The indignant wail of fiery youth,
    Its noble aspirations crushed,
Its generous zeal, its love of truth,
    Trampled by tyrants in the dust;
The aerial piles which fancy reared,
    And hopes too bright to be enjoyed,
Have passed and left his young heart seared,
    And all its dreams of bliss destroyed.
The shriek of virgin purity,
    Doomed to some libertine's embrace,
Should rouse the strongest sympathy
    Of each one of the human race;
And weak old age, oppressed with care,
    As he reviews the scene of strife,
Puts up to God a fervent prayer,
    To close his dark and troubled life.
The cry of fathers, mothers, wives,
    Severed from all their hearts hold dear,
And doomed to spend their wretched lives
    In gloom, and doubt, and hate, and fear:
And manhood, too, with soul of fire,
And arm of strength, and smothered ire,
Stands pondering with brow of gloom,
Upon his dark unhappy doom,
Whether to plunge in battle's strife,
And buy his freedom with his life,
And with stout heart and weapon strong,
Pay back the tyrant wrong for wrong,
Or wait the promised time of God,
    When his Almighty ire shall wake,
And smite the oppressor in his wrath,
And hurl red ruin in his path,
And with the terrors of his rod,
    Cause adamantine hearts to quake.
Here Christian writhes in bondage still,
    Beneath his brother Christian's rod,
And pastors trample down at will,
    The image of the living God.
While prayers go up in lofty strains,

And pealing hymns ascend to heaven,
The captive, toiling in his chains,
    With tortured limbs and bosom riven,
Raises his fettered hand on high,
    And in the accents of despair,
To him who rules both earth and sky,
    Puts up a sad, a fervent prayer,
To free him from the awful blast
    Of slavery's bitter galling shame—
Although his portion should be cast
    With demons in eternal flame!
Almighty God! 't is this they call
    The land of liberty and law;
Part of its sons in baser thrall
    Than Babylon or Egypt saw—
Worse scenes of rapine, lust and shame,
    Than Babylonian ever knew,
Are perpetrated in the name
    Of God, the holy, just, and true;
And darker doom than Egypt felt,
May yet repay this nation's guilt.
Almighty God! thy aid impart,
And fire anew each faltering heart,
And strengthen every patriot's hand,
Who aims to save our native land.
We do not come before thy throne,
    With carnal weapons drenched in gore,
Although our blood has freely flown,
    In adding to the tyrant's store.
Father! before thy throne we come,
    Not in the panoply of war,
With pealing trump, and rolling drum,
    And cannon booming loud and far;
Striving in blood to wash out blood,
    Through wrong to seek redress for wrong;
For while thou'rt holy, just and good,
    The battle is not to the strong;
But in the sacred name of peace,
    Of justice, virtue, love and truth,

We pray, and never mean to cease,
    Till weak old age and fiery youth
In freedom's cause their voices raise,
And burst the bonds of every slave;
Till, north and south, and east and west,
The wrongs we bear shall be redressed.

PHOEBE CARY

Phoebe Cary (1824–1871) is invariably linked with her older sister, Alice Cary, since the two lived and wrote together for most of their lives and even published together: their first book was entitled *Poems of Alice and Phoebe Cary* (1850), and a posthumous collection appeared as *The Last Poems of Alice and Phoebe Cary* (1873). Alice, however, is perhaps best represented in her prose, while Phoebe wrote poetry exclusively. Phoebe was well known for her clever wit, and her parodies and light verse complemented her more serious and often intensely religious poetry.

Phoebe Cary was born in Miami Valley, Ohio, near Cincinnati, which was then considered frontier country. She received little formal education but at home read deeply in the few books available, which included the Bible, Pope's essays, *Charlotte Temple*, and issues of the Universalist paper, the *Trumpet*. In 1833 two of Cary's sisters died, and in 1835 her mother died as well, all from tuberculosis. Phoebe and Alice both began publishing verses in periodicals, and together they appeared in Rufus Griswold's popular anthology, *Female Poets of America* (1848). With the help of Griswold *Poems of Alice and Phoebe Cary* was published in 1850. After these early successes Phoebe followed Alice to New York in 1851, where the two sisters earned a sufficient living from their writing to purchase a house on 20th Street. There they held their famous Sunday evening receptions, which drew many writers and public figures, John Greenleaf Whittier, Elizabeth Cady Stanton, and P. T. Barnum among them. Over cups of sweetened milk and water they talked of the literary, artistic, and social issues of the day. Both sisters supported reform movements, particularly abolitionism and women's rights. Phoebe worked briefly as assistant editor of *The Revolution*, a suffragist journal run by Susan B. Anthony. She published two collections of her own verse, *Poems and Parodies* (1854) and *Poems of Faith, Hope and Love* (1869). Neither Phoebe nor Alice ever married, though Phoebe apparently turned down several offers in order to remain with her sister. As Alice's health failed and she became an invalid, Phoebe nursed her in the remaining years. Following Alice's death from tuberculosis in 1871 Phoebe's own health declined rapidly, and she died five months later from hepatitis.

Jacob

He dwelt among "apartments let,"
    About five stories high;
A man I thought that none would get,
    And very few would try.

A boulder, by a larger stone
    Half hidden in the mud,
Fair as a man when only one
    Is in the neighborhood.

He lived unknown, and few could tell
    When Jacob was not free;
But he has got a wife,—and O!
    The difference to me!

Advice Gratis to Certain Women

By a Woman

O, my strong-minded sisters, aspiring to vote,
And to row with your brothers, all in the same boat,
When you come out to speak to the public your mind,
Leave your tricks, and your airs, and your graces behind!

For instance, when you by the world would be seen
As reporter, or editor (first-class, I mean),
I think—just to come to the point in one line—
What you write will be finer, if 'tis not too fine.

Pray, don't let the thread of your subject be strung
With "golden," and "shimmer," "sweet," "filter," and "flung;"
Nor compel, by your style, all your readers to guess
You've been looking up words Webster marks *obs.*

And another thing: whatever else you may say,
Do keep personalities out of the way;
Don't try every sentence to make people see
What a dear, charming creature the writer must be!

Leave out affectations and pretty appeals;
Don't "drag yourself in by the neck and the heels,"
Your dear little boots, and your gloves; and take heed,
Nor pull your curls over men's eyes while they read.

Don't mistake me; I mean that the public's not home,
You must do as the Romans do, when you're in Rome;
I would have you be womanly, while you are wise;
'Tis the weak and the womanish tricks I despise.

Women can't win?

On the other hand: don't write and dress in such styles
As astonish the natives, and frighten the isles;
Do look, on the platform, so folks in the show
Needn't ask, "Which are lions, and which tigers?" you know!

'Tis a good thing to write, and to rule in the state,
But to be a true, womanly woman is great:
And if ever you come to be that, 'twill be when
You can cease to be babies, nor try to be men!

Dorothy's Dower

In Three Parts

Part I

"My sweetest Dorothy," said John,
    Of course before the wedding,
As metaphorically he stood,
    His gold upon her shedding,
"Whatever thing you wish or want
    Shall be hereafter granted,
For all my worldly goods are yours."
    The fellow was enchanted!

"About that little dower you have,
    You thought might yet come handy,
Throw it away, do what you please,
    Spend it on sugar-candy!
I like your sweet, dependent ways,
    I love you when you tease me;
The more you ask, the more you spend,
    The better you will please me."

Part II

"Confound it, Dorothy!" said John,
    I haven't got it by me.
You haven't, have you, spent that sum,
    The dower from Aunt Jemima?
No; well that's sensible for you;
    This fix is most unpleasant;
But money's tight, so just take yours
    And use it for the present.
Now I must go—to—meet a man!
    By George! I'll have to borrow!
Lend me a twenty—that's all right!
    I'll pay you back to-morrow."

Part III

"Madam," says John to Dorothy,
    And past her rudely pushes,
"You think a man is made of gold,
    And money grows on bushes!
Tom's shoes! your doctor! Can't you now
    Get up some new disaster?
You and your children are enough
    To break John Jacob Astor.
Where's what you had yourself when I
    Was fool enough to court you?
That little sum, till you got me,
    'Twas what had to support you!"
"It's lent and gone, not very far;
    Pray don't be apprehensive."
"*Lent!* I've had use enough for it:
    My family is expensive.
I didn't, as a woman would,
    Spend it on sugar-candy!"
"No, John, I think the most of it
    Went for cigars and brandy!"

FRANCES ELLEN WATKINS HARPER

Frances Ellen Watkins Harper (1825–1911) was the most popular and best-known African-American poet of her time. Her books of poetry went through numerous editions and sold more than fifty thousand copies in her lifetime. She was also the second black woman to publish a full-length novel (*Iola Leroy; or, Shadows Uplifted* [1892]), the first to publish a short story ("The Two Offers" [1859]), and a premier speaker on the lyceum circuit.

Harper was born in Baltimore, the only child of free parents, and orphaned at the age of three. Raised by an aunt and uncle active in the abolitionist movement, she attended their school for free blacks until she was fourteen. She became a domestic in the home of a white bookseller in Baltimore and subsequently worked as a nursemaid and seamstress. In 1845 she published her first volume of poems, *Forest Leaves*, but no copies have survived. Harper moved to Ohio in 1850 to live in a free state and taught sewing at the Union Seminary, a school for free blacks near Columbus. She later taught at Little York, Pennsylvania, where she became active in the abolitionist cause. Moving to Philadelphia in 1854, she worked with William Grant Still for the Underground Railroad. That year she published her enormously popular second book, *Poems on Miscellaneous Subjects*, with a preface by William Lloyd Garrison, and delivered her first antislavery speech (in New Bedford, Massachusetts). Thereafter Harper lectured widely and frequently, first in New England and then in Canada and the West, all the while writing and publishing her poems, stories, and speeches.

Harper retired from lecturing in 1860 when she married a widower, Fenton Harper, and bore a daughter, Mary. However, upon the death of her husband in 1864 she resumed her activities, this time touring the southern states during Reconstruction. In 1869 Harper published a long narrative poem, *Moses: A Story of the Nile*, and in 1871 a collection entitled *Poems. Sketches of Southern Life* followed in 1872. Settling in Philadelphia, Harper founded a YMCA Sabbath school and worked energetically in many movements and organizations, including the Women's Christian Temperance Union, the National Council of Women, the American Association of Education of Colored Youth (which she directed in 1894), the American Woman Suffrage Association, the American Equal Rights Association, the International Council of Women, and the National Association of Colored Women, which she helped found in 1896. *Iola Leroy; or, Shadows Uplifted* appeared in 1892, and another collection of verse, *Atlanta Offering*, was published in 1895.

Harper was an extremely effective speaker and writer; her rhetorical skills and her fierce passion for justice, together with her dignified manner, stirred thousands of listeners and readers.

The Slave Mother

Heard you that shriek? It rose
    So wildly on the air,
It seem'd as if a burden'd heart
    Was breaking in despair.

Saw you those hands so sadly clasped—
    The bowed and feeble head—
The shuddering of that fragile form—
    That look of grief and dread?

Saw you the sad, imploring eye?
    Its every glance was pain,
As if a storm of agony
    Were sweeping through the brain.

She is a mother pale with fear,
    Her boy clings to her side,
And in her kyrtle vainly tries
    His trembling form to hide.

He is not hers, although she bore
    For him a mother's pains;
He is not hers, although her blood
    Is coursing through his veins!

He is not hers, for cruel hands
    May rudely tear apart
The only wreath of household love
    That binds her breaking heart.

His love has been a joyous light
    That o'er her pathway smiled,
A fountain gushing ever new,
    Amid life's desert wild.

His lightest word has been a tone
    Of music round her heart,
Their lives a streamlet blent in one—
    Oh, Father! must they part?

Bible Defence of Slavery

Take sackcloth of the darkest dye,
    And shroud the pulpits round!
Servants of Him that cannot lie,
    Sit mourning on the ground.

Let holy horror blanch each cheek,
    Pale every brow with fears;
And rocks and stones, if ye could speak,
    Ye well might melt to tears!

Let sorrow breathe in every tone,
    In every strain ye raise;
Insult not God's majestic throne
    With th' mockery of praise.

A "reverend" man, whose light should be
    The guide of age and youth,
Brings to the shrine of Slavery
    The sacrifice of truth!

For the direst wrong by man imposed,
    Since Sodom's fearful cry,
The word of life has been unclos'd,
    To give your God the lie.

Oh! when ye pray for heathen lands,
    And plead for their dark shores,
Remember Slavery's cruel hands
    Make heathens at your doors!

Lines

At the Portals of the Future,
    Full of madness, guilt and gloom,
Stood the hateful form of Slavery,
    Crying, Give, Oh! give me room—

Room to smite the earth with cursing,
    Room to scatter, rend and slay,
From the trembling mother's bosom
    Room to tear her child away;

Room to trample on the manhood
    Of the country far and wide;
Room to spread o'er every Eden
    Slavery's scorching lava-tide.

Pale and trembling stood the Future,
    Quailing 'neath his frown of hate,
As he grasped with bloody clutches
    The great keys of Doom and Fate.

In his hand he held a banner
    All festooned with blood and tears:
'Twas a fearful ensign, woven
    With the grief and wrong of years.

On his brow he wore a helmet
    Decked with strange and cruel art;
Every jewel was a life-drop
    Wrung from some poor broken heart.

Though her cheek was pale and anxious,
    Yet, with look and brow sublime,
By the pale and trembling Future
    Stood the Crisis of our time.

And from many a throbbing bosom
    Came the words in fear and gloom,
Tell us, Oh! thou coming Crisis,
    What shall be our country's doom?

Shall the wings of dark destruction
     Brood and hover o'er our land,
Till we trace the steps of ruin
     By their blight, from strand to strand?

Free Labor

I wear an easy garment,
     O'er it no toiling slave
Wept tears of hopeless anguish,
     In his passage to the grave.

And from its ample folds
     Shall rise no cry to God,
Upon its warp and woof shall be
     No stain of tears and blood.

Oh, lightly shall it press my form,
     Unladened with a sigh,
I shall not 'mid its rustling hear,
     Some sad despairing cry.

This fabric is too light to bear
     The weight of bondsmen's tears,
I shall not in its texture trace
     The agony of years.

Too light to bear a smother'd sigh,
     From some lorn woman's heart,
Whose only wreath of household love
     Is rudely torn apart.

Then lightly shall it press my form,
     Unburden'd by a sigh;
And from its seams and folds shall rise,
     No voice to pierce the sky,

And witness at the throne of God,
     In language deep and strong,
That I have nerv'd Oppression's hand,
     For deeds of guilt and wrong

Let the Light Enter!

The Dying Words of Goethe

"Light! more light! the shadows deepen,
    And my life is ebbing low,
Throw the windows widely open:
    Light! more light! before I go.

"Softly let the balmy sunshine
    Play around my dying bed,
O'er the dimly lighted valley
    I with lonely feet must tread.

"Light! more light! for Death is weaving
    Shadows 'round my waning sight,
And I fain would gaze upon him
    Through a stream of earthly light."

Not for greater gifts of genius;
    Not for thoughts more grandly bright.
All the dying poet whispers
    Is a prayer for light, more light.

Heeds he not the gathered laurels,
    Fading slowly from his sight;
All the poet's aspirations
    Centre in that prayer for light.

Gracious Saviour, when life's day-dreams
    Melt and vanish from the sight,
May our dim and longing vision
    Then be blessed with light, more light.

Bury Me in a Free Land

Make me a grave where'er you will,
In a lowly plain, or a lofty hill,
Make it among earth's humblest graves,
But not in a land where men are slaves.

I could not rest if around my grave
I heard the steps of a trembling slave:
His shadows above my silent tomb
Would make it a place of fearful gloom.

I could not rest if I heard the tread
Of a coffle gang to the shambles led,
And the mother's shriek of wild despair
Rise like a curse on the trembling air.

I could not sleep if I saw the lash
Drinking her blood at each fearful gash,
And I saw her babes torn from her breast,
Like trembling doves from their parent nest.

I'd shudder and start if I heard the bay
Of blood-hounds seizing their human prey,
And I heard the captive plead in vain
As they bound afresh his galling chain.

If I saw young girls from their mother's arms
Bartered and sold for their youthful charms,
My eye would flash with a mournful flame,
My death-paled cheek grow red with shame.

I would sleep, dear friends, where bloated might
Can rob no man of his dearest right;
My rest shall be calm in any grave
Where none can call his brother a slave.

I ask no monument, proud and high
To arrest the gaze of the passers-by;
All that my yearning spirit craves,
Is bury me not in a land of slaves.

JOHN ROLLIN RIDGE

John Rollin Ridge (1827–1867) was born into the Cherokee Nation before its forcible removal from its homeland by the U.S. government in 1838. Ridge's father and grandfather were key leaders of the Treaty party that negotiated the removal against the wishes of the majority of Cherokees, and both were murdered on the same day in 1839 for their apparent betrayal. Ridge, who witnessed his father's killing, believed throughout his life that the Treaty party was correct to have faced the inevitability of removal and that assimilation to white culture—known then as "civilizing"—was the only means of survival for Native Americans. His poetry reflects his own such acculturation.

Ridge grew up near Rome, Georgia, and was eleven when U.S. troops rounded up the Cherokees and deported them to Indian Territory (Oklahoma). After the retaliatory killings Ridge's mother fled to Fayetteville, Arkansas, where Ridge was tutored by missionaries, receiving a classical education. He spent some time at the Great Barrington Academy in Massachusetts but returned to Arkansas to complete his schooling and study law. Married in 1846, Ridge settled in the Indian Territory and took up farming. However, in 1849 he killed a Cherokee in an argument and had to flee to Missouri. By this time Ridge was fully involved in the factional disputes within the Cherokee Nation and at one point planned an invasion of the reservation. In 1850 Ridge traveled to California with other Cherokees to join the Gold Rush, leaving his wife and daughter behind in Arkansas. In California, Ridge became a miner and later worked for the Yoruba County government. He also began publishing poems and articles in local papers under the pseudonym Yellow Bird. Having sent for his family, Ridge eventually moved to San Francisco, where in 1854 he published a popular novel based on a true story, *Life and Adventures of Joaquin Murieta, the Celebrated California Bandit.*

From his earlier publications in Arkansas and the Indian Territory, Ridge already had something of a reputation as a poet, and in California he also became well known as a journalist. Between 1857 and 1863 Ridge edited successively the *Sacramento Bee*, the *California Express*, and the *San Francisco Herald.* Ridge supported the Confederate cause during the Civil War (as did most Cherokees) and was a member of a delegation that negotiated a peace treaty in Washington after the war. Ridge continued to agitate on behalf of his political faction among the Cherokee but was never able to prevail. After his death his poetry was collected and published as *Poems* in 1868. In recent years Ridge's poetry and prose have received renewed attention. Drawing on the romantic topoi of the period, his work intersects with Native American traditions in interesting ways.

Mount Shasta

Behold the dread Mt. Shasta, where it stands
Imperial midst the lesser heights, and, like
Some mighty unimpassioned mind, companionless
And cold. The storms of Heaven may beat in wrath
Against it, but it stands in unpolluted
Grandeur still; and from the rolling mists upheaves
Its tower of pride e'en purer than before.
The wintry showers and white-winged tempests leave
Their frozen tributes on its brow, and it
Doth make of them an everlasting crown.
Thus doth it, day by day and age by age,
Defy each stroke of time: still rising highest
Into Heaven!
Aspiring to the eagle's cloudless height,
No human foot has stained its snowy side;
No human breath has dimmed the icy mirror which
It holds unto the moon and stars and sov'reign sun.
We may not grow familiar with the secrets
Of its hoary top, whereon the Genius
Of that mountain builds his glorious throne!
Far lifted in the boundless blue, he doth
Encircle, with his gaze supreme, the broad
Dominions of the West, which lie beneath
His feet, in pictures of sublime repose
No artist ever drew. He sees the tall
Gigantic hills arise in silentness
And peace, and in the long review of distance
Range themselves in order grand. He sees the sunlight
Play upon the golden streams which through the valleys
Glide. He hears the music of the great and solemn sea,
And overlooks the huge old western wall
To view the birth-place of undying Melody!

Itself all light, save when some loftiest cloud
Doth for a while embrace its cold forbidding
Form, that monarch mountain casts its mighty
Shadow down upon the crownless peaks below,
That, like inferior minds to some great
Spirit, stand in strong contrasted littleness!
All through the long and Summery months of our
Most tranquil year, it points its icy shaft
On high, to catch the dazzling beams that fall
In showers of splendor round that crysal cone,
And roll in floods of far magnificence
Away from that lone, vast Reflector in
The dome of Heaven.
Still watchful of the fertile
Vale and undulating plains below, the grass
Grows greener in its shade, and sweeter bloom
The flowers. Strong purifier! From its snowy
Side the breezes cool are wafted to the "peaceful
Homes of men," who shelter at its feet, and love
To gaze upon its honored form, aye standing
There the guarantee of health and happiness.
Well might it win communities so blest
To loftier feelings and to nobler thoughts—
The great material symbol of eternal
Things! And well I ween, in after years, how
In the middle of his furrowed track the plowman
In some sultry hour will pause, and wiping
From his brow the dusty sweat, with reverence
Gaze upon that hoary peak. The herdsman
Oft will rein his charger in the plain, and drink
Into his inmost soul the calm sublimity;
And little children, playing on the green, shall
Cease their sport, and, turning to that mountain
Old, shall of their mother ask: "Who made it?"
And she shall answer,—"GOD!"

And well this Golden State shall thrive, if like
Its own Mt. Shasta, Sovereign Law shall lift
Itself in purer atmosphere—so high

That human feeling, human passion at its base
Shall lie subdued; e'en pity's tears shall on
Its summit freeze; to warm it e'en the sunlight
Of deep sympathy shall fail:
Its pure administration shall be like
The snow immaculate upon that mountain's brow!

The Rainy Season in California

The rains have come, the winds are shrill,
    Dark clouds are trailing near the ground;
The mists have clothed each naked hill,
    And all is sad and drear around.

The swollen torrents rapid rush,
    Far down the mountain gorges deep;
Now, falling o'er the jagged rocks,
    They thunder through the hollows steep.

Now, in a basin boiling round,
    They dance in maddest music high,
Or, with a sudden leap or bound,
    Dash on like bolts of destiny.

From mountain's side to mountain's side,
    The chasms vast in vapors lost,
Seem like a sea of darkness wide,
    Which fancy dreams can ne'er be crost.

Far off the loftier mountains stand,
    Calm, saint-like in their robes of white,
Like heaven-descended spirits grand
    Who fill the darkness with their light.

Black clouds are rolling round their feet,
    And ever strive to higher climb,
But still their mists dissolve in rain,
    And reach not to that height sublime.

Gone are the birds with sunny days,
    But flowers shall cheer us in their room,
And shrubs that pined in summer rays
    Shall top their leafy boughs with bloom.

The grass grows green upon the hills,
    (Now wrapt in thickly fallen clouds),
Which tall and beautiful shall rise
    When they have cast their wintry shrouds.

Then wandering through their thousand vales,
    Each flowery bordered path shall lead
To gardens wild, where nature's hand
    Hath nurtured all with kindly heed.

Her own voluptuous couch is spread
    Beneath the curtains of the sky,
And on her soft and flowery bed
    The night looks down with loving eye.

But Fancy paints the scene too fast,
    For thus she always loves to leave
The bitter present or the past,
    And rainbows from the future weave.

Lo! night upon my musings here,
    With rapid, stealthy foot hath crept
Unheard amid the sullen sounds
    Which o'er my head have lately swept.

The pouring rain upon the roof,
    The winds in wild careering bands,
Seem bent to see if tempest proof
    The building on its basis stands.

The fiend of this dark night and storm
    Stands howling at my very door—
I dread to see her haggard form
    Break in and pass the threshold o'er.

But hold your own my trusty door!
    Yield not an inch to's utmost might,
Nor let the hellish wild uproar
    That reigns without come in to-night.

It stands—my lonely candle burns,
    The single light for miles around;
Reminding me of some last hope
    That still will light life's gloom profound.

Howl on ye elemental sprites,
    And mutter forth your curses deep,
The anarchy that others frights,
    Shall rock me soundly into sleep.

For, oh, I love to slumber 'neath
    The tempest's wrathful melody,
And dream all night that on its wings
    My soul enchanted soareth free.

The Stolen White Girl

The prairies are broad, and the woodlands are wide
And proud on his steed the wild half-breed may ride,
With the belt round his waist and the knife at his side,
And no white man may claim his beautiful bride.

Though he stole her away from the land of the whites,
Pursuit is in vain, for her bosom delights
In the love that she bears the dark-eyed, the proud,
Whose glance is like starlight beneath a night-cloud.

Far down in the depths of the forest they'll stray,
Where the shadows like night are lingering all day;
Where the flowers are springing up wild at their feet,
And the voices of birds in the branches are sweet.

Together they'll roam by the streamlets that run,
O'ershadowed at times then meeting the sun—
The streamlets that soften their varying tune,
As up the blue heavens calm wanders the moon!

The contrast between them is pleasing and rare;
Her sweet eye of blue, and her soft silken hair,
Her beautiful waist, and her bosom of white
That heaves to the touch with a sense of delight;

His form more majestic and darker his brow,
Where the sun has imparted its liveliest glow—
An eye that grows brighter with passion's true fire,
As he looks on his loved one with earnest desire.

Oh, never let Sorrow's cloud darken their fate,
The girl of the "pale face," her Indian mate!
But deep in the forest of shadows and flowers,
Let Happiness smile, as she wings their sweet hours.

HENRY TIMROD

Henry Timrod (1828-1867) was known as the "laureate of the Confederacy," for much of his best poetry was written during the war and concerns the hopes, struggles and sufferings of his fellow Southerners. But Timrod was no mere propagandist or apologist; his poetry has a classical fineness and sensitivity even in its most passionate or public manner.

Timrod was raised in Charleston, South Carolina—in difficult circumstances after his father's death in 1838 (stemming from service in the Seminole War). Timrod was educated in the classics at school and went on in 1845 to attend Franklin College (now the University of Georgia) in Athens. Poor health and financial need forced him to withdraw in 1846, and he returned to Charleston to study law. He soon tired of the law and took up the study of classics once again, hoping for a position as a college professor. As no such job was forthcoming, Timrod eventually worked as a tutor on plantations in the Carolinas. During these years Timrod wrote and published poems in various Southern journals and newspapers. During holidays he returned to Charleston and associated himself with a literary group at Russell's Bookstore, helping to launch, in 1857, a short-lived journal, *Russell's Magazine*, to which he also contributed poems and articles (among them his well-known essay "Literature in the South").

In 1860 his first collection, *Poems*, was brought out by the prominent Boston publisher Ticknor and Fields, but national events quickly overtook literary ones, and the book received scant notice. Timrod himself, however, was soon caught up in the tide of passions as war approached, and his fervent belief in the Southern cause found expression in new poems of lyric power.

Deemed unfit to serve in the militia because of his poor health, Timrod later reenlisted as a regimental clerk in 1862, serving as a war correspondent for the *Charleston Mercury* during the retreat from Shiloh. Having contracted tuberculosis, Timrod was once again discharged from the army. At the same time plans for a new book of poems to be published in England fell through, to his "unspeakable disappointment." In 1864 Timrod moved to Columbia, South Carolina, where he worked on the *Daily South Carolinian* and married Katie Goodwin, a sister of his brother-in-law. In 1865 Sherman's army burned Columbia, and Timrod was thrown into severe poverty. He was now joined by his mother and his widowed sister with her four children. Soon after, Timrod's infant son died. His health failing, Timrod attempted various schemes to make money but in the end was forced to sell off his family belongings. In 1866, while recovering from an operation, he wrote his "Ode Sung on the Occasion of Decorating of the Confederate Dead, at Magnolia Cemetery." After a series of hemorrhages Timrod died of tuberculosis in 1867. His long-time friend, the poet Paul Hamilton Hayne, edited *The Poems of Henry Timrod*, published in 1873.

Dreams

Who first said "false as dreams?" Not one who saw
    Into the wild and wondrous world they sway;
No thinker who hath read their mystic law;
    No Poet who hath weaved them in his lay.

Else had he known that through the human breast
    Cross and recross a thousand fleeting gleams,
That, passed unnoticed in the day's unrest,
    Come out at night, like stars, in shining dreams;

That minds too busy or too dull to mark
    The dim suggestions of the noisier hours,
By dreams in the deep silence of the dark,
    Are roused at midnight with their folded powers.

Like that old fount beneath Dodona's oaks,
    That, dry and voiceless in the garish noon,
When the calm night arose with modest looks,
    Caught with full wave the sparkle of the moon.

If, now and then, a ghastly shape glide in,
    And fright us with its horrid gloom or glee,
It is the ghost of some forgotten sin
    We failed to exorcise on bended knee.

And that sweet face which only yesternight
    Came to thy solace, dreamer (did'st thou read
The blessing in its eyes of tearful light?)
    Was but the spirit of some gentle deed.

Each has its lesson; for our dreams in sooth,
    Come they in shape of demons, gods, or elves,
Are allegories with deep hearts of truth
    That tell us solemn secrets of ourselves.

"I know not why, but all this weary day"

I know not why, but all this weary day,
(Suggested by no definite grief or pain)
Sad fancies have been flitting through my brain
Now it has been a vessel losing way,
Rounding a stormy headland, now a gray
Dull waste of clouds above a wintry main;
And then, a banner, drooping in the rain,
And meadows beaten into bloody clay.
Strolling at random with this shadowy woe
At heart, I chanced to wander hither! Lo!
A league of desolate marsh-land, with its bush,
Hot grasses in a noisome, tide-left bed,
And faint, warm airs, that nestle in the hush,
Like whispers round the body of the dead!

Lines

Sleep sweetly in your humble graves,
    Sleep martyrs of a fallen cause!—
Though yet no marble column craves
    The pilgrim here to pause.

In seeds of laurels in the earth,
    The garlands of your fame are sown;
And, somewhere, waiting for its birth,
    The shaft is in the stone.

Meanwhile, your sisters for the years
    Which hold in trust your storied tombs,
Bring all they now can give you—tears,
    And these memorial blooms.

Small tributes, but your shades will smile
    As proudly on those wreaths to-day,
As when some cannon-moulded pile
    Shall overlook this Bay.

Stoop angels hither from the skies!
    There is no holier spot of ground,
Than where defeated valor lies
    By mourning beauty crowned.

HELEN HUNT JACKSON

Helen Hunt Jackson (1830–1885) is primarily known for her romantic novel *Ramona*, which concerns a Native American girl raised on a hacienda in California, and for her friendship with Emily Dickinson. However, in her time Jackson was considered by many to be America's finest woman poet, winning praise from Thomas Wentworth Higginson, Emerson, and others.

Jackson was born in Amherst, Massachusetts, and grew up knowing Dickinson well. Her father, a severe Calvinist, taught classics and moral philosophy at Amherst College, and the overbearingly pious atmosphere of the home prompted Jackson's revolt and distaste for the "pitiless community" she grew up in. Both of Jackson's parents, however, died of tuberculosis while she was still young, and Jackson was sent to live with relatives and educated at private schools near Boston and in New York. In 1852 she married Edward Hunt, an army engineer, and settled down to a domestic life, having given birth to two sons, but tragedy intervened. Her younger son died of a brain tumor in 1854; her husband was killed testing a torpedo in 1863; two years later her surviving son died of diphtheria. Jackson was so devastated by these losses that her friends feared for her sanity. Jackson, however, turned to writing verse in her bereavement and found ready acceptance for her poetry and prose in the periodical press. Jackson published under a series of pseudonyms, though increasingly she was known to be the author of her works. In 1870 she published *Verses*, which went through several expanded editions, and in 1872 *Bits of Travel*, a collection of her letters from Europe.

While convalescing in Colorado in 1873 Jackson met William Sharpless Jackson, a wealthy Quaker, and two years later they married. Her first novel, *Mercy Philbrick's Choice* (whose heroine bears a marked resemblance to her friend Dickinson), appeared in 1876, followed by two other novels in quick succession. In 1879 Jackson became outraged at the government's treatment of Native Americans and began a second career as an advocate for their rights. Writing now under her own name, Jackson brought out a nonfiction work, *A Century of Dishonor* (1881), followed by her *Report on the Conditions and Needs of the Mission Indians* (1883), which stemmed from an official investigation that she headed. In 1884 she published her popular novel, *Ramona*; another novel, *Zeph*, came out in 1885. Jackson was invalided from a severe fall, and soon her health began to fail. She died at the age of fifty-four in San Francisco. After her death a number of previously unpublished books appeared, including three collections of her verse. Scholars have recently given renewed attention to her poetry, and she is once again being read as a poet in her own right.

In Time of Famine

"She has no heart," they said, and turned away,
    Then, stung so that I wished my words might be
Two-edged swords, I answered low:—
                             "Have ye
Not read how once when famine held fierce sway
In Lydia, and men died day by day
Of hunger, there were found brave souls whose glee
Scarce hid their pangs, who said, 'Now we
Can eat but once in two days; we will play
Such games on those days when we eat no food
That we forget our pain.'
                    "Thus they withstood
Long years of famine; and to them we owe
The trumpets, pipes, and balls which mirth finds good
To-day, and little dreams that of such woe
They first were born.
               "That woman's life I know
Has been all famine. Mock now if ye dare,
To hear her brave sad laughter in the air."

Poppies on the Wheat

Along Ancona's hills the shimmering heat,
A tropic tide of air with ebb and flow
Bathes all the fields of wheat until they glow
Like flashing seas of green, which toss and beat
Around the vines. The poppies lithe and fleet
Seem running, fiery torchmen, to and fro
To mark the shore.

        The farmer does not know
That they are there. He walks with heavy feet,
Counting the bread and wine by autumn's gain,
But I,—I smile to think that days remain
Perhaps to me in which, though bread be sweet
No more, and red wine warm my blood in vain,
I shall be glad remembering how the fleet,
Lithe poppies ran like torchmen with the wheat.

Crossed Threads

The silken threads by viewless spinners spun,
Which float so idly on the summer air,
And help to make each summer morning fair,
Shining like silver in the summer sun,
Are caught by wayward breezes, one by one,
And blown to east and west and fastened there,
Weaving on all the roads their sudden snare.
No sign which road doth safest, freest run,
The wingèd insects know, that soar so gay
To meet their death upon each summer day.
How dare we any human deed arraign;
Attempt to reckon any moment's cost;
Or any pathway trust as safe and plain
Because we see not where the threads have crossed?

EMILY DICKINSON

Emily Dickinson (1830–1886) wrote—as far as we know—1,775 poems and published seven (all anonymously and none with her full consent). With the exception of a few friends she was entirely unknown as a poet. Although editions of her poetry began appearing shortly after her death, they were incomplete and poorly edited. It was not until 1955 that a complete and reliable text of Dickinson's poems became available, and yet by then she had already become one of the most popular and revered poets in the English language.

Dickinson grew up in Amherst, Massachusetts, the second of three children in a prominent family. Her grandfather founded Amherst College, and her father was a lawyer and at one time a congressman. Dickinson was educated at a local school and went on to study at Mount Holyoke Female Seminary in 1847. (She left, however, after one year.) Returning to the family house, Homestead, in 1848, she never left Amherst again except for one trip to Philadelphia and Washington in 1855 and an extended stay in Boston and Concord, for treatment of an eye ailment in 1864–1865. Indeed, in the last two decades of her life Dickinson rarely left the house and grounds at Homestead. She cultivated a close circle of friends, including her sister Lavinia, her older brother Austin, his wife Susan Gilbert (they lived in the house next door), Helen Hunt Jackson, and a very few others. Though Dickinson never married, she had intense friendships with a number of men (about which there has been considerable speculation)—but only one of them appears to have entertained thoughts of marrying her: Judge Otis P. Lord, an old family friend, with whom she had a romance late in life. All of Dickinson's friendships seemed to entail a curious mixture of intimacy and distance. One such relationship was with the literary critic Thomas Wentworth Higginson, who wrote for the *Atlantic Monthly*. Dickinson initiated a correspondence with Higginson by sending him some poems (asking if they were "alive"). Later, Higginson visited Dickinson on several occasions, and though she disconcerted and baffled him, they remained in contact until her death.

Dickinson wrote poems throughout her life, but her most intense years of inspiration were between 1858 and 1865, during which she composed over a thousand poems. In 1862 alone she wrote 366. It was during this time, too, that she began binding her poems into sewn packets (now referred to as "fascicles"). These were discovered only after Dickinson's death and became the basis for her initial posthumous collections. In her later years Dickinson was extremely reclusive and enigmatic, dressing only in white after her father's death in 1874 and rarely receiving visitors. After a three-year illness Dickinson died of Bright's disease in 1886.

67 "Success is counted sweetest"

Success is counted sweetest
By those who ne'er succeed.
To comprehend a nectar
Requires sorest need.

Not one of all the purple Host
Who took the Flag today
Can tell the definition
So clear of Victory

As he defeated—dying—
On whose forbidden ear
The distant strains of triumph
Burst agonized and clear!

130 "These are the days when Birds come back—"

These are the days when Birds come back—
A very few—a Bird or two—
To take a backward look.

These are the days when skies resume
The old—old sophistries of June—
A blue and gold mistake.

Oh fraud that cannot cheat the Bee—
Almost thy plausibility
Induces my belief.

Till ranks of seeds their witness bear—
And softly thro' the altered air
Hurries a timid leaf.

Oh Sacrament of summer days,
Oh Last Communion in the Haze—
Permit a child to join.

Thy sacred emblems to partake—
Thy consecrated bread to take
And thine immortal wine!

185 "'Faith' is a fine invention"

"Faith" is a fine invention
When Gentlemen can *see*—
But *Microscopes* are prudent
In an Emergency.

199 "I'm 'wife'—I've finished that—"

I'm "wife"—I've finished that—
That other state—
I'm Czar—I'm "Woman" now—
It's safer so—

How odd the Girl's life looks
Behind this soft Eclipse—
I think that Earth feels so
To folks in Heaven—now—

This being comfort—then
That other kind—was pain—
But why compare?
I'm "Wife"! Stop there!

214 "I taste a liquor never brewed—"

I taste a liquor never brewed—
From Tankards scooped in Pearl—
Not all the Vats upon the Rhine
Yield such an Alcohol!

Inebriate of Air—am I—
And Debauchee of Dew—
Reeling—thro endless summer days—
From inns of Molten Blue—

When "Landlords" turn the drunken Bee
Out of the Foxglove's door—
When Butterflies—renounce their "drams"—
I shall but drink the more!

Till Seraphs swing their snowy Hats—
And Saints—to windows run—
To see little Tippler
Leaning against the—Sun—

216 "Safe in their Alabaster Chambers—"

Safe in their Alabaster Chambers—
Untouched by Morning—
And untouched by Noon—
Lie the meek members of the Resurrection—
Rafter of Satin—and Roof of Stone!

Grand go the Years—in the Crescent—above them—
Worlds scoop their Arcs—
And Firmaments—row—
Diadems—drop—and Doges—surrender—
Soundless as dots—on a Disc of Snow—

241 "I like a look of Agony"

I like a look of Agony,
Because I know it's true—
Men do not sham Convulsion,
Nor simulate, a Throe—

The Eyes glaze once—and that is Death—
Impossible to feign
The Beads upon the Forehead
By homely Anguish strung.

249 "Wild Nights—Wild Nights!"

Wild Nights—Wild Nights!
Were I with thee
Wild Nights should be
Our luxury!

Futile—the Winds—
To a Heart in port—
Done with the Compass—
Done with the Chart!

Rowing in Eden—
Ah, the Sea!
Might I but moor—Tonight—
In Thee!

258 "There's a certain Slant of light"

There's a certain Slant of light,
Winter Afternoons—
That oppresses, like the Heft
Of Cathedral Tunes—

Heavenly Hurt, it gives us—
We can find no scar,
But internal difference,
Where the Meanings, are—

None may teach it—Any—
'Tis the Seal Despair—
An imperial affliction
Sent us of the Air—

When it comes, the Landscape listens—
Shadows—hold their breath—
When it goes, 'tis like the Distance
On the look of Death—

263 "A single Screw of Flesh"

A single Screw of Flesh
Is all that pins the Soul
That stands for Deity, to Mine,
Upon my side the Veil—

Once witnessed of the Gauze—
Its name is put away
As far from mine, as if no plight
Had printed yesterday,

In tender—solemn Alphabet,
My eyes just turned to see,
When it was smuggled by my sight
Into Eternity—

More Hands—to hold—These are but Two—
One more new-mailed Nerve
Just granted, for the Peril's sake—
Some striding—Giant—Love—

So greater than the Gods can show,
They slink before the Clay,
That not for all their Heaven can boast
Will let its Keepsake—go

280 "I felt a Funeral, in my Brain"

I felt a Funeral, in my Brain,
And Mourners to and fro
Kept treading—treading—till it seemed
That Sense was breaking through—

And when they all were seated,
A Service, like a Drum—
Kept beating—beating—till I thought
My Mind was going numb—

And then I heard them lift a Box
And creak across my Soul
With those same Boots of Lead, again,
Then Space—began to toll,

As all the Heavens were a Bell,
And Being, but an Ear,
And I, and Silence, some strange Race
Wrecked, solitary, here—

And then a Plank in Reason, broke,
And I dropped down, and down—
And hit a World, at every plunge,
And Finished knowing—then—

287 "A Clock stopped—"

A Clock stopped—
Not the Mantel's—
Geneva's farthest skill
Can't put the puppet bowing—
That just now dangled still—

An awe came on the Trinket!
The Figures hunched, with pain—
Then quivered out of Decimals—
Into Degreeless Noon—

It will not stir for Doctors—
This Pendulum of snow—
This Shopman importunes it—
While cool—concernless No—

Nods from the Gilded pointers—
Nods from the Seconds slim—
Decades of Arrogance between
The Dial life—
And Him—

288 "I'm Nobody! Who are you?"

I'm Nobody! Who are you?
Are you—Nobody—Too?
Then there's a pair of us!
Don't tell! they'd advertise—you know!

How dreary—to be—Somebody!
How public—like a Frog—
To tell one's name—the livelong June—
To an admiring Bog!

290 "Of Bronze—and Blaze—"

Of Bronze—and Blaze—
The North—Tonight—
So adequate—it forms—
So preconcerted with itself—
So distant—to alarms—
An Unconcern so sovereign
To Universe, or me—
Infects my simple spirit
With Taints of Majesty—
Till I take vaster attitudes—
And strut upon my stem—
Disdaining men, and Oxygen,
For Arrogance of them—

My Splendors, are Menagerie—
But their Competeless Show
Will entertain the Centuries
When I, am long ago,
An Island in dishonored Grass—
Whom none but Beetles—know.

303 "The Soul selects her own Society—"

The Soul selects her own Society—
Then—shuts the Door—
To her divine Majority—
Present no more—

Unmoved—she notes the Chariots—pausing—
At her low Gate—
Unmoved—an Emperor be kneeling
Upon her Mat—

I've known her—from an ample nation—
Choose One—
Then—close the Valves of her attention—
Like Stone—

313 "I should have been too glad, I see—"

I should have been too glad, I see—
Too lifted—for the scant degree
Of Life's penurious Round—
My little Circuit would have shamed
This new Circumference—have blamed—
The homelier time behind.

I should have been too saved—I see—
Too rescued—Fear too dim to me
That I could spell the Prayer
I knew so perfect—yesterday—
That Scalding One—Sabachthani—
Recited fluent—here—

Earth would have been too much—I see—
And Heaven—not enough for me—
I should have had the Joy
Without the Fear—to justify—
The Palm—without the Calvary—
So Savior—Crucify—

Defeat—whets Victory—they say—
The Reefs—in old Gethsemane—
Endear the Coast—beyond!
'Tis Beggars—Banquets—can define—
'Tis Parching—vitalizes Wine—
"Faith" bleats—to understand!

315 "He fumbles at your Soul"

He fumbles at your Soul
As Players at the Keys
Before they drop full Music on—
He stuns you by degrees—
Prepares your brittle Nature
For the Ethereal Blow
By fainter Hammers—further heard—
Then nearer—Then so slow
Your Breath has time to straighten—
Your Brain—to bubble Cool—
Deals—One—imperial—Thunderbolt—
That scalps your naked Soul—

When Winds take Forests in their Paws—
The Universe—is still—

327 "Before I got my eye put out"

Before I got my eye put out
I liked as well to see—
As other Creatures, that have Eyes
And know no other way—

But were it told to me—Today—
That I might have the sky
For mine—I tell you that my Heart
Would split, for size of me—

The Meadows—mine—
The Mountains—mine—
All Forests—Stintless Stars—
As much of Noon as I could take
Between my finite eyes—

The Motions of the Dipping Birds—
The Morning's Amber Road—
For mine—to look at when I liked—
The News would strike me dead—

So safer—guess—with just my soul
Upon the Window pane—
Where other Creatures put their eyes—
Incautious—of the Sun—

⭐328 "A Bird came down the Walk—"

A Bird came down the Walk—
He did not know I saw—
He bit an Angleworm in halves
And ate the fellow, raw,

And then he drank a Dew
From a convenient Grass—
And then hopped sidewise to the Wall
To let a Beetle pass—

He glanced with rapid eyes
That hurried all around—
They looked like frightened Beads, I thought—
He stirred his Velvet Head

Like one in danger, Cautious,
I offered him a Crumb
And he unrolled his feathers
And rowed him softer home—

Than Oars divide the Ocean,
Too silver for a seam—
Or Butterflies, off Banks of Noon
Leap, plashless as they swim.

341 "After great pain, a formal feeling comes—"

After great pain, a formal feeling comes—
The Nerves sit ceremonious, like Tombs—
The stiff Heart questions was it He, that bore,
And Yesterday, or Centuries before?

The Feet, mechanical, go round—
Of Ground, or Air, or Ought—
A Wooden way
Regardless grown,
A Quartz contentment, like a stone—

This is the Hour of Lead—
Remembered, if outlived,
As Freezing persons, recollect the Snow—
First—Chill—then Stupor—then the letting go—

435 "Much Madness is divinest Sense—"

Much Madness is divinest Sense—
To a discerning Eye—
Much Sense—the starkest Madness—
'Tis the Majority
In this, as All, prevail—
Assent—and you are sane—
Demur—you're straightway dangerous—
And handled with a Chain—

441 "This is my letter to the World"

This is my letter to the World
That never wrote to Me—
The simple News that Nature told—
With tender Majesty

Her Message is committed
To Hands I cannot see—
For love of Her—Sweet—countrymen—
Judge tenderly—of Me

448 "This was a Poet—It is That"

This was a Poet—It is That
Distills amazing sense
From ordinary Meanings—
And Attar so immense

From the familiar species
That perished by the Door—
We wonder it was not Ourselves
Arrested it—before—

Of Pictures, the Discloser—
The Poet—it is He—
Entitles Us—by Contrast—
To ceaseless Poverty—

Of Portion—so unconscious—
The Robbing—could not harm—
Himself—to Him—a Fortune—
Exterior—to Time—

465 "I heard a Fly buzz—when I died—"

I heard a Fly buzz—when I died—
The Stillness in the Room
Was like the Stillness in the Air—
Between the Heaves of Storm—

The Eyes around—had wrung them dry—
And Breaths were gathering firm
For that last Onset—when the King
Be witnessed—in the Room—

I willed my Keepsakes—Signed away
What portion of me be
Assignable—and then it was
There interposed a Fly—

With Blue—uncertain stumbling Buzz—
Between the light—and me—
And then the Windows failed—and then
I could not see to see—

508 "I'm ceded—I've stopped being Theirs—"

I'm ceded—I've stopped being Theirs—
The name They dropped upon my face
With water, in the country church
Is finished using, now,
And They can put it with my Dolls,
My childhood, and the string of spools,
I've finished threading—too—

Baptized, before, without the choice,
But this time, consciously, of Grace—
Unto supremest name—
Called to my Full—The Crescent dropped—
Existence's whole Arc, filled up,
With one small Diadem.

My second Rank—too small the first—
Crowned—Crowing—on my Father's breast—
A half unconscious Queen—
But this time—Adequate—Erect,
With Will to choose, or to reject,
And I choose, just a Crown—

510 "It was not Death, for I stood up"

It was not Death, for I stood up,
And all the Dead, lie down—
It was not Night, for all the Bells
Put out their Tongues, for Noon.

It was not Frost, for on my Flesh
I felt Siroccos—crawl—
Nor Fire—for just my Marble feet
Could keep a Chancel, cool—

And yet, it tasted, like them all,
The Figures I have seen
Set orderly, for Burial,
Reminded me, of mine—

As if my life were shaven,
And fitted to a frame,
And could not breathe without a key,
And 'twas like Midnight, some—

When everything that ticked—has stopped—
And Space stares all around—
Or Grisly frosts—first Autumn morns,
Repeal the Beating Ground—

But, most, like Chaos—Stopless—cool—
Without a Chance, or Spar—
Or even a Report of Land—
To justify—Despair.

528 "Mine—by the Right of the White Election!"

Mine—by the Right of the White Election!
Mine—by the Royal Seal!
Mine—by the Sign in the Scarlet prison—
Bars—cannot conceal!

Mine—here—in Vision—and in Veto!
Mine—by the Grave's Repeal—
Titled—Confirmed—
Delirious Charter!
Mine—long as Ages steal!

569 "I reckon—when I count at all—"

I reckon—when I count at all—
First—Poets—Then the Sun—
Then Summer—Then the Heaven of God—
And then—the List is done—

But, looking back—the First so seems
To Comprehend the Whole—
The Others look a needless Show—
So I write—Poets—All—

Their Summer—lasts a Solid Year—
They can afford a Sun
The East—would deem extravagant—
And if the Further Heaven—

Be Beautiful as they prepare
For Those who worship Them—
It is too difficult a Grace—
To justify the Dream—

613 "They shut me up in Prose—"

They shut me up in Prose—
As when a little Girl
They put me in the Closet—
Because they liked me "still"—

Still! Could themself have peeped—
And seen my Brain—go round—
They might as wise have lodged a Bird
For Treason—in the Pound—

Himself has but to will
And easy as a Star
Abolish his Captivity—
And laugh—No more have I—

615 "Our journey had advanced—"

Our journey had advanced—
Our feet were almost come
To that odd Fork in Being's Road—
Eternity—by Term—

Our pace took sudden awe—
Our feet—reluctant—led—
Before—were Cities—but Between—
The Forest of the Dead—

Retreat—was out of Hope—
Behind—a Sealed Route—
Eternity's White Flag—Before—
And God—at every Gate—

632 "The Brain—is wider than the Sky—"

The Brain—is wider than the Sky—
For—put them side by side—
The one the other will contain
With ease—and You—beside—

The Brain is deeper than the sea—
For—hold them—Blue to Blue—
The one the other will absorb—
As Sponges—Buckets—do—

The Brain is just the weight of God—
For—Heft them—Pound for Pound—
And they will differ—if they do—
As Syllable from Sound—

640 "I cannot live with You—"

I cannot live with You—
It would be Life—
And Life is over there—
Behind the Shelf

The Sexton keeps the Key to—
Putting up
Our Life—His Porcelain—
Like a Cup—

Discarded of the Housewife—
Quaint—or Broke—
A newer Sevres pleases—
Old Ones crack—

I could not die—with You—
For One must wait
To shut the Other's Gaze down—
You—could not—

And I—Could I stand by
And see You—freeze—

Without my Right of Frost—
Death's privilege?

Nor could I rise—with You—
Because Your Face
Would put out Jesus'—
That New Grace

Glow plain—and foreign
On my homesick Eye—
Except that You than He
Shone closer by—

They'd judge Us—How—
For You—served Heaven—You know,
Or sought to—
I could not—

Because You saturated Sight—
And I had no more Eyes
For sordid excellence
As Paradise

And were You lost, I would be—
Though My Name
Rang loudest
On the Heavenly fame—

And were You—saved—
And I—condemned to be
Where You were not—
That self—were Hell to Me—

So We must meet apart—
You there—I—here—
With just the Door ajar
That Oceans are—and Prayer—
And that White Sustenance—
Despair—

650 "Pain—has an Element of Blank—"

Pain—has an Element of Blank—
It cannot recollect
When it begun—or if there were
A time when it was not—

It has no Future—but itself—
Its Infinite contain
Its Past—enlightened to perceive
New Periods—of Pain.

657 "I dwell in Possibility—"

I dwell in Possibility—
A fairer House than Prose—
More numerous of Windows—
Superior—for Doors—

Of Chambers as the Cedars—
Impregnable of Eye—
And for an Everlasting Roof
The Gambrels of the Sky—

Of Visitors—the fairest—
For Occupation—This—
The spreading wide my narrow Hands
To gather Paradise—

664 "Of all the Souls that stand create—"

Of all the Souls that stand create—
I have elected—One—
When Sense from Spirit—files away—
And Subterfuge—is done—
When that which is—and that which was—
Apart—intrinsic—stand—
And this brief Drama in the flesh—
Is shifted—like a Sand—
When Figures show their royal Front—
And Mists—are carved away,
Behold the Atom—I preferred—
To all the lists of Clay!

709 "Publication—is the Auction"

Publication—is the Auction
Of the Mind of Man—
Poverty—be justifying
For so foul a thing

Possibly—but We—would rather
From Our Garret go
White—Unto the White Creator—
Than invest—Our Snow—

Thought belong to Him who gave it—
Then—to Him Who bear
Its Corporeal illustration—Sell
The Royal Air—

In the Parcel—Be the Merchant
Of the Heavenly Grace—
But reduce no Human Spirit
To Disgrace of Price—

712 "Because I could not stop for Death—"

Because I could not stop for Death—
He kindly stopped for me—
The Carriage held but just Ourselves—
And Immortality.

We slowly drove—He knew no haste
And I had put away
My labor and my leisure too,
For His Civility—

We passed the School, where Children strove
At Recess—in the Ring—
We passed the Fields of Gazing Grain—
We passed the Setting Sun—

Or rather—He passed Us—
The Dews drew quivering and chill—
For only Gossamer, my Gown—
My Tippet—only Tulle—

We paused before a House that seemed
A Swelling of the Ground—
The Roof was scarcely visible—
The Cornice—in the Ground—

Since then—'tis Centuries—and yet
Feels shorter than the Day
I first surmised the Horses' Heads
Were toward Eternity—

744 "Remorse—is Memory—awake—"

Remorse—is Memory—awake—
Her Parties all astir—
A Presence of Departed Acts—
At window—and at Door—

Its Past—set down before the Soul
And lighted with a Match—
Perusal—to facilitate—
And help Belief to stretch—

Remorse is cureless—the Disease
Not even God—can heal—
For 'tis His institution—and
The Adequate of Hell—

754 "My Life had stood—a Loaded Gun—"

My Life had stood—a Loaded Gun—
In Corners—till a Day
The Owner passed—identified—
And carried Me away—

And now We roam in Sovereign Woods—
And now We hunt the Doe—
And every time I speak for Him—
The Mountains straight reply—

And do I smile, such cordial light
Upon the Valley glow—
It is as a Vesuvian face
Had let its pleasure through—

And when at Night—Our good Day done—
I guard My Master's Head—
'Tis better than the Eider-Duck's
Deep Pillow—to have shared—

To foe of His—I'm deadly foe—
None stir the second time—
On whom I lay a Yellow Eye—
Or an emphatic Thumb—

Though I than He—may longer live
He longer must—than I—
For I have but the power to kill,
Without—the power to die—

799 "Despair's advantage is achieved"

Despair's advantage is achieved
By suffering—Despair—
To be assisted of Reverse
One must Reverse have bore—

The Worthiness of Suffering like
The Worthiness of Death
Is ascertained by tasting—

As can no other Mouth

Of Savors—make us conscious—
As did ourselves partake—
Affliction feels impalpable
Until Ourselves are struck—

822 "This Consciousness that is aware"

This Consciousness that is aware
Of Neighbors and the Sun
Will be the one aware of Death
And that itself alone

Is traversing the interval
Experience between
And most profound experiment
Appointed unto Men—

How adequate unto itself
Its properties shall be
Itself unto itself and none
Shall make discovery.

Adventure most unto itself
The Soul condemned to be—
Attended by a single Hound
Its own identity.

986 "A narrow Fellow in the Grass"

A narrow Fellow in the Grass
Occasionally rides—
You may have met Him—did you not
His notice sudden is—

The Grass divides as with a Comb—
A spotted shaft is seen—
And then it closes at your feet
And opens further on—

He likes a Boggy Acre
A Floor too cool for Corn—
Yet when a Boy, and Barefoot—
I more than once at Noon
Have passed, I thought, a Whip lash
Unbraiding in the Sun
When stooping to secure it
It wrinkled, and was gone—

Several of Nature's People
I know, and they know me—
I feel for them a transport
Of cordiality—

But never met this Fellow
Attended, or alone
Without a tighter breathing
And Zero at the Bone—

1072 "Title divine—is mine!"

Title divine—is mine!
The Wife—without the Sign!
Acute Degree—conferred on me—
Empress of Calvary!
Royal—all but the Crown!
Betrothed—without the swoon
God sends us Women—
When you—hold—Garnet to Garnet—
Gold—to Gold—
Born—Bridalled—Shrouded—
In a Day—
Tri Victory
"My Husband"—women say—
Stroking the Melody—
Is *this*—the way?

1099 "My Cocoon tightens—Colors tease—"

My Cocoon tightens—Colors tease—
I'm feeling for the Air—
A dim capacity for Wings
Demeans the Dress I wear—

A power of Butterfly must be—
The Aptitude to fly
Meadows of Majesty implies
And easy Sweeps of Sky—

So I must baffle at the Hint
And cipher at the Sign
And make much blunder, if at last
I take the clue divine—

1101 "Between the form of Life and Life"

Between the form of Life and Life
The difference is as big
As Liquor at the Lip between
And Liquor in the Jug
The latter—excellent to keep—
But for ecstatic need
The corkless is superior—
I know for I have tried

1129 "Tell all the Truth but tell it slant—"

Tell all the Truth but tell it slant—
Success in Circuit lies
Too bright for our infirm Delight
The Truth's superb surprise
As Lightning to the Children eased
With explanation kind
The Truth must dazzle gradually
Or every man be blind—

1545 "The Bible is an antique Volume—"

The Bible is an antique Volume—
Written by faded Men
At the suggestion of Holy Spectres—
Subjects—Bethlehem—
Eden—the ancient Homestead—
Satan—the Brigadier—
Judas—the Great Defaulter—
David—the Troubadour—
Sin—a distinguished Precipice
Others must resist—
Boys that "believe" are very lonesome—
Other Boys are "lost"—
Had but the Tale a warbling Teller—
All the Boys would come—
Orpheus' Sermon captivated—
It did not condemn—

1593 "There came a Wind like a Bugle—"

There came a Wind like a Bugle—
It quivered through the Grass
And a Green Chill upon the Heat
So ominous did pass
We barred the Windows and the Doors
As from an Emerald Ghost—
The Doom's electric Moccasin
That very instant passed—
On a strange Mob of panting Trees
And Fences fled away
And Rivers where the Houses ran
Those looked that lived—that Day—
The Bell within the steeple wild
The flying tidings told—
How much can come
And much can go,
And yet abide the World!

1651 "A Word made Flesh is seldom"

A Word made Flesh is seldom
And tremblingly partook
Nor then perhaps reported
But have I not mistook
Each one of us has tasted
With ecstasies of stealth
The very food debated
To our specific strength—

A Word that breathes distinctly
Has not the power to die
Cohesive as the Spirit
It may expire if He—
"Made Flesh and dwelt among us"
Could condescension be
Like this consent of Language
This loved Philology.

1732 "My life closed twice before its close—"

My life closed twice before its close—
It yet remains to see
If Immortality unveil
A third event to me

So huge, so hopeless to conceive
As these that twice befell.
Parting is all we know of heaven,`
And all we need of hell.

ADAH ISAACS MENKEN

Adah Isaacs Menken (1835–1868) is better known for her highly charged and scandalous life than for her poetry, and yet she was undoubtedly a talented woman whose flair for the dramatic effect is evident in both the work and the life. Menken's career as an actress made her notorious and wealthy—at one point, she was the highest-paid actress in the world—and the sensuousness she brought to the stage was mirrored in the romantic richness of her verse. *Infelicia* (1868), her only book, is full of extravagant gestures and fevered sentiments; and, though the volume was savagely reviewed by critics, it went through twelve editions and sold well.

Menken fabricated various versions of her early life—including five different accounts of her parentage—and for a long time was thought to be either Jewish or mulatto. It now appears that she was of Irish descent, born Ada McCord in Memphis, Tennessee, in 1835. Her father died in 1842, and her mother remarried, moving to New Orleans. Menken developed an interest in poetry and drama early on, learned several languages, and was adept at riding and shooting. In 1856 she married a musician, Alexander Isaacs Menken, and converted to Judaism. She soon began publishing poems with Jewish themes in the *Cincinnati Israelite*. The marriage broke up in 1859, and Menken moved to New York, where she took up her acting career and frequented Pfaff's beer cellar, where she associated with a bohemian crowd that included Walt Whitman. Menken published several articles extolling the poetry of Whitman and Poe, predicting that "the next century" would recognize their genius. She married (perhaps illegally) a prizefighter in 1859 but was later abandoned by him; she married again in 1861 and a fourth time in 1866.

Menken became famous for her theatrical role in Byron's drama *Mazeppa*, in which—dressed in a revealing bodystocking—she rode on stage chained to the back of a horse. Her subsequent acting career took her across the country and overseas, where she made the acquaintance of Bret Harte, Mark Twain, Dante Gabriel Rossetti, Algernon Charles Swinburne, Charles Dickens, George Sand, Théophile Gautier, and Aléxandre Dumas. Her liaisons with Swinburne and the aging Dumas caused scandal across Europe. Menken bore one child, a son, in 1866, but the boy died in infancy. Two years later Menken herself fell ill in Paris, where she died, apparently from cancer. Before her death Menken collected her poems in the volume *Infelicia*, dedicated to Charles Dickens. Of Menken Dickens once said, "she is a sensitive poet who, unfortunately, cannot write."

However, for all its faults, Menken's free-verse style is a conscious attempt to build on the work of Whitman, Poe, and Swinburne. For its passionate eclecticism alone it is remarkable.

Judith

"Repent, or I will come unto thee quickly, and will fight thee with the sword of my mouth." —Revelation ii. 16.

I.

Ashkelon is not cut off with the remnant of a valley.

Baldness dwells not upon Gaza.

The field of the valley is mine, and it is clothed in verdure.

The steepness of Baal-perazim is mine;

And the Philistines spread themselves in the valley of Rephaim.

They shall yet be delivered into my hands.

For the God of Battles has gone before me!

The sword of the mouth shall smite them to dust.

I have slept in the darkness—

But the seventh angel woke me, and giving me a sword of flame, points to the blood-ribbed cloud, that lifts his reeking head above the mountain.

Thus am I the prophet.

I see the dawn that heralds to my waiting soul the advent of power.

Power that will unseal the thunders!

Power that will give voice to graves!

Graves of the living;

Graves of the dying;

Graves of the sinning;

Graves of the loving;

Graves of the despairing;

And oh! graves of the deserted!

These shall speak, each as their voices shall be loosed.

And the day is dawning.

II.

Stand back, ye Philistines!

Practice what ye preach to me;

I heed ye not, for I know ye all.

Ye are living burning lies, and profanation to the garments which with stately steps ye sweep your marble palaces.

Your palaces of Sin, around which the damning evidence of guilt hangs like a reeking vapor.

Stand back!

I would pass up the golden road of the world.

A place in the ranks awaits me.

I know that ye are hedged on the borders of my path.

Lie and tremble, for ye well know that I hold with iron grasp the battle axe.

Creep back to your dark tents in the valley.

Slouch back to your haunts of crime.

Ye do not know me, neither do ye see me.

But the sword of the mouth is unsealed, and ye coil yourselves in slime and bitterness at my feet.

I mix your jeweled heads, and your gleaming eyes, and your hissing tongues with the dust.

My garments shall bear no mark of ye.

When I shall return this sword to the angel, your foul blood will not stain its edge.

It will glimmer with the light of truth, and the strong arm shall rest.

III.

Stand back!

I am no Magdalene waiting to kiss the hem of your garment.

It is mid-day.

See ye not what is written on my forehead?

I am Judith!

I wait for the head of my Holofernes!

Ere the last tremble of the conscious death-agony shall have shuddered, I will show it to ye with the long black hair clinging to the glazed eyes, and the great mouth opened in search of voice, and the strong throat all hot and reeking with blood, that will thrill me with wild unspeakable joy as it courses down my bare body and dabbles my cold feet!

My sensuous soul will quake with the burden of so much bliss.

Oh, what wild passionate kisses will I draw up from that bleeding mouth!

I will strangle this pallid throat of mine on the sweet blood!

I will revel in my passion.

At midnight I will feast on it in the darkness.

For it was that which thrilled its crimson tides of reckless passion
through the blue veins of my life, and made them leap up in the wild
sweetness of Love and agony of Revenge!

I am starving for this feast.

Oh forget not that I am Judith!

And I know where sleeps Holofernes.

Aspiration

Poor, impious Soul! that fixes its high hopes
    In the dim distance, on a throne of clouds,
And from the morning's mist would make the ropes
    To draw it up amid acclaim of crowds—
Beware! That soaring path is lined with shrouds;
    And he who braves it, though of sturdy breath,
May meet, half way, the avalanche and death!

O poor young Soul!—whose year-devouring glance
    Fixes in ecstasy upon a star,
Whose feverish brilliance looks a part of earth,
    Yet quivers where the feet of angels are,
And seems the future crown in realms afar—
    Beware! A spark *thou* art, and dost but see
Thine own reflection in Eternity!

Infelix

Where is the promise of my years;
    Once written on my brow?
Ere errors, agonies and fears
Brought with them all that speaks in tears,
Ere I had sunk beneath my peers;
    Where sleeps that promise now?

Naught lingers to redeem those hours,
    Still, still to memory sweet!
The flowers that bloomed in sunny bowers
Are withered all; and Evil towers
Supreme above her sister powers
    Of Sorrow and Deceit.

I look along the columned years,
    And see Life's riven fane,
Just where it fell, amid the jeers
Of scornful lips, whose mocking sneers,
For ever hiss within mine ears
    To break the sleep of pain.

I can but own my life is vain
    A desert void of peace;
I missed the goal I sought to gain,
I missed the measure of the strain
That lulls Fame's fever in the brain,
    And bids Earth's tumult cease.

Myself! alas for theme so poor
    A theme but rich in Fear;
I stand a wreck on Error's shore,
A spectre not within the door,
A houseless shadow evermore,
    An exile lingering here.

EMMA LAZARUS

Emma Lazarus (1849–1887) is the author of the inscription on the base of the Statue of Liberty, giving it, as James Russell Lowell said, its spiritual basis. "The New Colossus," from which the quotation is taken, would make a fitting emblem for her own work. Lazarus is a poet and writer whose dedication to the welfare of poor immigrants, especially Jews, gave her work intensity and urgency.

Lazarus's antecedents were Sephardic Jews, long established in New York. Her father was a wealthy merchant, and Lazarus grew up in cultivated circumstances, tutored at home in several European languages. Her first book was published when she was just eighteen; *Poems and Translations* (1867) contained some conventional romantic poems of her own as well as translations from French and German poets. Lazarus, who admired Emerson greatly, sent him a copy of her book, and his favorable response initiated a long friendship. Her second book, *Admetus, and Other Poems* (1871), was dedicated to Emerson, and in 1876 she spent a week with the Emersons in Concord. Lazarus was also befriended by Thomas Wentworth Higginson and other important writers and critics of the period. She began publishing poems widely and in 1874 brought out a novel, *Alide: An Episode in Goethe's Life*, and in 1876 a verse play, *The Spagnoletto*. She sent her novel to the Russian writer Turgenev, who responded with enthusiasm. Lazarus's fine translation of the German poet Heine, *Poems and Translations of Heinrich Heine*, appeared in 1881, at which point she was also working on translations from Hebrew poetry.

In the 1880s Lazarus was galvanized by the plight of Jews in Europe, who were persecuted in the pogroms, and by the struggles of Jewish immigrants and refugees in New York. She became active in Jewish causes and began writing with a new sense of purpose, contributing a weekly column to the *American Hebrew*. In 1882 Lazarus argued for the establishment of a Jewish homeland in Palestine. That year *Songs of a Semite* was issued in a cheap edition to make it more accessible. (It contained one of her most powerful works, "The Dance of Death," a verse drama about a medieval pogrom.) To help raise funds for the Statue of Liberty, Lazarus composed "The New Colossus." In 1883 she traveled to Europe, where she visited William Morris's workshops and met Robert Browning. Reading extensively in socialist and humanitarian works, Lazarus continued to urge reforms. Though she had contracted cancer, Lazarus made an extended trip to Europe from 1885 to 1887 and worked on a sequence of prose poems, "By the Waters of Babylon" (published in 1887). Upon her death tributes were offered by many fellow writers, including Whittier, Stowe, and Whitman. *The Poems of Emma Lazarus*, in two volumes, was published posthumously in 1889. In her short life Lazarus traveled great distances in her writing. As with most young poets, her early verse was largely derivative, but she quickly forged her own style. In the work of her last years, particularly the prose poems of "By the Waters of Babylon," Lazarus shows a remarkably innovative and experimental bent that anticipates twentieth-century modernist developments. Her work still awaits its proper appreciation.

Echoes

Late-born and woman-souled I dare not hope,
The freshness of the elder lays, the might
Of manly, modern passion shall alight
Upon my Muse's lips, nor may I cope
(Who veiled and screened by womanhood must grope)
With the world's strong-armed warriors and recite
The dangers, wounds, and triumphs of the fight;
Twanging the full-stringed lyre through all its scope.
But if thou ever in some lake-floored cave
O'erbrowed by rocks, a wild voice wooed and heard,
Answering at once from heaven and earth and wave,
Lending elf-music to thy harshest word,
Misprize thou not these echoes that belong
To one in love with solitude and song.

Venus of the Louvre

Down the long hall she glistens like a star,
The foam-born mother of Love, transfixed to stone,
Yet none the less immortal, breathing on.
Time's brutal hand hath maimed but could not mar.
When first the enthralled enchantress from afar
Dazzled mine eyes, I saw not her alone,
Serenely poised on her world-worshiped throne,
As when she guided once her dove-drawn car,—
But at her feet a pale, death-stricken Jew,
Her life adorer, sobbed farewell to love.
Here *Heine* wept! Here still he weeps anew,
Nor ever shall his shadow lift or move,
While mourns one ardent heart, one poet-brain,
For vanished Hellas and Hebraic pain.

1492

Thou two-faced year, Mother of Change and Fate,
Didst weep when Spain cast forth with flaming sword,
The children of the prophets of the Lord,
Prince, priest, and people, spurned by zealot hate.
Hounded from sea to sea, from state to state,
The West refused them, and the East abhorred.
No anchorage the known world could afford,
Close-locked was every port, barred every gate.

Then smiling, thou unveil'dst, O two-faced year,
A virgin world where doors of sunset part,
Saying, "Ho, all who weary, enter here!
There falls each ancient barrier that the art
Of race or creed or rank devised, to rear
Grim bulwarked hatred between heart and heart!"

The New Colossus

Not like the brazen giant of Greek fame,
With conquering limbs astride from land to land;
Here at our sea-washed, sunset gates shall stand
A mighty woman with a torch, whose flame
Is the imprisoned lightning, and her name
Mother of Exiles. From her beacon-hand
Glows world-wide welcome; her mild eyes command
The air-bridged harbor that twin cities frame.
"Keep, ancient lands, your storied pomp!" cries she
With silent lips. "Give me your tired, your poor,
Your huddled masses yearning to breathe free,
The wretched refuse of your teeming shore.
Send these, the homeless, tempest-tost to me,
I lift my lamp beside the golden door!"

From By the Waters of Babylon: No. V. Currents

1. Vast oceanic movements, the flux and reflux of immeasurable tides oversweep our continent.
2. From the far Caucasian steppes, from the squalid Ghettos of Europe,
3. From Odessa and Bucharest, from Kief and Ekaterinoslav,
4. Hark to the cry of the exiles of Babylon, the voice of Rachel mourning for her children, of Israel lamenting for Zion.
5. And lo, like a turbid stream, the long-pent flood bursts the dykes of oppression and rushes hitherward.
6. Unto her ample breast, the generous mother of nations welcomes them.
7. The herdsman of Canaan and the seed of Jerusalem's royal shepherd renew their youth amid the pastoral plains of Texas and the golden valleys of the Sierras.

NOTES ON THE POEMS

LYDIA HUNTLEY SIGOURNEY

"To a Shred of Linen"

l. 26   *hatchel-tooth*   A hatchel was a comb used on flax.

l. 28   *wheel*   Spinning wheel.

l. 45   *Hygeian*   Greek goddess of health.

l. 45   *harp*   The spinning wheel.

WILLIAM CULLEN BRYANT

"Thanatopsis"

title   *Thanatopsis*   Greek for "meditation on death."

l. 51   *Barcan*   Barca, in northeast Libya.

l. 53   *Oregan*   Oregon (now Columbia) River.

"To a Waterfowl"

l. 9   *plashy*   Marshlike.

"Sonnet—To An American Painter Departing for Europe"

l. 2   *Cole*   Thomas Cole (1801–1848), American painter and leader of the Hudson River School. He was a walking companion of Bryant's in the Catskill Mountains.

l. 3   *native land*   Cole was in fact born in England. Bryant later changed the line.

"The Prairies"

l. 21   *Sonora*   A river in northwest Mexico.

l. 42   *mighty mounds*   Native American burial mounds in Illinois, thought at the time to be the work of some other ancient race.

l. 48   *Pentelicus*   Mountain in Greece quarried for marble to build temples.

MARIA GOWEN BROOKS

from "Zóphiël, or the Bride of Seven"

title   *Zóphiël*   A book-length poem in six cantos, based on a story from the Apocryphal Book of Tobit in which Sara, the daughter of Raguel, "had been married to seven husbands, whom Asmodeus the evil spirit had killed, before they had lain with her." In Brooks's version Asmodeus becomes Zóphiël (the name comes from Milton's *Paradise Lost* VI, 535), a fallen angel in love with the young Hebrew woman Egla. In this excerpt from the first canto Zóphiël sees the beautiful Egla for the first time. She is unhappily betrothed to Meles, a noble man of the Medeans who had subjugated the Jews.

[I] l. 1   *Shade of Columbus*   "The remains of Columbus are preserved in the cathedral at Havana, beneath a monument and bust of very rude sculpture." [Author's note]

[II] l. 1   *Madoc*   The name of a Welsh prince in a poem by the English poet Robert Southey.

[L] l. 6   *sacrificed*   "The captive Hebrews, though they sometimes outwardly conformed to the religion of their oppressors, were accustomed to practise their own in secret." [Author's note]

[LI] l. 1   *complained*   Countered or rebutted.

[LVI] l. 3   *Sybyl's form*   Sibyl: a woman prophetess. Brooks adds the following note to this stanza: "The identity of Zóphiël with Appollo [sic] will be perceived in this and other passages."

[LIX] l. 7   *Endor*   Zóphiël identifies himself here as the Witch of Endor, who called up the dead prophet Samuel to answer King Saul's questions concerning the forthcoming battle in which he was to die. See 1 Samuel 28: 7.

[LXII] l. 2   *fleeting life*   Brooks adds the note: "Zóphiël, being one of the angels who fell before the Creation was completed, is not supposed to know anything of the immortality of the souls of men."

[LXII] l. 5   *the sprite*   Spirit (i.e., Zóphiël).

[LXII] l. 7   *Meles*   Egla has been persuaded by her mother to marry Meles; he will be the first of six husbands to die mysteriously.

"Composed at the Request of a Lady, and Descriptive of Her Feelings"

title   The poem was also known by the title "Farewell to Cuba."

l. 11   *Lethe*   The river of forgetfulness in Hades.

l. 22   *grenadilla*   A melon.

l. 30   *seguidilla*   A Spanish song form. The speaker in the poem is asking the muleteer to sing (frame) a song.

GEORGE MOSES HORTON

"On Hearing of the Intention of a Gentleman to Purchase the Poet's Freedom"

l. 29   *osiers*   Willow trees.

l. 30   *manumission*   A formal release from slavery.

RALPH WALDO EMERSON

"Each and All"

l. 1   *clown*   A peasant.

"The Problem"

l. 7   *vest*   Vestment.

l. 10   *Phidias*   Ancient Greek sculptor (c. 500?–432 B.C.). His colossal statue of Zeus was one of the Seven Wonders of the World.

l. 19   *the hand*   Michelangelo, the chief architect of St. Peter's Basilica in Rome.

l. 44   *Andes ... Ararat*   Andes: mountains in South America; Ararat: highest mountain in Turkey, where Noah's Ark is said to have landed.

l. 51   *Pentecost*   In Acts 2 of the New Testament, the Holy Spirit descends upon the apostles in the form of tongues of flame.

l. 58   *fanes*   Temples.

l. 65   *Chrysostom*   St. John Chrysostom (A.D. 345?–407) was admired for his eloquence (his name means "golden-mouthed").

l. 65   *Augustine*   St. Augustine (A.D. 354–430); Christian religious philosopher and formerly a teacher of rhetoric.

l. 68   *Taylor*   Jeremy Taylor (1613–1667); English bishop and theologian, known for his eloquence.

"The Visit"

l. 25   *rede*   A council in which one places trust.

"Uriel"

title   *Uriel*   The angel of the sun in Milton's *Paradise Lost*.

l. 7   *Pleiads*   Constellation of seven stars. In Greek mythology they were the daughters of Atlas and Pleione.

l. 8   SAID   Saadi, or sometimes Sa'dī (c.1215?–1292); Persian poet and popular moralist.

"Hamatreya"

title   *Hamatreya*   Variant of Maitreya, a character in the Hindu sacred text *Vishnu Purana*.

l. 1	*Minott . . . Flint*	Names of local landowners in Concord. Willard and Flint were among the founders of the town.
l. 8	*flags*	Sweet flag, a marsh herb.
l. 39	*In tail*	Entailed, a limitation on the inheritance of property, specifying an unalterable succession of heirs.

"The Rhodora"

title   *Rhodora*   A shrub related to the rhododendron; it flowers in spring before putting out its leaves.

"The Snow-Storm"

l. 18   *Parian*   Allusion to the ancient marble quarries on the Greek island of Paros; the white marble was valued by sculptors.

"Ode"

title   *W. H. Channing*   William Henry Channing (1810–1884), a clergyman and abolitionist who had urged Emerson to become active in the antislavery movement.

l. 21   *Contoocook*   River in southern New Hampshire.

l. 22   *Agiochook*   Mountain in New Hampshire.

l. 26   *little men*   New Hampshire had voted proslavery; Daniel Webster, senator from New Hampshire, had compromised with Southern demands.

l. 45   *neat*   Cow.

l. 63   *glebe*   Soil.

l. 70   *As Olympus follows Jove*   As the lesser gods follow the chief god.

l. 87   *Out of the lion*   Allusion to Judges 14: 8, where Samson discovers bees in the carcass of a lion.

l. 90   *Cossack eats Poland*   Russia was involved in the partition of Poland in the eighteenth century.

"Merlin I"

title   *Merlin*   Legendary Welsh poet (not the magician of King Arthur's court).

l. 32   *aye*   Always.

l. 49   *Sybarites*   Inhabitants of Sybaris, a Greek city in southern Italy notorious for its hedonism.

"Merlin II"

l. 41   *Nemesis*   In Greek mythology, a child of Night and the agent of retribution (establishing the just order of things).

l. 49   *Sisters*   The three Parcae, or Fates, of Greek mythology.

"Bacchus"

title   *Bacchus*   Roman name for Dionysius, god of wine and poetic inspiration.

l. 5   *scape*   Escape.

l. 9   *Styx and Erebus*   Styx is a river in Hades; Erebus is a region in the underworld that must be crossed before reaching Hades.

l. 39   *Chaos*   In Greek mythology, one of the oldest gods and a deity of the infernal regions.

l. 64   *lote*   Lotus, the fruit that brings forgetfulness.

l. 77   *Pleiads*   Constellation of seven stars. In Greek mythology, they were the daughters of Atlas and Pleione.

"Musketaquid"

title   *Musketaquid*   A river in Massachusetts.

l. 28   *sannup*   A married male Native American.

"Brahma"

title   *Brahma*   One of the supreme triad of Hindu gods, representing the creative aspect of ultimate reality.

l. 12   *Brahmin*   A member of the highest caste of Hindus in India.

l. 14   *sacred Seven*   The Seven Seers (or singers) of ancient Hindu poetry.

"Days"

l. 2   *dervishes*   Islamic ascetics or mystics.

l. 4   *diadems and fagots*   Diadems are royal headbands; fagots are bundles of sticks bound together.

l. 7   *pleached garden*   A garden underneath a slatted canopy or arbor.

l. 11   *fillet*   A narrow ornamental headband, usually a ribbon.

"Waldeinsamkeit"

title   *Waldeinsamkeit*   German for "forest solitude."

l. 35   *Chaos*   In Greek mythology, one of the oldest gods and a deity of the infernal regions.

"Compensation"

II. l. 4   *reave*   To carry off forcibly.

"Awed I behold once more"

l. 2   *blue river*   Concord River.

l. 10   *redundant*   The Latin root for "redundant" means "to overflow."

"Teach me I am forgotten by the dead"

title   This is one of several unpublished poems written soon after the death of Emerson's first wife, Ellen Tucker.

"Maia"

title   *Maia*   Maya, or illusion, in the Hindu system of thought.

HENRY WADSWORTH LONGFELLOW

"A Psalm of Life"

l. 1   *numbers*   Meter or rhythm in poetry.

l. 18   *bivouac*   A temporary encampment made by soldiers.

"The Wreck of the Hesperus"

title   *Hesperus*   Based on the actual account of the wreck of the ship *Hesperus*.

l. 11   *flaw*   A squall.

l. 28   *cable's length*   A unit of nautical length equal to over 600 feet.

l. 60   *Norman's Woe*   A reef off the coast of Massachusetts, near Gloucester Harbor.

"Mezzo Cammin"

title   *Mezzo Cammin*   Italian for "middle of the journey," from the opening line of Dante's *Inferno*.

subtitle   *Boppard*   A town on the Rhine River in Germany; a well-known tourist spot.

"The Jewish Cemetery at Newport"

l. 32   *Ishmaels and Hagars*   In the Old Testament, Ishmael and his mother Hagar were cast into the wilderness.

l. 34   *Ghetto and Judenstrass*   Jewish quarters and streets in European cities.

l. 40   *marah*   Bitter water. Marah was the first stopping place of the Israelites after crossing the Red Sea; the water there was bitter.

l. 41   *Anathema maranatha*   A double curse, or a curse intensified by a prayer.

l. 43   *Mordecai*   Here, a typical Jewish name.

"My Lost Youth"

l. 1   *beautiful town*   Longfellow is thinking of Portland, Maine, his hometown.

l. 13   *Hesperides*   In Greek mythology, islands where golden apple grew.

l. 37   *sea-fight*   During the War of 1812, the U.S.S. *Enterprise* fought the British ship *Boxer* near Portland. Both captains died.

l. 47   *Deering's Woods*   Woods near Portland.

"Aftermath"

title   *Aftermath*   The word means both "a consequence" and "a second cutting of grass in one season."

l. 11   *rowen*   A second crop in a season (similar in meaning to "aftermath").

"The Bells of San Blas"

l. 1   *San Blas*   Town on the west coast of Mexico, north of Guadalajara.

l. 3   *Mazatlan*   Town north of San Blas.

JOHN GREENLEAF WHITTIER

"The Hunters of Men"

l. 2   *cane-break*   A thicket of sugar cane.

"Ichabod!"

title   *Ichabod*   The name, which comes from 1 Samuel 4:21, carries the meaning "the glory is departed from Israel." Here it refers to Daniel Webster, who had helped pass the Fugitive Slave Law in 1850 (thereby alienating abolitionists).

l. 36   *shame*   An allusion to Noah's drunken nakedness after the Flood (see Genesis 9:20–25).

"Telling the Bees"

title   It was a New England custom to inform the bees immediately of a death in the family in order to keep the bees from swarming and seeking a new home.

"Barbara Frietchie"

title *Barbara Frietchie* The poem is based on a true incident, though, as Whittier himself noted, "the story was probably incorrect in some of its details."

"What the Birds Said"

l. 9 *bivouac* A temporary encampment made by soldiers.

l. 30 *clomb* Climbed.

"Snow-Bound: A Winter Idyll"

[p. 110] **epigraph** *Cor. Agrippa* Heinrich Cornelius Agrippa von Nettesheim (1486-1535), known as Agrippa, published his three-volume *De Occulta Philosophia* in 1531-1533.

 epigraph *Emerson.* The lines quoted are from Emerson's "The Snow Storm."

[p. 111] **l. 25** *stanchion rows* Vertical posts used to secure a cow's head during milking.

 l. 45 *pellicle* "A thin film or crust or crystallization."—[Whittier's note in a letter to his publisher]

[p. 112] **l. 63** *sweep* A long pole attached to a pivot, with a well bucket at one end.

 l. 90 *Amun* Egyptian deity with the head of a ram.

[p. 114] **l. 136** *trammels* Chain links and hook for lowering pots onto a fire.

 l. 137 *Turks' heads* Wrought-iron knots that look woven like a turban.

 l. 168 *couchant* In heraldry, lying down with the head raised.

[p. 115] **l. 207** *marbles* Marble headstones in the graveyard.

[p. 116] **l. 215** *Chief of Gambia* A line from "The African Chief," a popular antislavery poem by Sarah Wentworth Morton (not Dame Mercy Warren, as Whittier attributes it).

 l. 225 *Memphremagog's* A lake in Quebec that extends into Vermont.

 l. 226 *samp* A coarse hominy porridge.

 l. 229 *St. François'* Lake Saint François, north of Lake Memphremagog.

 l. 231 *Norman cap* French-Canadian hat worn by women.

 l. 237 *Salisbury's* Marshland near the town of Salisbury, in north-eastern Massachusetts.

 l. 242 *Boar's Head* Little Boar's Head, off the coast of New Hampshire.

 l. 243 *Isles of Shoals* Small islands off the coast of Maine and New Hampshire..

[p. 117] l. 254 *gundalow* A flat-bottomed boat.

l. 259 *Cochecho* Dover, New Hampshire, site of a Native American attack in 1689.

l. 270 *wizard's conjuring-book* Heinrich Cornelius Agrippa von Nettesheim's *De Occulta Philosophia*. See note for "epigraph" on p. 368.

l. 272 *Piscataqua* River in New Hampshire.

l. 286 *Sewell's* William Sewell (1654–1720), author of *The History, Rise, Increase and Progress of the Christian People Called Quakers*. The Quakers were often persecuted.

[p.118] l. 289 *Chalkley's Journal* Thomas Chalkley (1675–1741), a Quaker, published his *Journal* in 1766. It was reprinted many times.

l. 303 *"Take, eat"* Matthew 26:26. Jesus' words at Passover.

l. 306 *child of Abraham* See Genesis 22:13 for the story of Abraham and his son Isaac.

l. 310 *lyceum* Lecture hall. (See Introduction for discussion of lyceums.)

l. 315 *cunning-warded keys* Answers to secrets guarded cunningly by Nature.

l. 320 *Apollonius* Apollonius of Tyana (3 B.C.–A.D. 97); Greek mystic philosopher.

l. 322 *Hermes* Hermes Trismegistus, legendary occult philosopher of third-century Egypt.

[p. 119] l. 323 *Nilus* Nile River in Egypt.

l. 332 *White of Selborne's* Gilbert White (1720–1793); English naturalist and author.

[p. 122] l. 464 *whirling plate* A game where one spins a plate on edge for as long as possible.

l. 476 *Pindus-born Araxes* Meant to refer to a river that rises in the Pindus mountains of northern Greece.

[p. 123] l. 510 *Another guest* Harriet Livermore (1788–1867), an eccentric young woman who was a Second Advent believer (i.e., one who expected the imminent return of Jesus).

[p. 124] l. 523 *pard-like* Leopard-like.

l. 536 *Petruchio's Kate* Heroine of Shakespeare's *The Taming of the Shrew*.

l. 537 *Siena's saint* St. Catherine of Siena (1347–1380), a mystic.

[p. 125] l. 555 *Queen of Lebanon* Lady Hester Stanhope (1776–1839), who settled in a fortified estate in Lebanon where she ruled despotically over the local populace and proclaimed an occult mixture of Christianity and Islam.

[p. 128] l. 669   *mail* Armor.

l. 683   *Ellwood's* Thomas Ellwood (1639–1713), Quaker poet.

l. 693   *Creeks* Native American people of Alabama.

l. 694   *McGregor* Gregor McGregor, who fought under Simón Bolívar in South America and later set himself up as a potentate on a Caribbean island.

l. 696   *Taygetos* Mountains in southern Greece.

l. 697   *Ypsilanti's* Demetrios Ypsilanti (1793–1832); Greek revolutionary patriot who defeated the Turks at Taygetos.

[p. 129] l. 728   *amaranths* Flowers thought never to fade.

l. 739   *aloe* Century plant, thought to bloom once a century.

EDGAR ALLAN POE

"To Science"

[

l. 9   *Diana* Goddess of the moon in Roman mythology.

l. 10   *Hamadryad* Wood nymph in classical mythology.

l. 12   *Naiad* Water nymph in classical mythology.

"Romance"

l. 5   *paroquet* A wooden bird hung outside church towers to be shot at by archers.

l. 11   *Condor* Scavenging bird.

"To Helen"

l. 2   *Nicéan* Obscure name that is probably intended to suggest a classical reference.

l. 8   *Naiad* Water nymph in classical mythology.

l. 14   *Psyche* Greek goddess of the soul.

"Israfel"

title   *Israfel* "And the angel Israfel, whose heart-strings are a lute, and who has the sweetest voice of all God's creatures.— KORAN" [Poe's note].

l. 13   *Pleiads* Constellation of seven stars. In Greek mythology, they were the daughters of Atlas and Pleione.

l. 26   *Houri* In Islam a beautiful maiden waiting in paradise for devout men.

"The Valley of Unrest"

l. 16   *Hebrides*   Islands off the west coast of Scotland.

"The City in the Sea"

l. 18   *fanes*   Temples.

"The Sleeper"

l. 13   *Lethe*   In Greek mythology, the river of forgetfulness in Hazdes.

"Lenore"

l. 2   *Stygian river*   The river Styx in Hades.

l. 3   *Guy De Vere*   A character invented by Poe for dramatic effect.

l. 13   *Peccavimus*   Latin for "we have sinned."

l. 26   *Paean*   A song of praise.

"Dream-Land"

l. 3   *Eidelon*   A phantom.

l. 6   *Thule*   A legendary island to the north of Britain.

l. 10   *Titan*   The Titans were the original Greek gods.

l. 29   *tarns*   Small mountain lakes.

l. 42   *Eldorado*   Mythical city of gold in South America.

"The Raven"

l. 41   *Pallas*   Another name for Athena, the Greek goddess of wisdom and the arts.

l. 45   *craven*   A cowardly person. Craven knights had their heads shorn.

l. 47   *Plutonian*   Black and hellish. In classical mythology, Pluto is the god of the underworld.

l. 80   *seraphim*   An order of angels.

l. 82   *nepenthe*   A drink that induces oblivion.

l. 89   *Gilead*   From Jeremiah 8: 22: "Is there no balm in Gilead; is there no physician there?" Gilead was renowned for its medicinal plants.

l. 93   *Aidenn*   Eden, or some heavenly paradise.

"Ulalume—A Ballad"

l. 6   *Auber*   Invented place name (as are "Weir" and "Yaanek" in the following lines).

l. 8   *tarn*   A mountain lake.

l. 14   *scoriac rivers*   Rivers of lava.

l. 19   *Boreal Pole*   The north pole.

l. 37   *Astarte's*   Phoenician goddess of the moon.

l. 39   *Dian*   Diana, Roman goddess of the moon.

l. 44   *Lion*   The constellation Leo.

l. 46   *Lethean*   Referring to the river of forgetfulness in Hades.

l. 51   *Psyche*   Greek goddess of the soul.

l. 64   *Sybillic*   Sibyls were women with prophetic powers.

l. 103   *scintillant*   Shining.

OLIVER WENDELL HOLMES

"Old Ironsides"

title   *Old Ironsides*   The nickname of the frigate *Constitution*, which captured three British vessels during the War of 1812.

l. 15   *harpies*   Winged monsters in Greek mythology.

"The Chambered Nautilus"

title   *Nautilus*   A mollusk (Greek for "sailor") thought to have a membrane like a sail.

l. 26   *Triton*   Sea god whose trumpet was a conch shell. See William Wordsworth's sonnet "The World Is Too Much With Us" for the allusion to the line "Or hear old Triton blow his wreathèd horn."

MARGARET FULLER

"Sistrum"

title   *Sistrum*   An Egyptian ornamental instrument that jingled when shaken; it was used in the worship of the goddess Isis.

"Flaxman"

title   John Flaxman (1755–1826), English sculptor and illustrator.

FRANCES SARGENT OSGOOD

"Ah! Woman Still"

title   "A reply to one who said, 'Write from your heart'" [Author's note].

CHRISTOPHER PEARSE CRANCH

"Correspondences"

title   For more on the transcendentalist concept of correspondence, see section IV (Language) of Emerson's *Nature* (1836).

"Enosis"

    title   *Enosis*   Greek for unity. The poem was originally published in *The Dial* (July 1840) with the title *Stanzas*. Cranch later retitled it "Enosis," but it was consistently misspelled as "Gnosis" (knowledge) in reprintings.

"The Ocean"

    epigraph Quotation is from William Wordsworth's "Ode: Intimations of Immortality." The fourth line is slightly misquoted.

"In the Palais Royal Garden"

    title   *Palais Royal*   Seventeenth-century palace and gardens in Paris, originally built as a residence for Cardinal Richelieu, who left it to King Louis XIII.

    l. 3   *"Casta Diva"*   Italian for "chaste goddess." A famous aria sung by the heroine of *Norma*, an opera by the Italian composer Vincenzo Bellini.

"The Spirit of the Age"

    l. 5   *Auroral*   Flashing lights visible at night in northern skies, caused by the polar magnetic field.

JONES VERY

"The Columbine"

    l. 7   *honeybells*   Columbine blooms.

"Thy Brother's Blood"

    l. 7   *Abel's*   See Genesis 4.

HENRY DAVID THOREAU

"I am a parcel of vain strivings tied"

    title   "I have seen a bunch of violets in a glass vase, tied loosely with straw, which reminded me of myself" [Thoreau's note, from *A Week on the Concord and Merrimack Rivers*].

    l. 14   *Elysian fields*   In Greek mythology, the dwelling place of the blessed after death.

"Rumors from an Aeolian Harp"

    title   *aeolian Harp*   A wind harp, made by stretching strings across an open box.

"Light-winged Smoke, Icarian bird"

title   When first published in the *Dial*, Thoreau labeled this (and one other) poem "Orphics."

title   *Icarian*   In Greek mythology, Icarus attempted to escape Crete by flying with wings of wax and feathers. In flying too close to the sun his wings melted.

"When Winter fringes every bough"

l. 38   *faggot*   Variant of fagot; a bundle of sticks bound together.

WILLIAM ELLERY CHANNING

"A Poet's Hope"

title   This poem was written impromptu on a challenge from Channing's friend, Mrs. Samuel G. Ward.

l. 12   *alway*   Always.

l. 41   *bourne*   End of a journey, or a goal.

l. 52   *tesselate*   To form into a mosaic pattern.

l. 78   *bark*   Boat or sailing ship.

"Walden"

title   *Walden*   Walden Pond in Concord, Massachusetts, where Thoreau spent two years.

l.9   *one attracted*   Thoreau.

JAMES RUSSELL LOWELL

from "A Fable for Critics"

title   The following passages are excerpted from Lowell's poem. In it Apollo, the Greek god of poetry, is speaking about American literature. Other writers discussed in the poem are A. Bronson Alcott, William Cullen Bryant, John Greenleaf Irving. The first excerpt begins at line 523 of the complete poem.

l. 2   *gold nails*   See Ecclesiastes 12:11.

l. 24   *Exchange*   Stock Exchange.

l. 27   *Plotinus-Montaigne*   Plotinus (c. 205–270) was an idealist philosopher; Michel de Montaigne (1533–1592), a French ("Gascon") skeptical essayist.

l. 52   *Carlyle*   Thomas Carlyle (1795–1881); Scottish prose writer with whom Emerson corresponded.

l. 70   *transdiurnal*   Beyond the boundary of day.

l. 73   *à la Fuseli*   J. H. Fuseli (1741–1825); Swiss-born British painter.

l. 77   *Flaxman*   John Flaxman (1755–1826); sculptor and illustrator.

l. 93   *There comes_*   William Ellery Channing (see above).

l. 97   *rocket*   Fireworks rocket.

l. 102   *_has picked*   Probably Thoreau.

l. 104   *Hesperides*   In Greek mythology, islands where golden apples grew.

l. 117   *rathe*   Appearing early in the year.

l. 120   *John Bunyan Fouqué, a Puritan Tieck*   A conflation of different writers: John Bunyan (1628–1688), English didactic writer; Friedrich Heinrich Karl, Baron de la Motte-Fouqué (1777–1843), fanciful German romantic; Ludwig Tieck (1773–1853), unpuritanical German romantic.

l. 128   *Dwight*   John Sullivan Dwight (1813–1893); Boston poet and music critic associated with the transcendentalists.

l. 133   *Barnaby Rudge*   Title character in novel by Charles Dickens. Rudge's companion is Grip, a raven.

l. 139   *Matthews*   Cornelius Matthews (1817–1889); New York writer and editor who advocated a strong nationalist literature. Longfellow was attacked by Poe and others as too imitative of English models.

l. 152   *Collins and Gray*   William Collins (1721–1759) and Thomas Gray (1716–1771); famous English poets.

l.156   *Mr. Pope*   Alexander Pope (1688–1744); English poet who translated Homer into heroic couplets.

l. 158   *Melesigenes*   Ancient name for Homer (referring to the river Meles, near where he was born).

l. 163   *Strauss*   Johann Strauss (1804–1849); Austrian composer.

l. 166   *Theocritus*   Greek poet of the pastoral, from the third century B.C.

l. 168   *Evangeline*   Longfellow's famous long poem *Evangeline*, written in hexameters.

WALT WHITMAN

from "Song of Myself"

title   Excerpts from the text are taken from the original 1855 edition, in which *Song of Myself* was untitled. Section numbers (also added later) have been inserted in brackets. Notes correspond to line numbers within each separate section.

[3] l. 14   *entretied*   Cross-braced.

[3] l. 35   *cipher*   Figure out, calculate.

[5] l. 18   *kelson*   Keelson; timber bolted to a ship's keel to reinforce it.

[6] l. 15   *Kanuck, Tuckahoe, Congressman, Cuff*   Kanuck: French Canadian (Canuck); Tuckahoe: Virginian, from Tidewater area where tuckahoe grows; Cuff: African–American, from African word *cuffee*.

[24] l. 10   *afflatus*   Creative or divine inspiration.

[31] l. 2   *pismire*   Ant.

[35] l. 1   *frigate-fight*   Sea fight in 1799 between the American *Bon Homme Richard*, commanded by John Paul Jones, and the British *Serapis*.

[35] l. 16   *magazine*   Gunpowder room.

[35] l. 25   *grape and cannister*   Grapeshot (small iron balls) was packed in canisters and shot from cannons.

"The Sleepers"

[1] l. 9   *ennuyees*   French for "bored, life-wearied people."

[1] l. 40   *douceurs*   Sweets or sweet gifts.

[1] l. 41   *cache*   French for "to hide" or a "hiding place."

[5] l. 1   *defeat at Brooklyn*   Washington's defeat at Brooklyn Heights, 27 August 1776.

[5] l. 7   *southern braves*   Many of Washington's troops were volunteers from Virginia and other southern colonies.

[7] l. 35   *erysipalite*   Literally, "red skin." An acute inflammation of the skin caused by streptococcus.

"Crossing Brooklyn Ferry"

title   Originally published as "Sun-Down Poem."

[3] l. 13   *Twelfth-month*   December.

[3] l. 39   *lighter*   Barge used to tend cargo ships.

[9] l. 6   *Mannahatta*   Native American name for Manhattan island.

"Out of the Cradle Endlessly Rocking"

title   Originally published as "A Child's Reminiscence."

l. 25   *Paumanok*   Algonquian word for Long Island meaning "fish-shaped."

"As I Ebb'd With the Ocean of Life"

title   First published as "Bardic Symbols."

[1] l. 3   *Paumanok*   (see above)

[1] l. 13   *sea-gluten*   Sticky substance.

[1] l. 19   *types*   Likenesses.

[3] l. 4   *friable*   Crumbling.

"When Lilacs Last in the Dooryard Bloom'd"

title   This poem is an elegy for President Lincoln.

[1] l. 2   *star*   Venus.

[5] l. 7   *blows*   Blossoms.

[6] l. 5   *flambeaus*   Torches or large candles.

"The Last Invocation"

l. 3   *keep*   Underground vault of a fortress.

"So Long!"

l. 25   *adhesiveness*   A term used in phrenology to denote the propensity for friendship.

l. 62   *Camerado*   Comrade, friend.

l. 68   *tympans*   Tympanic membrane; eardrum.

l. 77   *avataras*   Sanskrit for incarnation or embodiment.

"Hours Continuing Long"

title   Originally published as number 9 of the "Calamus" poems but not reprinted in subsequent editions.

HERMAN MELVILLE

"The Portent"

l. 6   *John Brown*   John Brown's raid at Harper's Ferry, Virginia, took place in October 1859. He was hanged in December.

"A Utilitarian View of the Monitor's Fight"

title   On May 9, 1862, the Union ironclad *Monitor* fought a inconclusive battle with the Confederate ironclad *Virginia* (actually the rebuilt *Merrimack*) at Hampton Roads, Virginia.

l. 28   *operatives*   Factory workers.

"Malvern Hill"

title   *Malvern Hill*   Site in Virginia where the last fighting in the Seven Days' Battles took place. The retreating Union troops used artillery to repulse Confederate attackers.

l. 3   *McClellan*   General George B. McClellan, commander of the Union's Army of the Potomac.

l. 7   *cartridge*   Civil War rifles and muskets used gunpowder cartridges that were bit off and the gunpowder poured down the barrel.

"The Maldive Shark"

l. 2	*Maldive sea*	Southwest of India around the Maldive Islands.
l. 5	*charnel*	Charnel house, where the bodies of the dead are kept.
l. 8	*Gorgonian head*	In Greek mythology, the Gorgon's head could turn one to stone. It had snakes for hair.

"To Ned"

l. 1	*Ned Bunn*	A fictional name for Melville's shipmate Richard Tobias Greene (the character Toby in Melville's novel *Typee*).
l. 4	*Paul Pry*	A play by John Poole (1786–1872), and a name for someone who pries into others' affairs.
l. 4	*Pelf*	Wealth dishonestly gained.
l. 10	*Pantheistic*	Identifying God with nature.
l. 11	*Marquesas*	Islands in the South Pacific.
l. 15	*Typee-truants*	Typee: a fictional island in the Marquesas. A truant is an idle or lazy person.
l. 17	*Saturn's Age*	In Greek mythology, the Golden Age.
l. 18	*Syrian pilgrimage*	Difficult Christian pilgrimage through the world.

"After the Pleasure Party"

subtitle	*Amor*	Cupid, who speaks the italicized lines that follow.
l. 26	*ambuscade*	Ambush.
l. 29	*Vesta*	Chaste Roman goddess of house and hearth.
l. 29	*Sappho*	Ancient Greek lyric poet who wrote of erotic passions; she is said to have killed herself by leaping from a cliff into the sea.
l. 46	*Contemning*	Condemning.
l. 51	*Cassiopea in Golden Chair*	In Greek mythology, Cassiopeia was punished for proclaiming her beauty by being turned into a constellation; she hangs in the sky upside down in a chair.
l. 73	*Decameron folk*	Sophisticated characters in Giovanni Boccaccio's *Decameron* (1351–53), who tell each other stories.
l. 93	*Co-relatives*	In Plato's *Symposium* there is a legend that male and female split off from one spherical being (hence sexual attraction to reunite).

l. 111	*Urania*	The name of the unmarried female astronomer who speaks in the poem (lines 18–110 and 131–47); she is named after the Greek muse of astronomy.
l. 121	*Albani's porch*	Villa Albani (now Villa Torlonia) in Rome, known for its collection of fine statues.
l. 124	*Thomas à Kempis*	Thomas Hammerken von Kempen (c. 1380–1471); German monk and author of *Imitation of Christ*.
l. 138	*Virgin!*	Athena, Greek goddess of wisdom and warfare.

"Monody"

title		A monody is a poem of lament. This poem is thought by some to be about Hawthorne.

HENRY HOWARD BROWNELL

"Night-Quarters"

l. 2	*Sea-Hive*	i.e. the ship. (Brownell was serving under Admiral Farragut.)
l. 7	*steerage*	The ship had no light to steer by.
l. 8	*boot and hose*	Boots and socks.
l. 18	*taking of a lunar*	Determining the ship's position by the moon.
l. 22	*skulk*	One who evades work.
l. 24	*magazine*	Gunpowder room below decks.
l. 32	*brand*	Sword.
l. 33	*frog*	A loop on the belt that holds a sword.

FREDERICK GODDARD TUCKERMAN

"The Cricket"

[II] l. 22	*Winrows*	Windrow; a line of hay raked up to dry before stacking into ricks.
[III] l. 10	*seamew*	A variety of seagull that frequents coastal areas.
[IV] l. 5	*Caÿster*	River in Turkey, now called Küçük Menderes River.
[IV] l. 9	*Eurotas*	River in Greece.
[IV] l. 11	*Xenaphyle*	Possibly Xenophilus, an ancient Pythagorean philosopher from southeastern Greece who was also known as a musician.
[IV] l. 14	*Psammathe*	Possibly Psamathe, mother of Linus by Apollo.
[V] l. 4	*mandrake or dorcynium*	Mandrake: a plant, whose root resembles a human body, from which a narcotic is made; dorcynium: possibly leopard's-bane *(Doronicum)*, once thought to be poisonous to animals.

[V] l. 26 *euphorbias* A family of herbs and shrubs often used for medicinal purposes.

Phoebe Cary

"Jacob"

title The poem is a parody of Wordsworth's poem "She Dwelt Among the Untrodden Ways."

"Advice Gratis to Certain Women"

l. 12 *obs* Words in Webster's dictionary that are obsolete.

"Dorothy's Dower"

[III] l. 8 *John Jacob Astor* Wealthy American capitalist and philanthropist (1763–1848).

Frances Ellen Watkins Harper

"The Slave Mother"

l. 15 *kyrtle* Kirtle, a woman's long dress or skirt.

John Rollin Ridge

"Mount Shasta"

title Extinct volcano in the Cascades of northern California.
l. 19 *Genius* The resident spirit of the place.
l. 57 *ween* To suppose.

Henry Timrod

"Dreams"

l. 13 *Dodona* Site of an ancient Greek oracle. The sacred oaks and doves were said to deliver oracles.

Helen Hunt Jackson

"In Time of Famine"

l. 6 *Lydia* Ancient country in the center of western Asia Minor.

"Poppies on the Wheat"

l. 1 *Ancona* City on the Adriatic coast of central Italy.

Emily Dickinson

214 "I taste a liquor never brewed—"

l. 13 *Seraphs* Angels guarding God's throne.

216 "Safe in their Alabastor Chambers—"

l. 1 *Alabaster* Gypsum, used to make plaster of paris.

l. 9   *Diadems, Doges*   Diadem: a royal crown; doge: one of a group of rulers in Venice and Genoa in the sixteenth century.

287 "A Clock stopped—"

l. 3   *Geneva's*   Geneva, Switzerland, is famous for its clocks.

290 "Of Bronze—and Blaze"

l. 2   *North*   The aurora borealis ("northern lights") is being described.

l. 11   *stem*   One meaning of the word is "axis."

313 "I should have been too glad, I see—"

l. 11   *Sabachthani*   From Mark 15:34: "Eloi, Eloi, lema sabach-thani?" (Aramaic for "My God, my God, why has thou forsaken me?"), Christ's words on the cross.

l. 20   *Gethsemane*   Scene of Christ's agony in the garden (Mark 14:32).

328 "A Bird came down the Walk—"

l. 20   *plashless*   Splashless.

448 "This was a Poet—It is That"

l. 4   *Attar*   Perfume, especially that obtained from roses.

510 "It was not Death, for I stood up"

l. 6   *Siroccos*   Hot winds from North Africa.

l. 8   *Chancel*   Section of a church around the altar.

640 "I cannot live with You—"

l. 5   *Sexton*   Church custodian.

l. 11   *Sevres*   Fine French porcelain.

657 "I dwell in Possibility—"

l. 8   *Gambrels*   A gambrel is a ridged roof with a double slope on each side.

709 "Publication—is the Auction"

l. 6   *Garret*   Attic of a house.

712 "Because I could not stop for Death—"

l. 15   *Gossamer*   Very fine fabric.

l. 16   *Tippet—only Tulle*   Tippet: shoulder cape; tulle: fine starched silk net used for gowns and veils.

754 "My Life had stood—a Loaded Gun—"

   l. 11   *Vesuvian* Vesuvius is a volcano in Italy.

1072 "Title divine—is mine!"

   l. 8   *Garnet* Gemstone, usually dark red.

1545 "The Bible is an antique Volume"

   l. 15   *Orpheus' Sermon* Orpheus, legendary Greek poet and musician, could soothe wild animals and enchant nature.

1651 "A Word made Flesh is seldom"

   l. 15   *Philology* Study of words and literature

ADAH ISAACS MENKEN

"Judith"

   title   The Apocryphal book of Judith recounts the story of Judith's slaying of the Philistine general Holofernes, thereby saving her people.

   [I] l. 1   *Ashkelon* Ashkelon and Gaza were important Philistine cities in southwest Palestine.

   [I] l. 4   *Baal-perazim* Along with Rephaim, sites of victories by David over the Philistines.

   [III] l. 3   *Magdalene* A woman of Magdala, a city famous for its immorality. (The reference is not to Mary Magdalene of the New Testament.)

"Infelix"

   title   *Infelix* Latin for the unfortunate one.

EMMA LAZARUS

"Venus of the Louvre"

   l. 11   *Heine* Heinrich Heine (1797–1856), German Jewish poet who lived in Paris. His name at birth was Chaim Harry Heine.

"The New Colossus"

   title   The last five lines of the poem, in quotations, were inscribed on the base of the Statue of Liberty.

"*From* By the Waters of Babylon: No. V. Currents"

   l. 4   "These cities were the sites of some of the pogroms that started in Russia in 1879 and spread to other countries nearby." (Author's note)

ACKNOWLEDGEMENTS

The below-listed poems by Emily Dickinson indicated by their number were reprinted by permission of the publishers and the Trustees of Amherst College from *The Poems of Emily Dickinson*, Thomas H. Johnson, ed., Cambridge, Mass.: The Belknap Press of Harvard University Press, Copyright © 1951, 1955, 1979, 1983 by the President and Fellows of Harvard College: 67, 130, 185, 199, 214, 216, 241, 249, 258, 263, 280, 287, 288, 290, 303, 313, 315, 327, 328, 341, 435, 441, 448, 465, 508, 510, 528, 569, 613, 615, 632, 640, 650, 657, 664, 709, 712, 744, 754, 799, 822, 986, 1072, 1099, 1101, 1129, 1545, 1593, 1651, and 1732.

All other poems by Emily Dickinson are from *The Complete Poems of Emily Dickinson* edited by Thomas H. Johnson. Copyright © 1929, 1935 by Martha Dickinson Bianchi; Copyright © renewed 1957, 1963 by Mary L. Hampson. By permission Little, Brown and Company.

"Awed I behold once more," "Teach me I am forgotten by the dead," and "Maia," by Ralph Waldo Emerson from *The Poetry Notebooks of Ralph Waldo Emerson* edited by Ralph H. Orth, copyright © 1986 by The Ralph Waldo Emerson Memorial Association. Reprinted by permission of The Ralph Waldo Emerson Association.

"Oh could I raise the darken'd veil," "The Ocean," and "Oh, Man can seek the downward glance" by Nathaniel Hawthorne from *Nathaniel Hawthorne: Poems* edited by Richard E. Peck, copyright © 1967 by The Bibliographical Society of the University of Virginia. Reprinted by permission of the Phillips Library, Peabody Essex Museum, Salem, Massachusetts.

"'Alone'" and "Israfel" by Edgar Allan Poe are from *The Collected Works of Edgar Allan Poe*, edited by Thomas Ollive Mabbot, copyright © 1969 by the President and Fellows of Harvard University, published by The Belknap Press of Harvard University Press.

"Dream-Land" and "Ulalume—A Ballad" by Edgar Allan Poe are from the following volume: Stovall, Floyd, ed. *The Poems of Edgar Allan Poe*. Charlottesville: University Press of Virginia, 1965. Used by permission of the University Press of Virginia.

"Music" by Henry David Thoreau: The Pierpont Morgan Library, New York. MA920.

"On fields oer which the reaper's hand has passed" by Henry David Thoreau from *The Collected Poems of Henry David Thoreau* edited by Carl Bode, copyright © 1964 by the Johns Hopkins University Press. Reprinted by permission of the Johns Hopkins University Press.

"The Cricket" and "Sometimes I walk where the deep water dips" from *The Complete Poems of Frederick Goddard Tuckerman*, edited by N. Scott Momaday, copyright © 1965 by Oxford University Press, Inc. Reprinted by permission of Oxford University Press.

All poems by Jones Very included in this volume are from *Jones Very: The Complete Poems*, edited by Helen Deese, copyright © 1993 by Helen R. Deese, published by The University of Georgia Press.

My thanks to Dustin L. Kirkpatrick for his assistance in correcting this revised edition.